TOO
COOL

TOO COOL

COOL

EDITED BY GENE SCULATTI

St. Martin's Press
New York.

Design by Harry Chester, Inc.

Library of Congress Cataloging-in-Publication Data

Too Cool/edited by Gene Sculatti.
     p. cm.
   ISBN 0-312-08915-5
    1. United States—Popular culture. I. Sculatti, Gene.
  E169.12.T654 1993   92-36037
  306′.0973—dc20   CIP

First edition: February 1993
10 9 8 7 6 5 4 3 2 1

Edited by Gene Sculatti

Associate Editor: Dick Blackburn
Art Direction: Alex Soma for Harry Chester Inc.
Photography (front cover, product shots, fumetti):
    Bruce Malone
Contributing Editors: Bob Merlis
                        Davin Seay
                        Ronn Spencer
                        Jim Trombetta
                        Tom Vickers
                        Danny Weizmann

Editor at large: Dave Stuckey
Contributing Writers: Ken Barnes, Bill Bentley, David Chute, Chris Davidson, Dr. Demento, Michael Dolan, Art Fein, Phil Freshman, Tim Hathaway, Alan Karp, J.D. King, Mike Koehn, Amy Linden, Alan Nahigian, Domenic Priore, Rube Ruben, Metal Mike Saunders, Swamp Dogg, Chuck Thegze, Nick Tosches, Ed Ward, Tim Warren

All unsigned material was written by the editor

Frontispiece illustrations: *Screen:* Rick Altergott
                                    Sounds: J.D. King
                                    Ink: Chris Cooper
                                    Talk Talk: Peter Bagge
                                    Good Looks: Doug Erb
                                    Tube: Drew Friedman
                                    Tall Cool Ones: Carol Lay

Additional illustrations: Chris Cooper, Alex Jones, J.D. King
Models: Audrey Moorehead, Chris "Like Mad" Cooper

ACKNOWLEDGEMENTS:

Thanks to Jim Stein and Tim White for the introductions, Alex and Bruce for the execution, Marsha for the patience, Jim Fitzgerald for the interest. Special thanks to Chuck Thegze, for being there in the first place. And...

Applehead Man
James Austin
Steve Barilotti at *Surfer*
Eric Caidin at Hollywood Book & Poster
Porky Chedwick
Al "Jazzbeaux" Collins
Jef "Doc" Feldman
Gregg Geller
Jeff Gold
Roger Heartsner
Larry's Photo Lab
Major Bill Liebowitz
P.J. McArdle
Eric Monson
Louis Nye
Michael Ochs and Lynne Richardson
Chris and Mary Rawson
Jeff Rosen
Charles Schneider
Gordon Skene

Their Beat Goes On:
Mark Edmunds, Lee Eakle, John Cipollina

TABLE OF CONTENTS

Chapter 4: TALK TALK

Chapter 5: GOOD LOOKS

Chapter 6: TUBE

Chapter 7: TALL COOL ONES

Callin' Out Around the World

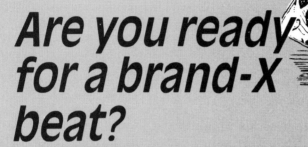

Are you ready for a brand-X beat?

"Stay awhile!" cries Alf.
"Stay awake," purrs Sweet Alyssum, pulling him to the party in progress. "Man," swings Frank to no one in particular, "they got a gang of coffee in Brazil!"
Jus' then Coffin Ed & Gravedigger Jones fall by for a cup 'n' spy Sgt. Frank Smith, corner booth, sweet-talkin' Jim Dean's date into closin' up the candy store/going to a-go-go. Getting late, yes, but in the fiberglass jungle Big Daddy Roth burns moonlight oil, lacquering the Beatnik Bandit's right front fender with coat #10.
"You got collision?" wonders Alf.
"That's what the party's all about," Alyssum jumps, applying a fresh streak of Great Granny Red: a trans-generational junction function that would, you know, "be like Cream of Nowhere without the crash..." Alf is still yeah-butting about when do we get there as they breeze past Safe As Milk, where Snowman 'n' wife're debating what's hotter: a new cyber-cop sequel with soft-drink tie-ins or a new alternative band with tattoos on its soles.
"S'anybody got the time?" blurts Alf.

"Follow that dream!" shouts Alys, hailing a truck fulla smogballs climbing Cahuenga Pass bound f'r Jack Isadore's recappery up north. They're moving pards now, A & A: graspin' that smogtruck tailgate w/ white knuckles 'n' wonderin' Who'll Be There as the two-four wheeler blasts through Tie City, Point Blank, Flibberty Jib ... Downtown it's darker/in B'klyn & East Los silent except for the eternal "Deserie" sweeping streets with mystery.

POW! North Beach jumps into sight, the truck skiddin' into B'way's blaze on its inside two. Crowds, loudness, scientific delirium madness: 100's of flamekeepers queue up in Clubland to dig the rich licks of this subcult fire-sale—in a sea of frug & sharkskin Bobby Freeman swims in Betty Lou's shoes, sayin' a taste ("But Aloe," implores Alfa, "what time is it *now?*") ... Hysteric Bunker Hill bleats "Little Red Riding Hood," Babs Gonzales bops between raindrops — Up on th' roof the ceiling falls away t' reveal Frank Smith doing a mad mambo w/ Mustang Sally, Lenbruce tossing wordsalad on tourists two floors below and—in the main room — Untamed Youth burnin' down the house with that Rollerland thing.

Alyssum looks up from all this, turns to anxious Al in a trice. "There! Right there," she sez, adjusting her wig-hat for max reception, "*that's* what time it is..."

THE CALENDAR OF COOL
Some Significant Haps In The History Of Hip

525-549 A.D.
Seeking an alcohol substitute, Chinese Buddhists take tea and see

150,000 B.C.
Wooly Bully: First mammoths roam

Before The Beginning:
Universe cools . . . atoms form . . . Antarctica freezes

1862
First appearance of the martini, in *The Bon Vivant's Companion*

1519
Coffee introduced to Europe from Arabia

1198
Bohemia becomes a kingdom

1885
First sunglasses for sale, Philly

1876
Edison invents phonograph

1904
Salvador Dali born

1871
Lewis Carroll writes *Through the Looking Glass*

1905
Neon signs first displayed

Mama Mia!

1895
Marconi invents radio

10

Illustrations: J .D. King

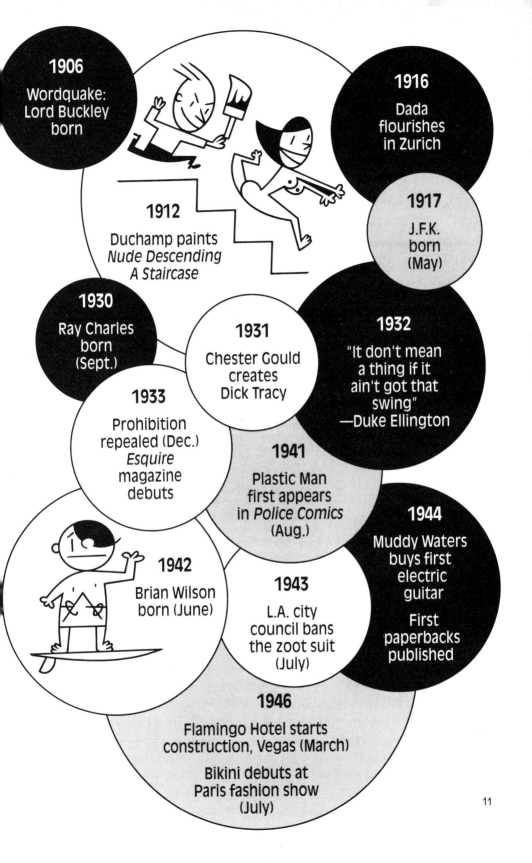

1906
Wordquake:
Lord Buckley
born

1916
Dada
flourishes
in Zurich

1917
J.F.K.
born
(May)

1912
Duchamp paints
*Nude Descending
A Staircase*

1930
Ray Charles
born
(Sept.)

1931
Chester Gould
creates
Dick Tracy

1932
"It don't mean
a thing if it
ain't got that
swing"
—Duke Ellington

1933
Prohibition
repealed (Dec.)
Esquire
magazine
debuts

1941
Plastic Man
first appears
in *Police Comics*
(Aug.)

1944
Muddy Waters
buys first
electric
guitar

First
paperbacks
published

1942
Brian Wilson
born (June)

1943
L.A. city
council bans
the zoot suit
(July)

1946
Flamingo Hotel starts
construction, Vegas (March)

Bikini debuts at
Paris fashion show
(July)

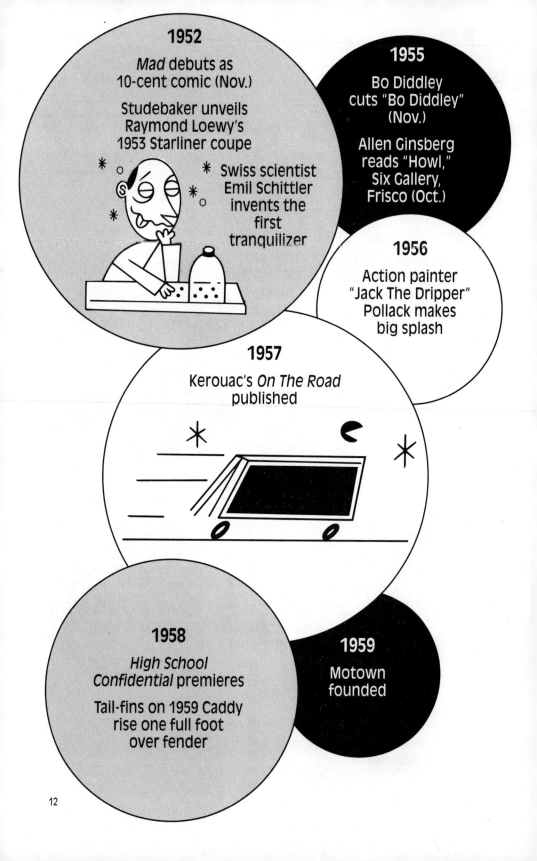

1952

Mad debuts as 10-cent comic (Nov.)

Studebaker unveils Raymond Loewy's 1953 Starliner coupe

Swiss scientist Emil Schittler invents the first tranquilizer

1955

Bo Diddley cuts "Bo Diddley" (Nov.)

Allen Ginsberg reads "Howl," Six Gallery, Frisco (Oct.)

1956

Action painter "Jack The Dripper" Pollack makes big splash

1957

Kerouac's *On The Road* published

1958

High School Confidential premieres

Tail-fins on 1959 Caddy rise one full foot over fender

1959

Motown founded

1961

Bob Dylan arrives in N.Y. City from Hibbing, Minnesota (Jan.)

1962

Primetime TV lineup includes *Naked City* and *Route 66*

1963

First pop art show at Guggenheim (Warhol, Rauschenberg, Johns) (May)

Phil Spector cuts "Be My Baby," "Da Doo Ron Ron," "Then He Kissed Me," "Today I Met The Boy I'm Gonna Marry"

Dr. Strangelove premieres

1965

Velvet Underground debuts at Jersey highschool gig (Nov.)

Tom Wolfe's *Kandy-Kolored Tangerine-Flake Streamline Baby* published

1966

First appearance of Vincent Price as *Batman* villain Egghead, ABC TV

1969

Jack Kerouac dies while watching *The Galloping Gourmet* (Oct.)

1973

Mean Streets premieres

1974

Ramones first play CBGB (Aug.)

RIchard Price's *The Wanderers* published

1976

Sex Pistols begin residency at 100 Club, London

1977

Fine programming: SCTV debuts

1980

Hernandez Bros. begin publishing *Love & Rockets* comics

1984

"The Cool And The Crazy" radio show debuts

1985

Nicholas Pileggi's *Wiseguy* published

1990

The Plot Against Harry released after 21 years in the can

2992

Hell freezes over

Courtesy: Showtime Archives

INTRODUCTION

> "I owe a lot of who I am and what I've done to the beatniks of the Fifties and to the poetry and art and music that I've come in contact with…I can't even imagine life without that stuff…We all have those things, those pillars of greatness. And if you're lucky, you might find out about them, and if you're not lucky, you don't."
> —Jerry Garcia, *Rolling Stone*, Oct. 31, 1991

You just got lucky. It may not feel like it, but you're holding two hundred-plus pages of pillars and irrepressibly swingin' things, of "entities," as *downbeat* (1948) defined the objects of cool, "which, in colloquial terms, 'gas' the witness." Here we're gassed & testifying, about Bobby Bland and B-3 organ trios, about *Route 66*, lipstick and coffee, wiseguys, Ann Savage in *Detour*, and Dyl's Eskimo encomium.

The party started ten years ago. We published THE CATALOG OF COOL to celebrate all the riffs and artifacts that we felt retained the power to shake and stomp beyond their time. We wanted to share the stoke about cool folks and their deeds—Harvey Kurtzman founding *Mad* magazine, Terry Southern scripting *Dr. Strangelove*, Lenny Bruce shpritzing, the Stones rolling.

Now there's TOO COOL, because space constraints forced us to leave so much out of the CATALOG, and because—if you know where to look—the intervening ten years have produced plenty of grooved goods that need a nod.

15

Michael Ochs Archives

"What key? What key?"

As before, our selections are highly subjective, and more pre-New Age-ishly engaged than post-modernistically detatched. Jerry Lee's the house pianist in this joint, not George Winston. At the same time, our rave-ups are free-range and roam unconfined over seven chapters—from the sly jive of Forties hepcat Louis Jordan (See SOUNDS) to the novelistic futureturf of Michael Swanwick and Samuel R. Delany (see INK). We'll fill you in on the heavy-detail jones of Victorian painter Richard Dadd (GOOD LOOKS) and the bad-dame excesses of *Bloody Mama* (a Seventies flick about a Thirties femme, from our SCREEN chapter), point you toward the alchemical mysteries of Trip Shakespeare (SOUNDS) and that incandescent Roy Head *Shindig* clip (TUBE).

We think all of these things belong together. Each one, and the hundreds of other subjects saluted in TOO COOL, carves its own niche, and says something smart or weird or uncannily appropriate or tosses some genuine joy at the world. Collectively they suggest just the opposite of the

popular definition of cool. There's nothing trendy or temporary about a tradition that embraces solid style wherever it's found, and realizes that this spirit swings through all ages.

Wade in the Water

A logical question, as you sit there, hands full of pillars, contemplating your lucky strike, is: why would anyone bother to undertake writing (or reading) such a book as TOO COOL? In 1930, the compilers of the dictionary of *American Tramp and Underworld Slang* located what they felt were the origins of the word "hip." According to jazzbos of the day, the adjective derived from "having one's hip boots on—i.e., the way in which they protect the wearer from bad weather or dangerous currents is analogous to the way in which awareness or sophistication arms one against social perils."

Obviously, the currents aren't that deep or dangerous around here, and we've got no eyes for any kind of arms sales. Nonetheless, the popcul-tural stream is where we all swim these days, and it's rarely been grayer or more muddied. TOO COOL is about vision enhancement, about seeing things that really stand out, often, but not neces-sarlly, at the edges, in the corners. Its premise is that there's more to appreciate than this week's Hottest Author, Fastest Selling Record or Top Grossing Movie. (TV's entertainment magazines recite these breathlessly, like you're dying to find them out, dying to participate in the statistical pole vault of one product-stack over another, or dead in the water because you haven't read/heard/seen them all yet.)

You'll probably have the most fun with TOO COOL if you look at it as a combination guidebook, catalog and family album. If we've done our job, the book will suggest some trips, put you in touch with some goods and services (check our *Shop Around* buying leads at the end of each chapter), and hold its heroes fast, capturing their best moments in sharp focus.

Better still, dig this book as paper radio. It's night. Signals crackle through whitenoise and storm static. You punch a dashboard button and tune in, somewhere between pages 1 and 220 on the dial, and dive into surprise broadcasts from the Big "E" over Elsewhere. Thousands of watts 24 hours a daydream. Buzz a while 'cos you're what's hap-pening, baby.

We should sign off. So you can go now, like that tambourine man, wandering. Now's the time, as Louis Nye's Mad Ave ad-man so coolly observes, to "toss it down the well and check it for splash."

G.S.

Shop Around product-info guides are placed at the end of the SOUNDS, SCREEN, INK and TUBE chapters. In addition, each SOUNDS entry cites the latest available recordings by the respective artists; SCREEN entries give the year of each film's release followed by its current videocassette distributor, and INK listings provide the year of each book's original publication and the most recently available edition. Within the GOOD LOOKS, TALK TALK and TALL COOL ONES chapters, product information is given at the end of each entry or feature.

SOUNDS

Your feet start tappin'
And you can't seem to find
How you got there
So just blow your mind
– *"Do You Believe in Magic,"
The Lovin' Spoonful*

Music's always been the hippest trip & transport. And the coolest disks fly forever: their ear fare stays fresh and solid no matter what the Seiko says. Meet their makers . . .

ACAPELLA. Doowop's bride stripped bare. All-mouth American music that heals heart and soul and knocks most solidly on Heaven's door. Like the Belmonts' awesome *Cigars, Acapella, Candy* (cut in 1972, reissued as an Elektra cd last year), or anything by the Zircons, Chessmen, the Blue Stars, or Patty & the Street-Tones. (See this chapter's Shop Around guide.)

THE ANIMALS. Don't let them be misunderstood. Both as intercontinental mod-gods and Love Gen petal-pushers, they could never hide the fact that they were actual pub thugs who brawled for the sheer pleasure of it. On "Gin House Blues," Burdon vows "I'll fight the army and Royal Navy if I don't get some gin tonight." Acid-housekeeping: Burd's pre-War "Girl Named Sandoz."
Cassette only: *Animals' Greatest Hits* (Mercury), and original albums (MGM).
Best of the Animals (ABKCO), *Best of Eric Burdon & the Animals* (PolyGram). D.W.

TONY BENNETT. Prince of the city, with coffee-rich chops. Even as a "kid," the king of grown-up songstuff—love lost and found, bucking traffic on the Street of Dreams, the warmth of the sun on faces in the September of their years. He swings on *Jazz*, revisits the nabe on *Astoria: Portrait of the Artist*. The box: *Forty Years: The Artistry of Tony Bennett* (features "Rags To Riches," etc.) (all CBS/Sony).

RICHARD BERRY. Oblivious to the danger to himself, Berry—the menacing voice on the Robins' "Riot in Cell Block No. 9" and writer of the R&B cult gem "Oh! Oh! Get Out of the Car"—entered his L.A. laboratory late one night in 1955. When he emerged, he brought the world something more profound than Einstein's theory or Jeckyll's practice: a thing called "Louie Louie."
LP only: *Louie Louie* (Earth Angel). R.S.

Tony Bennett (Columbia Records)

BLUES. It tossed America the keys to the highway and threw in a roadmap for the soul. Behind the wheel: Muddy Waters, Howlin' Wolf, Elmore James, Sonny Boy Williamson, Buddy Guy, Junior Wells, all of whom are represented by currently available, immeasurably boss disks. (Check out Down Home Music's blues catalogs. See Shop Around.)

GARY U.S. BONDS. Duly acclaimed for such Sixties revels as "Quarter To Three" and "Dear Lady Twist," this Virginia creeper had to wait till 1990 and a Rhino *Best Of* to get his greatest achievement before the public. Not only is "I Wanta Holler (But the Town's Too Small)" his toughest tribal stomp, it seems to cry like freedom's chimes for all those too hung up or shut out to make the party. Soul for sure.

BOW WOW WOW. The world's first & only jungle-surf group was fronted by a snotty 14-year old Burmese nymph whom Malcom McLaren discovered in a laundromat. "I can't dance and I can't sing/ I can't do anything," squeals Annabella Lewin. "I can't even find my way around town!" Paris match: Annabella gets hot for architecture in "Sexy Eiffel Towers."
Top dog sets: *See Jungle! See Jungle! Go Join Your Gang Yeah! City All Over, Go Ape Crazy* (RCA), *12 Original Recordings* (EMI), *Best of Bow Wow* (RCA). —D.W.

CHARLIE BURTON. Nutso garageabilly from Nebraska. Play the cut "Roadkill" on a car stereo and you'll swear you ran over something big. CB's "Breathe For Me Presley" steals the royal crown from Mojo Nixon's "Elvis Is Everywhere" when it comes to king things.
Albums (both on Wild): *I Heard That* (feat. "Roadkill"), *Is That Charlie Burton - Or What?!?!* ("Breathe"). D.B.

CALIFORNIA PUNK. The Feel Bad Music of the Big Zilch Generation was a gas, and left behind enough shrapnel to repave the Hollywood Fwy. Today, the best of it sounds better than ever: alive, kicking, fast, funny, remarkably light on its feet. "It all sounds the same," until you listen. Every suburb had a different take on the three-chord model, from the ridic bopper snot-punk of Red Cross ("I Hate My School") to the raging malevolent thunderball of the Germs ("Land Of Treason"). As Fear so succinctly put it, "I don't want no satisfaction/ I just wanna get some action."

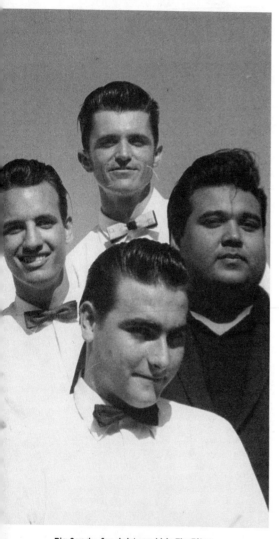

Big Sandy, far right, and his Fly-Rites.

BIG SANDY & THE FLY-RITE TRIO. Thoroughly modern, timelessly sharp "rockabilly" in the purest sense of the word, live from Orange County. Think of Vincent's Blue Caps crossed with Willie Dixon's Big Three, blowin' like a hurricane.

LP: *Fly Right with Big Sandy & the Fly-Rite Trio* (Dionysius, P.O. Box 1975, Burbank, CA 91507).

Get started: *Dangerhouse: Volume One* and *Weird World: The Weirdos 1977-1981*, *Group Sex: The Circle Jerks* (all Frontier). *Los Angeles/Wild Gift: X* (Slash) D.W.

WYNONA CARR. Unsung shouter of Fifties R & B, Carr's the earthy equal of such tough mamas as Ruth Brown and Lavern Baker. Whether cryin' or drivin', she kept a frog in her throat and her eyes on the prize. "I'm gon' let go now!" she announces at the top of "Ding Dong Daddy," then proceeds to go for goods over gold: "You know that I don't want his money/ He may not have a cent/ But if he rings my ding dong bell/ I'd live with him in a tent!"
LP only: *Jump, Jack, Jump!* (Ace import).

RAY CHARLES. The Genius hits the road, invents soul music ("The Right Time," 1959), flies his tour plane. What'd he say? Early: *The Birth of Soul* (Atlantic box). Later (ABC sides): *Anthology* (Rhino).

Jungle-surf squealer: Bow Wow Wow's Annabella.
RCA Records photo by David Bailey.

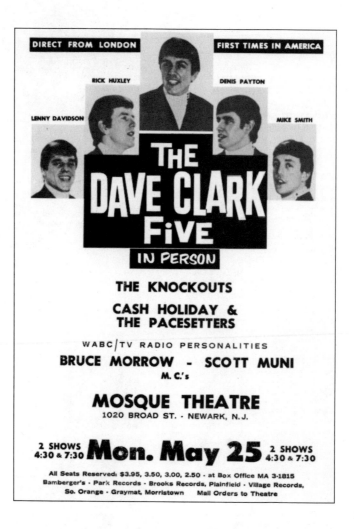

THE DAVE CLARK FIVE. The Fab Four's most significant rival during the British Invasion, the DC5 eschewed arty affectation and intellectual pretension, and were therefore dismissed by revisionist historians and every overinflated music crit who ever slopped at the trough of Jann Wenner. Truth is, "Any Way You Want It" is one of the most relentlessly perfect, tear-the-house-down rock 'n' roll records ever committed to carnuba. And "Try Too Hard," "Glad All Over," "Bits & Pieces," "I Really Love You" and "All Night Long" surpass any of the lovable Moptops' early attempts to simulate an actual no-holds-barred r'n'r band.
(Original U.S. albums on Epic.) R.S.

BOOTSY COLLINS. Yabbadabbadoozibubba! Of course Bootsy's a player. By 21 he'd already put James Brown on the jungle groove and launched Clinton's Mothership. He also invented the funky bass as we now know it, crafted a whole new kind of Stoopid, and wrote the first dancemusic plumbing metaphor ("roto-rooter, bubba/trouble shooter!").
Essential: *Player of the Year, Stretchin' Out in Bootsy's Rubber Band, Ahhh, The Name is Bootsy, Baby*(Warner Bros.).
D.W.

WILLY DE VILLE. As Mink De Ville, he was the Romeo of Loisada, marrying junkie romance with Ben E.

King passion. Big in France (where they dig drama-
tics) but unsung on the homefront, he's an R & B
singer with a poet's heart who made theme music
for well-intentioned fuckups—guys who wear
their hearts on their sleeves & burn holes in your
sofa. These days, he lives in N'awlins, where
dressing like Zorro-meets-Shaft is appreciated,
and where amor and mystery rule. His debut,
Cabretta (Capitol 1977), is NYC on a platter. *Le Chat
Bleu* (Capitol '81) mixes chemicals, Edith Piaf and
Doc Pomus. —Amy Linden.

ROKY ERICKSON. "My eyes are filled with coral
snakes and liquid plastic castles/ Her daily life
revolves around a thousand petty hassles." Before
cool was cool, Roky was Hi-cool. He had to be: his
Sixties band, the 13th Floor Elevators, was
routinely dogged by several Texas law enforce-
ment agencies who loved to take apart the Els'
amps in their zealous herb-search. After such

Willy DeVille

Roky Erickson

dayglo classics as "You're Gonna Miss Me" and
"Reverberation," Roky tumbled downhill. In '72,
after four years at TX's Hospital for the Criminally
Insane, he emerged as the Rev. Roky Erickson,
publishing a book of poetry prayers, *Openers*. By
the time he formed the Bleib Alien combo ("Two-
Headed Dog"), it looked like he was never coming
down. In '89, the law nabbed him again, for collect-
ing his neighbors' mail and nailing it to his wall.
Don't knock the Rok.
Psychedelic Sounds / 13th Floor Elevators Live
(Charly import); *You're Gonna Miss Me: The Best
of Roky Erickson*(Restless). *Where the Pyramid
Meets the Eye: A Tribute to Roky Erickson* (Sire).
-Bill Bentley.

FINE YOUNG CANNIBALS. It's no mystery why the
trio took its name from a (1960) flick inspired by
the life of Chet Baker. Like West Coast jazz, FYC's
rock uses leanness and Lo-sweat to max effect
("She Drives Me Crazy"). The chord changes to
"Don't Look Back" and "I'm Not Satisfied" feel like
the sleeves of a silk suit, with lots of cuff.
Fine Young Cannibals, The Raw And The Cooked
(IRS)

Ella Fitzgerald

ELLA FITZGERALD. What you should do: go buy these Verve albums (cds), mostly cut in L.A. in the 1950's . . . *The Gershwin Songbook* and *The Johnny Mercer Songbook* (both arranged by Nelson Riddle); *The Harold Arlen Songbook* (arranged by Billy May); *Clap Hands, Here Comes Charlie.* I have never heard, nor do I expect to hear, so much emotion and heart delivered in a song. Ella brings the life of Ella Fitzgerald to the words & melodies; her thoughts and feelings of so many people she has known and cared about come pouring through. And sitting there, listening intently, you recognize those emotions as your own. As I write this, she is singing Ellington's "Don't Get Around Much Anymore." It's coming from KJAZ, the jazz station in San Francisco. I've heard 50 songs on the radio this afternoon. This is the only one that stops me. I didn't even realize it was her. I just knew that something was happening.—Chuck Thegze.

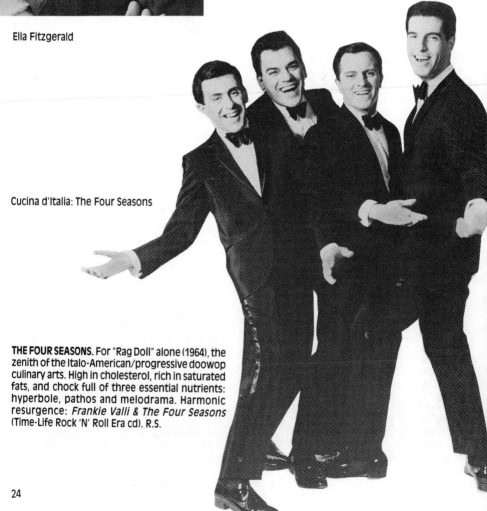

Cucina d'Italia: The Four Seasons

THE FOUR SEASONS. For "Rag Doll" alone (1964), the zenith of the Italo-American/progressive doowop culinary arts. High in cholesterol, rich in saturated fats, and chock full of three essential nutrients: hyperbole, pathos and melodrama. Harmonic resurgence: *Frankie Valli & The Four Seasons* (Time-Life Rock 'N' Roll Era cd). R.S.

the FUGS

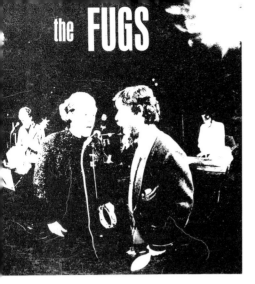

THE FUGS. Twixt '65 and '67 these Lower East Side college rockers consistently combined sub-Velvets primitivism with supra-Mothers dada to flip the Brain Police a stiff digit ("Kill For Peace," "Johnny Pissoff Meets the Red Angel"). Inspirational Verse: "I ain't never gonna go to Vietnam / I prefer to stay right here and screw your mom." *The Fugs* and *Virgin Fugs* (Base / ESP Folk Archive). Out of print: *It Crawled Into My Hand, Honest* (Reprise).

TINY GRIMES. The greatest unknown amplified guitar in the world. T.G. started in the late Thirties with jive group The Three Cats And A Fiddle, laid down some heavy sides with Bird, crossed over to R&B aided by his kilted Rocking Highlanders (featured vocalist: Screamin' Jay Hawkins), and returned to jazz in his last years before a surfeit of reefer and Southern Comfort caught up with him. An American classic; various sets on Oldie Blues, Krazy Kat, Prestige, etc. D.B.

THE GUESS WHO. These Canadians were one of those faceless hitmaker bands like Jay & the Americans, Three Dog Night or Creedence—all of them might be sitting across from you on the bus and you'd never know it. Burton Cummings was their driving force, and his quirkiness, like his voice, was a wonder to behold during the band's Seventies heyday. He followed hostility ("American Woman") with pity for nine-to-fivers ("Bus Rider"), hippie Communism ("Share The Land"), droll gun-control ("Rain Dance"), and such innocently Out There fare as "Glamour Boy" (an anti-Bowie ballad) and "Life In The Bloodstream" (achingly beaut doowop from the POV of a contraceptive pill!).
RCA cd: *Track Record.*—Art Fein.

WYNONIE HARRIS. How many of the Byrned-out globetrotters pushing musical multiculturalism have spent a scant five minutes in their own backyard digging Omaha's coarse boogie king? When Mr. Blues came to town (late Forties), America jumped back and got rhythm. "Everything about Wynonie was strong," recalled one theater manager of the man behind "Sittin' On It All The Time" and the torrid "Christina," "...strong language, loud clothes, potent whiskey, and a set of vocal chords seemingly made of steel." Hard stuff: WH lp's on Route 66, Charly. T.H.

HYPER-SOUL. A kind of musical grand-theft auto with multiple counts of speeding. Usually, it's a Vandellas rip ("Heat Wave"), over-revved and driven to exhaustion. Prime: the Butlers' breathless "She Tried to Kiss Me," Tina Britt's "The Real Thing" (both reissued as Lost-Nite singles). The down-tempo variety pirates ballad structure, but shoves it wondrously out of shape with scorching vocal/instro perfs. Bonnie & Clyde's "I Want A Boyfriend (Girlfriend)" is 2:04 of raw power (In-Sound 45). So sharp.

CHRIS ISAAK. Only the lonely know the way he feels tonight. A terminally lovesick rocker who makes beauty from bruises and surfs the Sea of Heartbreak in Orb's wetsuit ("Wicked Game," "Forever Young").
Heart Shaped World, Silvertone (Reprise).—Tim Hathaway

WANDA JACKSON. "Her voice, a wild-fluttering thing of sexy subtleties and sudden harshnesses, feral feline purrings and raving banshee shrieking, was a vulgar wonder to hear"—Nick Tosches, *Unsung Heroes of Rock 'n' Roll*. Dig "Let's Have A Party" and "Fujiyama Mama" from *W.J.: Rockin' in the Country* (Rhino cd).

Wanda Jackson (Capitol Records)

25

Jan And Dean

JAMC: Gabba Gabba Hum

JAN AND DEAN. Their blatant faddism beat PoMo's eclecticism by a quarter century. Bright, busy *faux* Beach Boys tracks that skipped effortlessly from Surf to Drag to "Folk City," from leftover *Batman* camp to right-wing protest ("Universal Coward"). Jap imports of original lps are dear, but where else to cop "Surfin' Hearse" or "Horace, The Swingin' School Bus Driver"? Gremmy set: *Surf City* (EMI Legends of Rock n' Roll cd).

JESUS AND MARY CHAIN. An entire band-unit dedicated to the (fairly supportable) proposition that "Sweet Jane" is the coolest tune of all time. All four JAMC cd's burn like one sustained ultra-Velvet ray, though the debut *Psycho Candy* and 1990's *Automatic* buzz best. Interpretive cool: *Automatic*'s "Head On" recasts the Ramones' "I Wanna Be Your Boyfriend" as 60-cycle hum. *Psycho Candy*, *Darklands*, *Automatic* (Reprise).

JOAN JETT. The czarina of crunch and high priestess of the power chord, she formed the first all-girl band with any juice (Runaways) and hasn't slowed since. Her taste in covers is on the money ("Little Drummer Boy," "Starfucker," "I Wanna Be

Your Dog"), she produced the Germs, and has resisted all attempts to girly up her 4/4 manifesto. First and best: *Bad Reputation* (Boardwalk 1981, feat. "You Don't Own Me"). Also bad: *Up Your Alley* (CBS Associated 1988). A.L.

BILLY JOEL. For the fashion sense to know that hearts sometimes go well with sleeves (he sent doowop a bouquet in "The Longest Time" and saluted the Seasons like a fanboy in "Uptown Girl" on '83's *An Innocent Man*). As a rock crit, he's no slouch. Ronnie Spector's voice on "Be My Baby," he writes, "just oozes sex. I mean, it sounds almost lubricated. It's got a smell to it, like sweat and garlic."

RAHSAAN ROLAND KIRK. Of all the Sixties jazzbo iconoclasts, the late RRK was consistently the wiggiest *and* the most listenable. Starting out in his teens as a honkin' R & B sax man, he matured into a virtuoso jazz performer who, on one occasion, blew three horns simultaneously for nearly 2 1/2 hours. Eccentric on and off stage, Kirk, in an attempt to illustrate his blindness, once wrapped his record producer's head in masking tape, held a gun to the guy's mummified noodle and said, "I just want you to know how I feel all the time." New live cd: *The Man Who Cried Fire* (Nite). Vintage: *Volunteered Slavery*, *Blacknuss* (Atlantic). R.S.

IRY LeJEUNE. With Coke-bottle glasses and a penchant for howling, Fifties accordion great LeJeune is the spiritual link between the Evangeline Oak and the zydeco washboard. Pass the pepper. *The Legendary Iry LeJeune, Vols. 1 and 2* (Goldband). D.S.

Rahsaan Roland Kirk

Iry LeJeune on squeezebox: sans specs and blind as a *Chauve-souris*.

ROCK AND ROLL MUSIC FOR KIDS OVER SIXTEEN
JACK E. LEONARD

LX-1080

Vik

A PRODUCT OF RADIO CORPORATION OF AMERICA
A "NEW ORTHOPHONIC" HIGH FIDELITY RECORDING

JACK E. LEONARD. The comic's 1956 send-up *Rock And Roll Music For Kids Over Sixteen* (Vik lp) throttles rock's corpse so thoroughly, one listen to it could've saved Einsturzende Neubaten and PIL years of wasted effort. And, since Fat Jack's naturally overwrought style suited early R & R's (groovy) excess so well (dig "Boll Weevil" and "Why Do Fools Fall In Love"), he manages to simultaneously beat the beast and ride it with more gusto than Don Henley, say, ever could.

LITTLE RICHARD. He put a wild face on rock 'n' roll. His left hand is a five-piece rhythm section (try "Lucille"), and he admits he can "scream like a white lady" (ask "Miss Ann"). Big Little: *The Specialty Sessions*, and various Ace imports. B.M.

THE LOVIN' SPOONFUL. Unique and unalloyed, a band whose origins (b. 1965, New York City, same as the V.U.) now seem as distant as archduke Ferdy. Warmer than the Byrds, more worldly than the Beach Boys, the last hip pre-hippie act radiates morning glory ("Daydream"), bright lights-big city optimism ("Summer In The City"), and so much more ("Full Measure," etc.). Slip on *Anthology* (26 tracks, Rhino), watch the shadows scatter.

BIG JAY McNEELY. One screams, the other doesn't. *This* Jay's a honker, *the* most unhinged R&B tenor saxist around. Since the Forties he's been hopping on tables, walking the bar, Pied Piping audiences out the door and into orbit. Bonus: somewhere along the line, he found time to pen the cosmos-probing "There Is Something On Your Mind (Parts I & II)."
Vintage honk: *Live at Birdland* (Big J). Recent: *Jay Walkin'* (ABC Australian import, 1990). R.S.

VAN MORRISON. Heavy on the heaven and earth tones, Belfast's lonely bluesboy dances with melody, writes automatic valentines to G-L-O-R-I-A and Madame George, and keeps on pushin', 30 years into one of the most idiosyncratic styles ever. It's too late to stop now. Thank you, baby.
Basics: *Moondance, Astral Weeks* (Warners), *Best of Van Morrison, Enlightenment* (Mercury), *Them* (London).

MOTOWN. Back in the days before Berry Gordy crossed grits off his grocery list (pre-'67), the Sound of Young America was really sayin' some-thin.' Which is to say, it's Reeves over Ross any day, Contours rule, and "Little" meant a lot more before he called to say whatever.
Individual artist collections; *Motown: The First Decade*, etc.

RON NAGLE. Somewhere between scoring the gut-

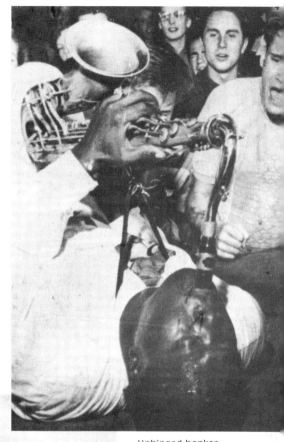

Unhinged honker:
Big Jay McNeely
(Courtesy Jim Dawson)

29

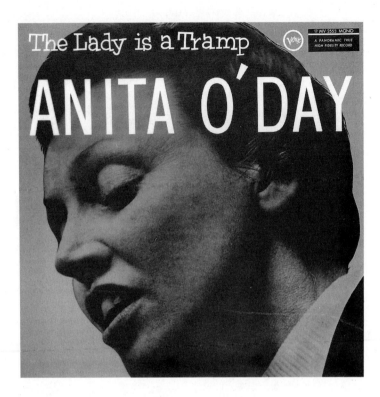

wrench sound effects for *The Exorcist* and penning tunes for (among others) Babs Streisand, this San Fran Renaissance Man got tagged "a cynical misanthrope" (BAM mag) and "the best undiscovered writer around" (Jack Nitzsche). Cool proof of both: Nagle's 1970 lp *Bad Rice* (Warners; reissued on Edsel). Faith healers, a boy seduced by his nanny, and a kid who "kicks in [his mom's] head with his wing-tips" people an album that fuses pre-punk rage with *Pet Sounds* romanticism. Kissin' cousin: Nagle and Scott Matthews' dark-humored, Spectorian debut as the *Durocs* (Capitol lp, 1979).

ANITA O'DAY. On her (Fifties) Verve sessions, a stylist supreme who transforms class ("Love For Sale") and corn alike ("Strawberry Moon") into prime movers. Lush and drowsy, the voice is late-afternoon cool, and when she digs the good word from that kicky bluebird in "Ain't This A Wonderful Day," the lady's a champ, jack. See INK.

ROY ORBISON. Of course the voice is paramount: growling, keening, vaulting to the heavens. But don't shortchange the songs, perfectly tailored for that magnificent vocal instrument. Byzantine plots, melodrama, heartbreak larger than life—if

Spector's records were "little symphonies for the kids," Orb's were little operas. On "In Dreams," "Crying," and the ineffable "It's Over" (elegy for the end of the world as we know it), R. O., wallowing in the depths of earthly sorrow, at the same time transcends and soars above it. *All-Time Greatest Hits Vol. 1* (Monument).—Ken Barnes.

GRAM PARSONS. Rock 'n' roll's trailblazing country-rock alchemist years before the Eagles turned it into a mewling, self-conscious embarrassment. Two decades dead, the bitter-sweet Byrd/Burrito lives, on forever young reissues.
G.P./Grievous Angel (Reprise CD); *Farther Along: Best of the Flying Burrito Bros.* (A&M); *The Byrds* box (Columbia).—R.S.

JOHNNIE RAY. Elvis may have invented white rock 'n' roll, but there was someone ahead of him. In 1951, Johnnie Ray, a lean, tormented torch singer—with a hearing aid—fell to his knees sobbing when he sang his double-sided hit "Cry" and "Little White Cloud That Cried," and teenagers went wild. His fame was quick and fleeting. By 1956 rock 'n' roll left him in its wake, despite the fact he had cut his teeth in R&B clubs in Detroit. Pre-echoing Presley's status as a circus clown led by Col.

30

Parker, Ray danced to Columbia Records' A&R chief Mitch Miller's baton, cutting such creaky pop as "Walking My Baby Back Home." When he died of a liver ailment in 1989, J.R. was a forgotten man, his only recent mention being in "Come On, Eileen" by Dexy's Midnight Runners: "He was the one our grandmothers pined for."
Greatest Hits (Columbia Special Products). A.F.

SADE. Neo-classic cool, as in understated, effortless and sexy. She sounds like she looks (transcendently sensual), but could swing just as easily if she were Hazel or Gertrude. Three Epic cds, including 1986's *Promise*, which includes "The Sweetest Taboo." Whew. B.M.

DOUG SAHM (SIR DOUGLAS QUINTET). The most important C & W synthesist since Bob Wills, Sir Doug (assisted by keyboardist Augie Meyers) fused San Antonio R & B, Mexican norteño, Western swing, blues and rock into one of popular music's few Whole New Things, first served on the '65 single "She's About A Mover." Menus change, but the meal's always the real deal.
Best of Sir Douglas Quintet 1968-75 (Polygram), *Best of SDQ* (Tribe/Crazy Cajun), *Texas Tornados* and the TT's *Zone Of Our Own* (Reprise). R.S.

Pre-Presley torcher-er: Johnnie Ray
(RCA Victor Records)

Sir Douglas Quintet

SAM THE SHAM AND THE PARAOHS. Rock 'n' roll might have been a revolution, but Sam went to great lengths to prove it could be every bit as cornball as vaudeville. "You can't turn me off," torched Sam, "'cos you didn't turn me on!" *Pharaohization* (Rhino; featuring "Wooly Bully," "Ju Ju Hand," etc.). D.W.

JACK SCOTT. Once Presley parted the waters, rockabilly ran off in two directions. Conway Twitty went over the falls in a torrent of rococo self-pity ("It's Only Make Believe," "Lonely Blue Boy"). Scott swam for cool water with stark, equally dramatic sides that flashed hick soul ("My True Love") and hip affirmations ("The Way I Walk Is Just The Way I Walk"). Colossal. *J.S. Greatest Hits* (Curb).

SEX PISTOLS. Every year that separates us from their legacy makes them seem that much more prophetic. You have to dig that Trump, Arnold Schwarzenegger, Party Naked and "greedworks" hadn't happened yet when J. Rotten opened up their first American lp by screaming "Cheap holiday in other people's misery." *Never Mind the Bollocks, Here's the Sex Pistols* (Warners); *The Great Rock 'n' Roll Swindle* (Virgin import). D.W.

DEL SHANNON. His unbridled emotions—paranoia ("Stranger In Town"), vengefulness ("Hats Off To Larry"), obsession ("Keep Searchin'")—were chilling, all the more so in the sunnier '61-65 timespan. He was the first Yank to cover the Beatles ("From Me To You," 1963); what could be

Everyhood: Jack Scott, affirming (Capitol Records)

The Sex Pistols (Warner Bros. Records)

more appropriate, considering he practically invented Merseybeat and folk-rock in the same song, 1962's "Little Town Flirt." Come to think of it, he practically invented synth-pop too ("Runaway's" musitron solo is surely the ancestor of all subsequent synth doodlings). He rocked when few would or could rock with him. Though the fervidly inventive early Sixties were far from the unjust musical desert promulgated by hordes of superficial hack historians, they were short on rock hits. His were the exceptions. And he left a sufficient body of simple but oddly tormented, compelling music, in his heyday on through his last recordings, to merit a historical place far more substantial than that of a "Runaway" success story.
Greatest Hits (Bug). *The Liberty Years* (EMI). K.B.

SOUTH AFRICAN ROCK 'N' ROLL. Township rock ruled eons before Paul parted the fronds and brought it back to *Graceland*. When Kwela, the local tinwhistle blues 'n' boogie jazz, hit in the mid-Fifties, its popularity encouraged Benoni Rocket, the Pretty Dolls and other acts, awash in Yankee R & R 78's, to test their tonsils on the new sound. Result: a nonsensical shuffling of the lyrics to "Be-Bop-A-Lula" and similar hits that created tracks of staggering surrealism. Get down with this stuff and you'll think you're on a palm-wine bender. Cassette only: *Flying Rock* (Global Village). D.B.

STEELY DAN. Mistakenly tarred as members of the criminal Seventies-rock burnout, Fagen & Becker in truth pushed the most potent lyric pills since mid-Dyl. Sleek ball-bearing grooves hide a rogues gallery of creeps 'n' cons who come on more twisted than Vegas at dawn. In "Haitian Divorce" Babs ditches Clean Willy for "the Charlie with the lotion and the kinky hair." "Kid Charlemagne" buys confidence, sells satori out of a spotless kitchen. MCA cds: *Countdown To Ecstasy / Can't Buy A Thrill*; *Royal Scam / Katy Lied*; *Pretzel Logic*. Side trip: Donald Fagen's *The Nightfly* (Warners), a balmy evocation of Camelot culture that floats on ironic optimism ("I.G.Y.") and bops between raindrops. D.W.

BILLY STEWART. At a soulful 300 lbs., he didn't need no doctor or 12-step program to come to grips with his avoirdupois ("She even said I was her pride and joy/ And that she was in love with a Fat Boy"). Really big: his stuttering, un-standardized version of Gershwin's "Summertime" (1966), one of the world's wickedest covers and the obvious thread between Nappy Brown's and Van Morrison's glottal gumbos.
Chess set: *One More Time.*

33

Surf-rocking Pyramids say "Later for hair bands."
(Courtesy John Blair)

SURF MUSIC. Hendrix was wrong. That stuff about "You'll never hear surf music again" ("Third Stone From the Sun") dropped no science. Nowadays, those lean instro wipeouts rip with freshness. Heavy metal, of which Jim was the progenitor, decays on the beach.
Wet sets (cds): *The Surfaris Play/ Fun City USA* and *Pipeline/ Two Sides of the Chantays* (Rooster imports). *Surfin' With the Astronauts/ Competition Coupe* (Bear Family import). *The Lively Ones; Surf Rider/Surfin' Drums* (Ace import). *King of the Surf Guitar: The Best of Dick Dale* and *Surfin' Hits* (Rhino).
Wet Ink: *The Illustrated History of Surf Music*—

John Blair (Popular Culture, Ink; 1-800-678-8828 to order).

T.V. SLIM. Downhome Louisiana blues-rocker who used intense personal experiences as a small-screen repairman, both sexual ("T.V. Man") and sociological ("Don't Knock The Blues"), to turn life into art. "Lady called me up the other day on the outskirts of town/ Said she had a picture but she didn't have no sound/ When I got there and I walked through the door/ I began to work on that set right on the floor."
TV Slim: 'Flat-foot Sam' (Moonshine lp). D.B.

THROW THAT BEAT IN THE GARBAGECAN. After, what—5000 Velvets-ripoffs from Steve "never heard 'em" Wynn's Dream Syndicate to any dork on your block—finally an unashamed Reed-inspired pastiche band (Sixties garage, deadpan Lou vocals, gonzo late Seventies punk energy levels when required) that derives from the AM, Top 40, bubblegum side of things. Per Chiz of the Memphis 'zine *Way Out*, these Germans are "led by the singing of lead guitar wiseacre Klaus Cornfield and Beatle-haired gal Lotsi Lapislasuli," and play "beautiful songs through tiny amps."
Import lps: *Large Marge Sent Us*; *Tweng LP* (September Gurls). -Metal Mike Saunders.

T.REX (MARC BOLAN). It never really was about boppers or androgyny. In the midst of early Seventies pomp and prog-rock, way pre-Pistols, M.B. stripped the r 'n' r chassis down to basic moving parts to give it an overdue tuneup. Inspirational Verse: "I have never kissed a car before/ It's like a door" - "The Slider."
T. Rextasy: The Best of T. Rex 1970-1973 (Warner Bros.) R.S.

TRIP SHAKESPEARE. At a time when pop iconoclasm is defined by Prince's butt cheeks, this quartet of Twin City surrealists is the genuine article. Anchored to the formidable songwriting skills of bros. Matt and Dan Wilson (along with bassist John Munson and drummer Elaine Harris), the Trippers gather the precious shards of psychedelia and refract them through a scintillating, pun-dappled prism of dangling metaphors and dangerous dreams. The group's gorgeous gift for harmonic convergence and melodic alchemy brings the feverish fun of their song-stories to life: small moments, keenly observed, become the substance of resonant epiphanies celebrating the sensational weirdness of reality.

Trip S's handful of albums yield nary a clunker, with a spread of musical style and lyric substance that suggests a grand unifying theory binding the infinitesimal to the infinite. "Your mouth is my apartment in the evening," declare the Wilsons in "Your Mouth," their slithering ode to a sensual soulmate. In the harrowing "The Nail," the narrator, on a mysterious mission, travels from Min-

Trip Shakespeare (A&M Records)

nesota to California. Somewhere in transit, lost along the highway, "running from the truth," he dreams that "times have changed," a reverie no doubt born of "the nail in my head." In the hilarious "Slacks," the brothers argue over who actually wore the magic pants in a failed attempt to seduce the "one-eyed lady from France," while Mrs. Braintree, the "chilly Northern woman" of the ethereal "Snow Days," is invited to "go down to yonder bus stop" where there's a "blessing on the ground." The dreaded subject of "Toolmaster," we are told, is returning to "the creamery" to "start up the old machinery," a prospect greeted with a mix of loopy horror and curious desire.

On albums like *Are You Shakesperienced* (Clean), *Applehead Man* (Gark), *Lulu* and *Across the Universe* (both A&M), Trip S decant a magical, mordant and mesmerizing elixir, daring us to drink deep and laughing, both with and at us, as we reel, intoxicated, through their hall of mirrors. (See Shop Around.) D.S.

UNTAMED YOUTH. The next square who reviews 'em as "roots" or "retro" gets a Moon-equipped knuckle-Manwich. The Rill Thing is a more apt designation for what this hi-volt combo from the Show Me state puts down. The gods whose grooves they hammer home are the stars on a hundred forgotten 45's, their sacred texts "Surfin' Hearse" and "Go Go Ferrari." They're best live, but

their Nineties lps *Some Kinda Fun* and *More Gone Gassers* (Norton) surge with power; do not run other appliances when playing these in your home. Groovy older cousins: THE SKELETONS (*In The Flesh*, ESD cd), world's hippest cover band bar none.

WAS (NOT WAS). They came out, walked the dinosaur, felt better than James Brown. Guest vocalist Mel Torme's "Zaz Turned Blue" was a collision of beauty and freakery at the corner of Smart & North Whack. They're workin' double shifts down at the Burning Idea Factory.
Was is: *Born To Laugh At Tornadoes* (feat. "Zaz"), *What Up, Dog?* and *Are You Okay?* (Chrysalis).

THE WHO. Forgive them *Tommy*, *Quadrophenia*, the reunions, the latter-day bloat. Cherish them for three singles that rocked the world, instilling an element of danger that opened new possibilities of chaos and disorder within the rock 'n' roll framework. In the beginning, the earth had been shaken by the deepest Muddy/Wolf/Bo blues, early Elvis, Little Richard. Long after this revolutionary trinity (the fathers, the Sun, and the wholly gross), the Kinks caused tremors with their first two hits. Then came the Who, debuting in January '65 with "I Can't Explain," not a million miles away from the Kinks' "All Day And All Of The Night" and relatively tame until guitar break #2.

U. Youth

Brinksmanship: Who's Moon. (MCA Records)

Suddenly guitars and drums threatened to teeter off the rails, Townshend and Moon restoring equilibrium just in time for a safe return to previously scheduled song structure. A tantalizing glimpse into the abyss.

The portentous opening chords of "Anyway Anyhow Anywhere" signaled a new magnitude of abandon to come. Roger Daltrey raged and strutted while guitars shrieked and shuddered, beeped and divebombed. It was unprecedented, profoundly disturbing, galvanizing; electric instruments weren't supposed to sound like this.

O.V. Wright (Photo: Benna A. Joseph Sr. Courtesy Bill Bentley)

Everything on "My Generation" was infused with the anarchy of "Anyway's" instro excess. The ominous two-chord riff, the pissed-off, pilled-up, incoherent, contemptuous vocal, the old bondage-up-yours message—all were pushed to the brink by bass, guitar, and especially the deranged drums until, sound and fury extinguished just before meltdown looms, it simply stopped. Nothing left to say. Nothing left to do. The subsequent tragedy of the Who.
Magic Bus/Who Sings My Generation (MCA). K.B.

MAURICE WILLIAMS. It could be argued that his definitively cool "Stay" (1960) said everything that rock 'n' roll would ever have to say about desire, in a minute and 37 seconds. On numerous cd anthologies.

O.V. WRIGHT. Texas soul cryer who missed the brass ring when his label deemed him "too ugly to tour." That didn't stop the Stones and Otis Redding from covering his "That's How Strong My Love Is," or a Tokyo bar from naming itself The O.V. Room (on the jukebox: O.V. only). His "Eight Men And Four Women" is the hippest love-on-trial song, and "Nickel And A Nail" ends with O wailing "I can spend the nickel, nail won't spend." So Wright: *O.V. Wright: The Complete Recorded Works by the Boss of Southern Soul* (Japanese MCA box). Starter kit: *That's How Strong My Love Is* (Hi UK).—B.B.

ZZ TOP. On the surface a Coral Waxed Canned Heat for the Eighties. Under the hood, an ultra-funky combo unbeatable at low yo-yo stuff, with an innate sense of the humor inherent in honky blues ("LaGrange," "Little Hippie Pad," "Cheap Sunglasses"). Modern mojo for the masses. Various cds (Warners). T.H.

REET PETITE AND GONE

Louis Jordan Let the Good Times Roll, With Clowning, Pride and "Caldonia"

By Swamp Dogg

Michael Ochs Archives

As though it was yesterday, I remember a seven-year old boy being escorted to the Groove Record Shop on High Street in Portsmouth, Virginia, by one of show business' most provocative and gorgeous shake dancers, Flash Gordon, my make-believe-aunt and family friend. It was 1949 and this trek involved the buying of my very first record, "Run Joe," by the man who had already etched his music indelibly on my mind, Louis Jordan.

From my first recollection while crawling across the floor, I was inundated with Louis Jordan belting out "(Come On Baby And) Knock Me A Kiss," "Five Guys Named Moe," "What's the Use of Get-

ting Sober (When I'll Only Get Drunk Again)," "Stone Cold Dead in the Market" (a duet with Ella Fitzgerald), and, of course, "Caldonia (What Makes Your Big Fuckin' Head So Hard)."

Portsmouth was a great place to live if you were a Louis Jordan fanatic. Louis and his Tympany Five made frequent appearances at the Cotton Club (which was upstairs from Ziv's drugstore and across from the black-owned Safeway Taxi stand on Chestnut St.), Grogan Hall on London St., and just six miles across the Elizabeth River by ferry at the Palace Royal, on Church St. in Norfolk. I was too young to frequent these dancehalls and clubs, but I was blessed with the curse of segregation.

There weren't but two hotels in Portsmouth and Norfolk where blacks could stay, the black-owned Omicron, and Bonnie McEachen's Plaza. Because of this, many acts were room-and-boarded in private homes, of which my aunt's house at 843 Duke St. was one of the favorites. Louis Jordan would stay at the Plaza, but members of his band like Dallas Bartley (bass) and Eddie Roane (trumpet) would be on Duke St., thus occasioning a better-than-fair chance meeting with Mr. "Beware" himself, which I had several times when he came by in what seemed to be a block-long 1941 stretch Chrysler station-wagon to retrieve them for rehearsals and shows. On one such occasion, I met his piano player, Bill "Honky Tonk" Doggett, seven or eight years before he catapulted to stardom playing organ for King Records.

Freakin' with the Deacon

The Cancerian from Brinkley, Arkansas, was a taskmaster. He did not tolerate sloppy attire, lateness, absenteeism, or half-hearted performances . . . ask Johnny Otis. No, he never fired Otis, but the young musician witnessed quite a few bandmates getting chewed out, thrown out or both.

Michael Ochs Archives

When Jordan reached his twelfth birthday, he ran away from home and toured with the Silas Green Review and the Ma & Pa Rainey Rabbit Foot Minstrels. Minstrel shows later became the target of the colored bourgeois, who labeled these performers Uncle Toms, something Jordan took as a personal affront. In his words, "Clowning is an honorable tradition."

Louis modeled his career after Cab Calloway, with the clowning, dancing and use of hip street vernacular. He sang black songs in a proud black manner that broadcast to everyone that he knew who he was and was not ashamed of same. "Ain't Nobody Here But Us Chickens," "Beans And Cornbread," "Fat Sam From Birmingham," "Saturday Night Fish Fry" and "Deacon Jones"—with that lyric: "Who gets all the chicken breast and leaves all the gizzards for the rest/ Deacon Jones, yes yes yes . . . And when a sister's feeling blue, who's always there to woo/ Deacon Jones, oh yeah . . . And before any of the church money is spent, who takes out his usual ten per cent/ You guessed it. . .Deacon Jones"—were some of his greatest ethnic performances, but they transcended race and made him a superstar with whites as well as blacks.

Jordan wasn't shy when it came to getting political with his lyrics. He sang about the futility and tragic ironies of World War II, in songs such as "G.I. Jive," "Ration Blues" (which poked fun at the stampbooks that were issued for food purchases), and "Inflation Blues," in which he appealed to the human side of F.D.R. to cut the price of sugar, make butter available for every American table, and stop the dollar from shrinking. The song contains the classic "I know what you're doing to the country" line "When you started rationing, you really played the game/ But prices are going up and my check remains the same."

Ella's Beaut, Chick's Boot

Louis Jordan impressed and influenced many musicians. One of them was Bill Haley, who said that Jordan's music provided him with the prototype he needed for his C&W group to evolve into an R&B aggregation. Ironically, or quite possibly by design, all of Haley's hits were picked and produced by Milt Gabler, the same man who produced Jordan's hits.

The old saying about being a hard act to follow must have originally applied to Jordan's live stage performances, because just about every great act of his day—from Peggy Lee to Lionel Hampton to the Mills Brothers—refused to close a show if Jordan was the act in front of them.

Not only was he loved for his music, he was loved for himself. Women would not leave him alone, and "no" was not in his vocabulary when it came to them. As a result of jealous and possessive women, he lost one eye early in life and sported a number of razor cuts on his face, bestowed on him by his second wife of three, who became enraged at the sight of lipstick on his lips when he arrived home one night. The story goes that she waited until he got into bed, turned out the light and closed his eyes, then she commenced to locate him in the dark with a swinging straight-edge. Louis felt the breeze of the swing, jumped out of bed bleeding, and ran for his life and a divorce lawyer, in that order.

His irresistible charm is the reason he was fired from Chick Webb's band. Stock documentation has it that Louis joined Webb's outfit in 1936, and left in '38 to form his own group. The truth is that he did join Webb in 1936, who happened to have a strict no-fraternizing rule when it came to band members and his female vocalists, a rule Louis completely ignored. Like most women who met him, Webb's singer Ella Fitzgerald was smitten upon her first encounter. Louis reciprocated the feelings . . . but only when they were traveling. Once they arrived in a town, he took off after the local beauties and ignored Ella. This type of behavior caused problems, and instigated intra-band tiffs on a regular basis. When Webb booted Jordan, he then formed the Louis Jordan Elks Rendezvous Band, the forerunner of the Tympany Five.

My life and music are still based on many things I learned from Louis Jordan. Play a strong song, sing a lyric that's relevant and hits home, then temper it with humor so it'll be palatable, keep 'em dancing, take the chance when the chance comes, and, most of all, believe in yourself. That was Jordan.

At least once a month I pull out a Jordan recording and introduce someone else to the man. Sometimes when I listen I dance. Other times I have a perpetual smile on my face . . . and there are times I cry because he brings back some of the greatest memories of my childhood when the bulk of my family was young, living and loving me. My Aunt Libby holding me in her arms and dancing off "Open The Door, Richard" . . . the weekend parties that looked as though the U.S.S. Missouri had docked in our living room. The sailors, my father Chief Petty Officer Jerry Williams included, the women, the food, the liquor, the gambling, the dancing and laughing as Jordan sang the very political "Reconversion Blues," "Let The Good Times Roll," and "If You're So Smart How Come You

Ain't Rich?" He was part of my family, the invisible guardian who sat with me sometimes when I was alone, filling the room with his voice that boomed out of our big Motorola combination radio-record player. The compartment at the bottom held all of his Decca black and blue-label 78's, which I used to pull out and stare at and imagine myself inside the record performing with him. I can still smell the shellac on those heavy monster discs . . . that's what Jordan did, has done, and still does for me.

What we see on MTV was pioneered by Jordan. The first music video was produced in the Forties by Jordan with his manager Berl Adams, to introduce his recording of "Caldonia." They convinced BMI to underwrite this venture, based on the pair's being able to contract theaters across the country to show the musical short between features. They called these little films "soundies" and they became a great promotional tool for Louis and later a multitude of artists. Jordan's "soundies" included "Fuzzy Wuzzy," "Old Man Mose," "Down Down Down" and "Five Guys Named Moe"—the inspiration for the long-running London musical of the same name. (Ten of these shorts are collected on *Louis Jordan And The Tympany Five*, BMG Video 1992.)

Although Jordan appeared in musical cameos in over 20 films, including *Miss Bobby Sox* and *Follow The Boys*, he had a full-length motion-picture starring career—in *Reet Petite And Gone*, *Look Out, Sister*, *Beware* and *Caldonia*. Unfortunately, these classics aren't all available, but there are people trying to secure the prints and rights to eventually make them available. I happen to have seen them, and I would love to have them run on every VCR in the world. Until you see them, please take my word: they're great!

Louis Jordan succumbed to a heart attack at the age of 66 in 1975, ending the illustrious career of the world's greatest performer, musician, songwriter, father of video recording, movie star, and my hero.

Sounds All Reet: *Louis Jordan: Five Guys Named Moe—Original Decca Recordings, Vols. 1 & 2* (MCA); *One Guy Named Louis* (Blue Note/Capitol).

Six guys named Slick: Jordan and orchestra.

ORGAN GRINDER SWING

by Tom Vickers

In the Sixties, the Beatles, Velvets, Dyl and other rockers were stuffing pop's new bag by wording up: defining cool with all sorts of lyrical landmarks. Across town, on the jazz side of the tracks, it was another story. There, the Hammond B3 organ (and its amplified antecedent the Leslie speaker) was staking out a whole new groovespace, one soulful and intimate enough to accommodate but three players: the organ trio (gtr/org/drms).

Let's go back to a time when the Moog, the Arp, and the DX7 didn't exist. The technological ad-

Key Cat: Jimmy Smith (Courtesy Blue Note Records)

vance that the Hammond Organ Company out on West Diversey Avenue in Chicago came up with was awesome for its time: a self-contained keyboard instrument that put the power of a full-sized big band in the hands of one musician. Add the whirling Leslie speaker (kind of like what the wah-wah pedal did for the guitar only infinitely hipper), and you had a king-sized sound at your fingertips.

Sure, there were respected keyboardists who had worked with organ sounds. Fats Waller utilized a Wurlitzer for some Twenties and Thirties sides, as did Count Basie. But up until the late Forties, the organ was relegated to the squarest cribs of the L7 world: churches and roller rinks.

As the big bands faded after the Big Deuce, piano players switched over to the then-burgeoning Hammond sphere. The drag was that most of them approached the instrument as a mere piano extension, and that early Hamms didn't have the range of sound that came about when the first B3's hit the production line.

Things changed fast. Suddenly, guys like Wild Bill Davis and Milt Buckner were cutting sides that not only swung but had this big fat funky sound that pulled both listeners and musicians into the B3 swirl. And, in the most 'down' jazz clubs and lounges, customers were crawlin' en masse, martinis in hand, to hear such cats as Brother Jack McDuff, Richard "Groove" Holmes, Jimmy Smith, and other practitioners of this (now) lost art, wailing like few have wailed before or since.

Mr. Smith Goes To Town

The most famous of the early grinders was Philadelphia's Bill Doggett, who recorded instrumentals for King Records in the early Fifties. Lesser known but equally cool: Hank Marr, another King find. Dave "Baby" Cortez opened it up on the rock 'n' roll front with "The Happy Organ" (1959), and then came Jimmy McGriff, and then the bossest organ swinger yet, Jimmy Smith.

Smith had done some Fifties sides for Blue Note ("The Sermon" is probably the best known), but he really hit his stride in the early Sixties with his Verve records. On "Hobo Flats," "The Cat," and "Walk On The Wild Side," he truly cool-fused jazz and blues. ("Walk" was one of several Smith collabs with arranger Oliver Nelson; almost as killer is the team's "Slaughter On Tenth Avenue," available on Verve's budget disk *Compact Jazz: Jimmy Smith*.) While the other Jimmy (McGriff, ex-cop and Big Maybelle bassist who hit with a version of Ray Charles' "I've Got A Woman" in '62) was more soulful and churchy, Smith took jazz and blues,

(and its flip "Cool Turkey"). 1961: Ray Charles' bacon-fat noodling on "One Mint Julep." '62: Booker T & the MGs' "Green Onions," and Joey Dee & the Starliters' "Peppermint Twist" (with future Rascal Felix Cavaliere on B3). '66-'67: Stevie Winwood, just 16, hammered Hammond and vocals on the Spencer Davis Group hits "Gimme Some Lovin'" and "I'm A Man." The Godfather himself even got in on the act; James Brown cut several organ instrumentals for King, and often solo'ed on organ when he wanted to get off the good foot during live shows.

The Hammond even became a staple for hippie bands in the late Sixties—the best work including Gregg Allman's dixie-rock, Mark Naftalin's jazzy outings with the Butterfield Blues Band ("Thank You Mr. Poobah"), and the speedy psyching of Linn County's Stephen Miller (their 1968 Mercury album *Proud Flesh Soothseer*). That taffy-thick B3 sound was great for ballroom lightshows or shadowy jazz dives, and for a brief moment in time, whether your drug of choice was Swiss-bred psychotropic or domestic gin-and-vermouth (stirred, not shaken), the warm rush of the Hamm 3 rocked the world.

Tough 'Duff:
Brother Jack

Smith off duty (Courtesy MGM/Verve Records)

put a pop thang on it, and rocked righteously on his rendition of Muddy Waters' "I've Got My Mojo Workin.'"

Southpaw Soul & "Misty" Grease

Behind Smith came a flood of former piano jazzbos who thought that getting organized would be a snap. Wrong. The B3 required not only a strong left hand, but killer coordination on those foot pedals to really get the bass groove percolating. Most pianists couldn't cut it, but those who could became legends on the jazz club/lounge circuit. The simmering "gutbucket" style of Brother Jack McDuff achieved the greasiest of Hammond sounds while the jazzier Shirley Scott (for a while Mrs. Stanley Turrentine) made some boss organ/tenor noise with Eddie "Lockjaw" Davis. Richard "Groove" Holmes, bass pedals to the floor, combined McDuff's grit with Jimmy Smith's pop leanings, and flipped Erroll Garner's "Misty" (1966) into B3 godhead.

None of this was being lost on rock 'n' roll hipsters. After Cortez's "Happy" discovery, the Sixties enjoyed a bumper crop of organic material. 1960: James Booker's air-conditioned "Gonzo"

Unfortunately, the moment came and went. As technology moved forward into the world of synthesizers (*Switched-On Bach*, anyone?), the juicy sound of the B3 was replaced by cold slabs of Arps and Moogs. Today, the organ grinders' swing is a tragically underpracticed art. Most young keyboard cats are more adept at pushing computer buttons than working the pedals, but there are still a few 'kids' coming on. On a neighborhood level, there's Lady Margaret, working her B3 weekly at Esther's Orbit Lounge in East Oakland. And Philly's Joey De Francesco has put out some boss jams on (four) Columbia cd's, though none as wild-sided as those hip purrs that J. Smith could coax out of his B3. But Smith and McGriff are still recording, and gigging live, and that's a groove.

Philly's De Francesco

To transport you instantly into that latenight, forever hip world of organ jazz, here's a guide to some prime grinders:

Jimmy Smith : *Compact Jazz: Jimmy Smith, The Cat*, and *I've Got My Mojo Workin'* (all Verve); *The Sermon* and *House Party* (Blue Note).

Richard "Groove" Holmes: *Soul Message* (Prestige, feat. "Misty"), and *Groovin' With Jug* (Capitol/Pacific Jazz).

Don Patterson *Hip Cake Walk* (Prestige)

. . . And virtually any recording by Bill Doggett, Shirley Scott, Hank Marr, and Brother Jack McDuff. Prestige reissues: *Tough 'Duff, Brother Jack Meets the Boss* (McDuff and Gene Ammons), *Blue Flames: Shirley Scott and Stanley Turrentine*. Recent decent: Jimmy McGriff's *Countdown*, and *Soul Survivors* (w/ Hank Crawford; both Milestone).

BOBBY BLAND

Squallin' with the Boss of the Blues

by Bob Merlis

Here's the Man! None other than Mr. Bobby "Blue" Bland, the reignin,' squallin' "king of all blues singers." It's not specifically known who conferred the title on him, but here in this ghettodelic New Orleans joint *way* off the tour bus path, the former Robert Calvin Brooks has no challengers. Midway through tonight's after-hours set, the downhome sovereign is approached by a lithe young female admirer so engaged by the smoldering soundstorm pouring from the legendary larynx that she jumps onstage to gyrate before him as he wails "I'll Take Care Of You." Next, in an apparent act of supplication, she becomes intimate with the regent's pant leg. Bobby Bland can, quite literally, move an audience.

Years earlier, during one of his famed Christmas Eve gigs at Houston's Civic Auditorium (where his Duke Records labelmate Johnny Ace lost that last round of Russian roulette), another facet of Bland's crown shines forth. At the prelude to prayer passage in "St. James Infirmary" (sung "St. Jameses'"), Mr. Triple B goes full Method, dropping dramatically to his knees, then pausing to *check himself*—the trouser crease sharp enough to cut timber, his haberdashery so immaculately turned out—he stops mid-crouch, the orchestra vamping on, then carefully unfolds his breast-

pocket handkerchief (cravat-coordinated, of course), and drops the silk square to the stage floor—to assure a hygenic landing place for the royal kneecaps when the much anticipated moment of funky pathos finally arrives. Style, or what?

No-Juice Adonis

Though hardly handsome by conventional standards, Bobby, with his majestic "conk" hairstyle, manicured digits and casually confident microphone caress, has been, almost from the start, a romantic figure who, as the New Orleans scenario proves, gets over with the gals. The phenomenon is illustrated on the cover of his classic *Call On Me* album, which depicts a bevy of Blandished beauts accessing Bobby on their rotary phones. The die for the smoldering stud character played to varying effect by Teddy Pendergrass, Barry "Beluga" White, Al Green, and even caucasoid crooners like Robert Palmer and Michael Bolton, was, for all intents and purposes, cast by Bobby "Blue" Bland decades before many of these pretenders experienced their first schoolboy crush. His facial features may be on the coarse side, his physique distinctly non-Adonis, and his approach low key, but the Blue One's got It, and the big girls understand.

Maybe, too, he's king because he's so far removed from the stereotypical blues singer: a wizened geezer with a beat-up guitar, porkpie hat, a juice jones and a repertoire rerunning that durable *dum de dum de dum de dum dum dum dum* pilot first screened eons ago in that cottonfield south of Clarksdale. Bland broke the mold and cast himself as a sophisticate, thus infusing the rural-route genre with the kind of upscale, urban class more often associated with Tony Bennett or Billy Eckstine than Lightnin' Hopkins.

In by Ten, Out by Four

If he were just so much style without the content, Bobby'd be a mere poseur with a heavy dry-cleaning habit, but the truth is: musically he's sayin' more than a little taste. The secret of his success: "the Squall"—his uncanny ability to wring transcendent testifying from a unique epiglottal gargle. Many have imitated the Squall and some have come close (Little Milton; BBB impersonator Geator Davis), but most walk away from the attempt with sore throats and empty clubs. The fact that the Squall even has a name (like guitarists tagging their axes "Lucille") underscores its independent nature. Hearing the Squall isolated from a song, one could be excused for thinking its origin not human. Scary stuff . . . what you'd call "big mojo" if you didn't know any better. (And we haven't even brought up the Squall's mutation into porcine root-riffing on the chorus of "Sunday Morning Love".)

Obviously, there's more to Bland's art than phenomenal phlegm juggling. His blues include echoes of T-bone Walker's jazz-tinged approach, especially on cuts featuring the guitar of the great Wayne Bennett. The omnipresent, fiercely arranged brass accompaniment also set him off from his Chicago-based contemporaries, who tended to limit themselves to harmonica or a single sax. Credit here goes to longtime Bland bandman/ orchestrator Joe Scott. Dig the buildup and spooky drama of his "Blind Man" arrangement, those contrapuntal horn fills that set off the fiery "That Did It" and the smoldering "I Pity The Fool." In the presence of greatness, everybody's inspired.

Though gospel (through Brother Ray, the Isleys, etc.) is credited with laying the structural groundwork for Sixties soul, Bobby Bland's boss blues furnished much of the emotional underpinning. In the pre-Soul period of 1961-63, half a dozen of them became Top 50 pop hits, a crossover fantasy few other Delta cats dared dream. Today, while most bluesmen who haven't been relegated to obscurity altogether work predominantly white crowds, Bland holds his black demogs. The appeal of a disheveled wretch wailing about how his baby left him is simply no match for the eternally suave lothario Squallin' out "Turn On Your Love Light," "Don't Cry No More" and the cosmic inevitability of "Ain't Nothin' You Can Do." And there ain't. You either get Bobby "Blue" Bland or you don't. Take it from The Man himself. In his live shows, after an effusive intro delineating his many accomplishments, delivered in rapid-fire Federal Expressive succession by the emcee, he takes the stage, brings the band down, and confides to the anxious audience, "It's time to get down to cases . . ."

Bobby Bland drives several hundred miles a year bringing his blues to a club, concert hall, hotel ballroom or chicken shack near you. See him. Till then, try these:

The Best of Bobby "Blue" Bland (MCA). Essential: the cream of the early Duke years, including "Cry Cry Cry," "Love Light," "If You Could Read My Mind," "Farther On Up The Road," "Ain't Nothin' You Can Do."

The Best, Vol. II (MCA). More Duke: "Blind Man," "Two Steps from the Blues," "36-22-36."

The 3B Blues Boy: The Blues Years (1952-1959) (Ace UK import). This 25-track cd chronicles his early heavy blues sides, some only recently unearthed.

His California Album (MCA). Originally on ABC, the post-Duke era's most consistent set; tasty production and gobs of (understated) Squallin' Soul.

ALEX JONES

Lou's right. It's time to cool it down, slow the pace and restore some decorum to this chapter. And who better to tackle the task than Crypt Records prexy & CEO Tim Warren? Here're his tastefully appointed

GRUNGIEST GARAGE~ROCK GASSERS

1. The Keggs "To Find Out" / "Girl" (Orbit).
   Outa tune Detroit caterwaul, and a lot cooler than *any* Stooges discs cuz 1) they didn't play pals with Bowie, and 2) they made one great record & quit! A band so hated in Detroit, they had to change their name after every show they played! The guitarist met with an evil demise: on his way to practice on his motor-bike, he got hit by a truck and knocked into a metal rail which lopped his head off 'n' ended the Keggs' wicked career. Only 75 copies pressed, so forget about scoring one. Hear both sides on *Back From The Grave*, Vols. 5 and 6.

2. The Rats "Rats' Revenge, Parts 1 and 2" (Black Cat).
   Preceding rap by a good 15 years was this wiseacre chunk of hilarity from Akron, consisting of *inept* guit-bass-drums riff topped w/ high braggadocio about how you shouldn't f**k with the fabled "leader of the Rats." Inspired by Harv Lembeck's immortal charac-

terization of Eric Von Zipper in AIP's dorky beach pix. Teasing a truly lame guitar "solo" is the God-like intro "This time don't use yer feet!"

3. The Beachnuts "My Iconoclastic Life" (Show-case).
   For sheer lyrical genius, try this: "My life is nil, I just take pills/ And sit for hours, watching the flowers." And this ain't no mindbending "hip-pie" psuckadelia; the guy's lost his mind cuz his fave gal done left him, so he's screamin' his lungs out!

Upper Division Grunge: For further study, Mr. Warren recommends the Dirty Wurdz' "Why," the Groupies' "Primitive," the One Way Streets' "Jack The Ripper," and the Aztex' "I Said Move," some of which are currently available on lp compilations.

Kicks magazine covers garage-punk (and surf, rockabilly and even more disreputable genres) like an oil slick on a slab floor. Write P.O. Box 646, Cooper Station, New York City 10003.

48

BEYOND REBEL ROUSER

Mood Swingin' at the Outer Edges of Instro Cool

by Dick Blackburn

Later for Worldbeat. Many of the world's most exotic (and clandestine) aural kicks are right here in our own backyard. Namely, mood instrumentals. "Smooth Grooves," and their sometimes noisier twin "Exotica Neuroticas," often ride a wilder range of interior landscapes than their more rockin' cousins. If you dig 'em, that's what you gotta do: dig 'em. These records aren't just lying around on the surface. The bad news: they're mostly available only on originals. The good news: they're cheap.

To get grounded, let's check some of the major riffs laid down by mood music's founding dads. The categories and the cats . . . Sentimental Kitsch: Percy Faith's blissful "Theme from *A Summer Place*," 1960; Acker Bilk's gull-strewn "Stranger on the Shore," '62) . . . Ethereal Romance: Santo & Johnny's "Sleep Walk," 1959 . . . Spooky Menace: Link Wray's "Rumble" ('58) and the Viscounts' "Harlem Nocturne" ('59) . . . Jungle Paradise: Martin Denny's "Quiet Village" ('59) . . . Western Adventure: Jorgen Ingmann's "Apache," '60) . . . and Outer Space: the Tornadoes' "Telstar" (1962). These sides, and more in such sub-mood genres as Bogue Oriental, Faux Latin, and Middle Eastern—done in various pop and R&R styles, provided soundtracks for most folks' imaginary mini-movies in the days before MTV. The ultimate audio-cinematic classic has got to be the Lost Ones' obscure "Trouble in the Streets" (Valiant), where sound effects are used to produce a condensed juvenile delinquent exploito-flick.

Where the origins of Smooth Groove are pretty obvious (lots of saxy jazz/R&B ballads, blues and honky gee-tar laments), Exotica Neurotica's beginnings are more diverse. In the Fifties, Fantasy Records' Korla Pandit, resplendent in jeweled turban, conjuring up the Mysterious East on his mighty Wurlitzer . . . Mexican mambo king Prez Prado's wiggier RCA outings ("Marilyn Mon-

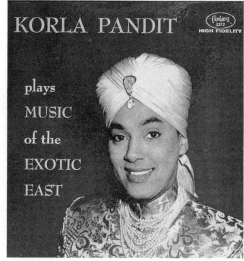

Turban-charged Exotica Neurotica

roe Mambo") . . . Anton Karas' sinister zither on "The Third Man Theme," and the first tinny African hit "Skokiaan" by Rhodesia's Bulwayo Sweet Rhythm Band (both on London).

Sonic Wallpaper for Bachelor Pads

Mood-musicologist Byron Werner has lately identified the Fifties Smooth Groove subgenre Space Age Bachelor Pad Music. Per Werner, this stuff existed largely for lonely guys out to impress women with their big stereo rigs. Lots of ping-ponging between speakers, oddball percussion, drippy Theremin, etc. The works of SABPM's main man, Jean Esquivel (on RCA), were often album best-sellers (*Other Worlds, Other Sounds, Infinity in Sounds, Vol.s 1 and 2*). Like pianists Ferrante & Teicher (their London lp *Soundproof*), Bernie Green (*Futura* RCA lp), and other craft-masters, Esky went for technical wizardry over soulfulness—not unlike, come to think of it, most of the best-selling rock acts of the Seventies and Eighties.

Ear-grabbing effects really are the soul of Space Age Bach Pad action, though—bent strings on Ricki Starr's "Shooting Star" (RCA), Fender Guitar Slim's tension-heavy intro to "Atomic Blues" (Enrica), the Volcanos' bass-distorted mauling of "Stardust" on Epic.

When SABPM melted into Atmospheric Rock (late Fifties-early Sixties), weird swipes and hybrids abounded. Glen Gray's "Surfer's Mood" (Dot) is

The Big "E" invited lonely guys to stand and show their rigs.

ESQUIVEL AND HIS ORCHESTRA Infinity IN SOUND VOLUME 2

LSP-2296

Produced by NEELY PLUMB

Recorded at RCA Victor's Music Center of the World, Hollywood, California.

Recording Engineer: JOHN NORMAN

SIDE 1

Jalousie *(Jealousy)* ASCAP 1:31
Time on My Hands ASCAP 2:25
Bye Bye Blues ASCAP 2:11
Baia BMI 2:46
Who's Sorry Now? ASCAP 2:36
Anna *(El Negro Zumbon)* BMI 2:44

SIDE 2

España Cañi BMI 2:57
Sentimental Journey ASCAP 2:38
Cherokee ASCAP 2:08
Lullaby of Birdland BMI 2:36
La Bamba BMI 2:08
Limehouse Blues ASCAP 2:16

Other RCA Victor albums by Esquivel you will enjoy:

Exploring New Sounds LPM-LSP-1978
Four Corners of the World LSP-1749
Infinity in Sound LPM/LSP-2225
Other Worlds, Other Sounds LPM/LSP-1753
Strings Aflame LPM/LSP-1988

© by Radio Corporation of America, 1961

TMK(S) ® Radio Corporation of America • Marca(s) Registrada(s)

Once again, Esquivel pushes and extends the outer limits of recorded sound. With imagination and daring, he fashions musical arrangements of vast depth and scope. His impeccable taste combines exciting rhythms, seldom-heard instruments and inventive harmonics in a kaleidoscopic variety of colors.

Although his humor and boldness create an illusion of carefree abandon, no arranger ever wrote with more meticulous and loving care than Esquivel. Each musical effect and passage is carefully designed to make full and creative use of high fidelity and stereophonic equipment, both from the standpoint of recording and sound reproduction. Every arrangement is thoughtfully prepared to evoke the maximum emotional response and excitement.

This album is the continuation of a musical experience which was begun with the first volume of INFINITY IN SOUND (LPM/LSP-2225). As in that collection, Esquivel here acts as guide through further adventure into the limitless universe of fine music. No trip could be more satisfying.

BILL OLOFSON

MIRACLE - SURFACE
This record contains the revolutionary new antistatic ingredient 317X which helps keep the record dust free, helps prevent surface static, helps insure faithful sound reproduction.

IMPORTANT NOTICE
This is a TRUE STEREOPHONIC RECORD specifically designed to be played only on phonographs equipped for stereophonic reproduction.

---

basically a salt-water "Rumble," and the Holidays' brooding "Dark Valley" (Santo) is Wray all the way. Harold & Bob's "Jungle Beat" (Delta) is only one of many hip re-groovings of M. Denny, while Cal & Ivan's "Lazy, Parts 1 & 2" (Skoop) pads softly down the hall after Santo & Johnny.

Most Outer Spacial mood music orbits around "Telstar." Bob and Jerry's "Ghost Satellite" (Rendezvous) and the Thunderbolts' "Lost Planet" (Dot) take it straight. The Valiants and the Invictas add more liquid—the former's "Moon-flight" (Amcan) and the latter's "Breakout/Missing" (20th Century) sound like surf music being played inside space capsules. Meanwhile, back on Earth, Middle Eastern mood-stuff is the sand-pitted version of something that first stalked out of the Pacific. Dick Dale's ripping "Misirlou" was such a monster, the surf bands went overboard on the exotic, yielding gone gassers like Dave and the Customs' "Ali Baba," or Sandy Nelson's one good record, "Casbah." (Thanks to the revival of interest in surf music, these sides are now easier to find on compilations.)

SABPM from F&T.

51

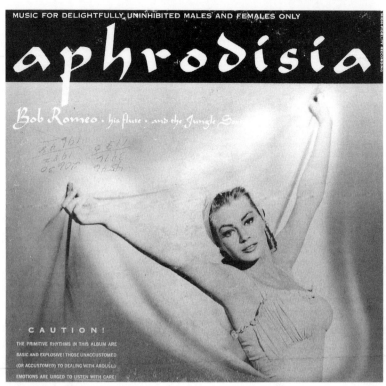

MUSIC FOR DELIGHTFULLY UNINHIBITED MALES AND FEMALES ONLY

aphrodisia

Bob Romeo · his flute · and the Jungle Band

CAUTION!

THE PRIMITIVE RHYTHMS IN THIS ALBUM ARE
BASIC AND EXPLOSIVE! THOSE UNACCUSTOMED
(OR ACCUSTOMED) TO DEALING WITH AROUSED
EMOTIONS ARE URGED TO LISTEN WITH CARE!

What "Quiet Village" wrought...

Searchin' For Squareness

All this mood swinging begs an obvious question: is it the passage of time alone that makes square cool? Not really. To dig a thing's weird (unintentional/eccentric) squareness can be cool, but the thing itself remains a cube. And so with Smooth Groove and Exotica Neurotica. Often the trick is to come up to a hair's breadth away from squareness in cool appreciation. F'rinstance, although Nels Riddle mined the same TV/movie theme landfill as Hank Mancini, "Lolita Ya Ya" and "The *Route 66* Theme" are definitely cool, while "Baby Elephant Walk" and "The Pink Panther" are debatable (no argument, though, on Hank's "Peter Gunn"). Larry Welk is not. In fact, Welk, bless him, seems to exist not just as a goofing stock for L. Bruce, but as an enduring symbol of middle-of-the-road square-ness, the L7 yardstick.

Like the (very) early days of Seventies punk, instro cool is one of the few genres where you can choose by title alone and be reasonably assured of getting your buck's bangsworth. It won't cost much, and who could pass up stuff like "Cool Martini" by the Blue Jeans (Souvenir), Jan Davis' "Snow Surfing Matador" (Smash), or "Theme from

The Fuzzy Ones" by the Mysterians (Jorel)? It would take a *real* square to comb a dusty thriftshop bin and not spring for "Saturday Night at the Duckpond" (the Cougars, on Parlophone) or the truly boss "Wolf Call" by Lord Dent & the Invaders (Shelley).

These days, the mood instro remains almost as closet-bound as it did 30 years ago. Ennio Morricone and Nino Rota get their ink and tribute albums. The late, lamented Raybeats did some cool things, and Michael Rother's decadent Euro-trash wallpaper deserves mention, as does Joel Zorn's *film noir*-ish *Spillane* (Elektra/Nonesuch) and some of the cuts on Denny Freeman's *Out of the Blue* (Amazing).

MOOD SHOP: Some of the sleazier Exoticas can be found on the *Vegas Grind* compilations (three volumes, on Strip Records), and on *At The Party* (Candy), while King Records' recent comp *After Hours* features good, smoky R&B Smooth Grooves. Ink-wise, the intermittently published newsletter *Audio Carpaetorium* keeps tabs on some of the deeper mood digs. Write Jerry Nutter, 111-32 112th St., South Ozone Park, N.Y. 11420-1026.

SHOP AROUND

Lots of the preceding soundstuff is easily obtainable, but some isn't. To help you connect with some of the less accessible, and to hip you to wider inventories of similar music (much of it available by mail order), we direct your attention to the following sources.

For more info on acapella and doowop in general, write Ronnie "I" at the non-profit United in Group Harmony Association, P.O. Box 185, Clifton, N.J. 07011. Phone: 201-470-UGHA. His Clifton Records is a solid source of new and vintage vocal-group sounds (the *Starlight Serenade* series features fresh-minted acapella in superb cd sound).

Frontier Records' mail catalog gets deep into California (and other forms of classic) punk rock. P.O. Box 22, Sun Valley, CA 91353-0022.

Big Jay McNeely's sax sounds are available from Big J Records, 6520 Selma Ave., No.442, Hollywood, CA 90028.

To learn more about Trip Shakespeare, write Shakespearicon, P.O. Box 8656, Minneapolis, MN 55408.

The Untamed Youth hang with good company; their Norton Records labelmates include the best (classic and current) practitioners of surf, garage and grunge-rock. For a catalog: P.O. Box 646, Cooper Station, New York City 10003. Phone: 718 789-4438. Fax: 718 398-9215.

The following general catalogs are a gaseous twin-spin: indispensable guides to the type of coolsounds covered here, and groovy reads in and of themselves. . .

Ace Records Ltd.:48-50 Steele Road, London NW 10 7AS.
    U.K. fax no. (081) 961-8725.

Demon Records Ltd., Canal House, Stars Estate, Transport Ave., Brentford, Middlesex, TW8 9HF, England. U.K. fax no. (081) 568-8223.

Roots & Rhythm, 6921 Stockton Ave., El Cerrito, CA 94530. Phone: 510 525-1494. Fax: 510 525-2904.

Fantasy Records (including Prestige, Riverside, Milestone, and other jazz and blues labels), 10th and Parker Sts., Berkeley, CA 94710.

Midnight Records, P.O. Box 390, Old Chelsea Station, New York City 10011. Phone: 212 675-2768. Fax: 212 741-7230.

Rhino Records, 2225 Colorado Ave., Santa Monica, CA 90404-3555.

Roundup Records, P.O. Box 154, No. Cambridge, MA 02140. Phone: 800 44-DISCS.

Sundazed Music, P.O. Box 85, Coxsackie, N.Y. Phone: 518 731-6262. Fax: 518 731-9492.

Ink:The See Hear mail-order catalog offers a wide variety of books about music. 59 East 7th St., New York, N.Y. 10003. Voice/fax: 212 982-6968.

Associate Editor Dick Blackburn sells rare 7-inch wax. For his list, write 1218 N. LaCienega Blvd., West Hollywood, CA 90069.

Courtesy Louis Nye.

Ten All-time
Wig-Flippin' Discs

WiG RECORDS

103 A
Far-Out
Pub. Corp.
BMI
Time 1:54

TEENAGE BEATNIK
(Pintoff, Stone & Kelly)
LOUIS NYE

THE HAYWIRE HALL OF FAME

by Dick Blackburn

1. "HELLO LUCILLE. ARE YOU A LESBIAN?" by T. Valentine (Val). A *magnum opus* probably inspired by the world's worst date. Mightily frustrated, T. unloads in nonlinear fashion and goes for Big Questions: e.g., "They say her hair ain't no longer than his. Why do he take her out?" Available on *The Big Itch 3* compilation (Mr. Manicotti).

2. "SCREAM" by Ralph Nielsen & the Chancellors (Surf). The title does not lie. This primal New Jersey hurricane came yowling down the turnpike to land on *Back From The Grave Vol. 2* as well as a 45 reissue (both on Crypt). In the same banshee bag: the Gentrys' "Wild" (same series, Vol. 7).

3. "THE GIRL CAN'T DANCE" by Bunker Hill (Mala). Ultimate napalm-lunged black screamer

backed by the "Rumble" Man. A low-fit temper tantrum in an orange juice can. On *Link Wray: Vol. 3* (Norton).

4. "TEENAGE BEATNIK" by Louis Nye (Wig). Sounding like a crazed fruit—but not a teenager or a beatnik—screwy Louie rings more changes on the chorus line "I don't dig squares, man, they're really a drag" than Bird did on "How High the Moon." Lou also likes to "cha cha in bermuda shorts." Produced by Steve Lawrence. Further study: "Hi Ho Steve-O" (Coral).

5. "BABY" by Marty Roberts (Arc). This minimalist masterpiece has a one-word lyric. "Baby," a sort of rockabilly mantra, is endlessly hiccupped, stuttered, crooned or caressed. Like, uh, redneck zen. Honorable mention: "Oh Baby!" by Harvey & Doc (Annette), a wacky piece of Spectoriana that doubles the voices and word count.

54

6. "SHE SAID" by Hasil Adkins (Judy). West Virginia ridge runner gets hitched during a booze spree, then faces his mate in the cold light of day. Incomprehensible lyrics and fractured vocalizing ensue, giving dark hints as to his beloved's ancestry. Scary, by gum. On Haze's *Out To Hunch* set (Norton).

7. "NINA-KOCKA-NINA" by the Dinks (Sully). Okie garage band gets into a ceaseless Nipponese (?) rant interspersed with anti-high school diatribe. On the follow-up (!) "Kocka-Mow-Mow," group commits mass careericide by ranking out deejays who refused to play their first side. "N-K-N" is on both the *Madness Invasion 1* comp (GMG) and *The Big Itch 2* (Mr. Manicotti), "K-M-M" on *Big Itch 3*.

8. "ROCKIN' OUT THE BLUES" by the Musical Linn Twins (Blue Feather). Frothy, near-epileptic Elvis impersonation. Singer's overwhelming emotional involvement allows only a few gasped phrases to be heard. On *That Good Ol' R & R Sound* (White Label).

9. "WOMBAT TWIST" by Glenn & Christy (Sonic). Somewhat irrational saga of yokel pursuing Greenwich Village chick. She buys it under the wheels of a bus, inspiring admirer to follow suit so they can twist together in Beatnik Heaven. Presence of wombat not fully explained. See *Big Itch 3*.

10. "HIPPIE IN A BLUNDER" by Johnny Buckett. Forget Muskogee's Okie. This is the ultimate shitkicker diatribe against the Love Gen. Buckett's flower-kid target "looked like a hog in a fattening pen" and "took LSD and benzedrine too/ Smoked marijuana and sniffed a little glue." Disc unravels completely by the end: "Shave and a haircut, two bits/ Hippie in a rat hole, tight fit!" On the Torture comp *Bent, Batty & Obnoxious*.

SCREEN

R. Altergott

The following motion pictures have been rated T.C., and may contain elements of subzero stylishness which have been been determined to cause cool spells in laboratory animals.

Frosted Flicks

ABSOLUTE BEGINNERS (1986; HBO/Cannon Video). Fast, if flawed, musical on the (late Fifties) coming-of-age of Brit teen culture, with visual-din art direction straight out of early *Mad*. Bop saint Slim Gaillard revs a wild party with "I'm Selling Out." D. Bowie, as ad-man Vendice Partners, resembles Edd Byrnes' evil twin and does a mean Gene Kelly on giant typewriter keys. Sounds: EMI's original soundtrack (Gil Evans, Sade's "Killer Blow"). Ink link: Colin MacInnes' original novel (1959, available as Penguin paperback).

BABY DOLL (1956; Warner Home Video). Down in the Delta, frustrated Karl Malden (hot 'n' sweaty) and vengeful Eli Wallich (cool 'n' greasy) both put the moves on airhead Carroll Baker (blonde 'n' sexy). Penned by Tenn. Wms, directed by Elia Kazan. Amazing soundtrack by Kenyon Hopkins with New Orleans great Smiley Lewis rockin' out on "Shame, Shame, Shame." Addled value: Mildred Dunnock as bird-brained Aunt Rose Comfort. D.B.

THE BEATLES: THE FIRST U.S. VISIT (1991; MPI Home Video). Armed with only a dorky stage presence and a kit bag full of simpy tunes, the loveable moptops came to conquer the colonies and the Maysles bros. get it all down on film. In the process, they leave behind a riveting Beatles documentary and, more importantly, a chronicle of cultural extinction circa 1964.

The New Wave is represented by a treacly Paul McCartney incessantly and narcissistically mugging for the camera, a model of premeditated spontaneity. The Old Guard is personified by New Yawk disc jockey Murray the K, the legendary sweater smoothie and patron saint of indigenous American cool. At stake is Greaseball Culture U.S.A. and its rock 'n' roll Maginot Line—a chain link fence festooned with pinkie rings and ID bracelets, defended by a million pompadoured wiseguys who'd sooner wear women's clothing than comb their hair into bangs.

In the end, Beatlemania proves to be more virulent than botulism in a half-opened tin of tuna. Even Mr. K turns fifth columnist and Fifth Beatle, spreading the word to the unconverted from his powerful podium at WINS 1010. But before the fall we get a cherished last look at America unsullied by the British invasion...

There's Murray himself in the studio, immaculate in a pair of H.I.S. creaseless and an oversized Russian fur hat. There's the Peppermint Lounge crammed to the limit with continental hipsters and transistor sisters all razor-cut and Fabu-lashed, moving

Absolute Beginners: David Bowie places £200 bid on rare Tin Machine acetate.

and grooving to the Push and Shake. And over by the bandstand with the Fab Four, there's Murray again, toupee askew, hully gullying with a bevy of capri-clad Ronettes clones as the band blasts "Money."

The Beatles and the new music explosion of the Sixties irrevocably changed American rock 'n' roll subculture, ushering in notions of high art, big ideas, sophistication and sensitivity that were previously confined to folk, jazz and classical scenes. If you'd like to take a look at the cuddly Liverpudlians who set it all in motion, scope out *The Beatles: The First U.S. Visit* and return to the very beginning of the end. R.S.

Baby Doll drew a "Condemned" rating for its frank treatment of phonephobia. (Editors' Archives)

Bedlam's bad Boris K: "Milady, you are *inthane!*"
(Hollywood Book & Poster)

BEDLAM (1946; Fox Hills Video, Image Video). Producer Val Lewton's best. Sinister Boris Karloff runs the madhouse & supplies loonies for a lord's party. Inmates portray various qualities. Due to *Goldfinger* type gilding, "Reason" expires in a jelly. D.B.

A "maaan" and a woman: Forrest Whittaker and Diane Venora in *Bird*.

THE BIG PICTURE (1989; RCA/Columbia Home Video). Small, supersharp satire on the movie biz from some of the same folks who gave you *Spinal Tap*. When his student flick cops the film school prize, Kevin Bacon rises high, falls hard. Heights: the head of a cheapo studio suggests Kev revise his script into a buddy pic about a Civil War president and a baseball legend, and we actually see a clip from *Abe And The Babe*; Martin Short as Bac's superfey agent, J.T. Walsh as the delectably smarmy film exec who greenlights his film.

BIRD (1988; Warner Home Video). As Charlie Parker's long-suffering wife Chan, Diane Venora is a pixie-cut dream Beat Girl. Hers is the coolest pronunciation of the word "man" in a major motion picture. "I don't want to make anybody peaceful, maaan."

THE CHASE (1946). Fractured *film noir* based on Cornell Woolrich's typically paranoiac Forties novel *The Black Path of Fear*. An abstracted, comic-book nightmare. Rich hood Steve Cochran gets his kicks beating up his manicurist and racing trains—goosing the speed of his chauffeur-driven car by a hidden gas pedal in the back seat. Confidant Pete Lorre scores big as a bummed-out psycho-hipster. Haunted Bob Cummings and Michelle Morgan stumble through dark-as-death photography desperately trying to wake up. Available through Sinister Cinema in a less-than-perfect but better-than-average print. D.B.

THE COBWEB (1955; no-rent). Supreme Fifties Technicolor neurotica from Vince Minelli. The plot? A power struggle to choose the curtains in a nuthouse. For real. With Oscar Levant singing "M-O-T-H-E-R" in wetpack, sensitive John Kerr obsessed with Van Gogh, and Charles Boyer as a washed-up dipso shrink trying to bed unhappily married Gloria Grahame: "Boat Kah-ren, I taught we would 'ave ahn *ah*-ffair!" Nervous. D.B.

COOGAN'S BLUFF (1968; Vestron Home Video). Stalking bad acidhead Don Stroud in Manhattan, Arizona deputy Clint E goes to a go-go discotheque. On the floor, crowds frug to "The Pigeon Toed Orange Peel," performed by The Pigeon Toed Orange Peel.—Tim Hathaway

DANCE HALL RACKET (1956; see "The Fang" in Shop Around guide). Lenny Bruce wrote, produced and acted in this exploito oddity that features his mother Sally Marr lecturing his wife Honey Harlow on how to strip. As giggling killer Vinnie, Len tries to turn the page of a stroke mag a thug is perusing while being talked to by his boss. "Hey! I ain't finished reading this!" "What's to read, stupid?" replies the future comickaze, "it's only pictures!" D.B.

DEMON (originally GOD TOLD ME TO; 1977). Blasphemy, anyone? The inimitable Larry Cohen (*Q, Maniac Cop*) outdoes himself with the tale of a scary alien invader who presents himself as J. Christ. He fools eminent businessmen ("He wants to deal with the leaders of society this time") and *Superfly* pimps alike. Final confrontation between

Boozed but priapic, the Chucker comes on strong in *The Cobweb*.

false messiah and tough cop Tony LoBianco who proves to have alien blood himself (his mom was raped by a flying saucer) is worth the price of admission. J.T.

EASY MONEY (1983; Orion Home Video). In the ultimate wiseguy nightmare, pot-head baby photographer Rodney Dangerfield is forced into

Regular Guy: Rodney passes the pepperoni in *Easy Money*.

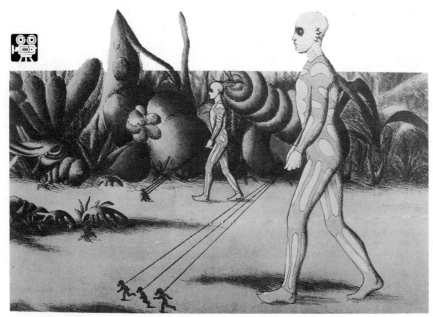

On the *Fantastic Planet*, Drogs use domesticated Ohms in genocide attempt.
(Hollywood Book & Poster)

sobriety and clean living for a solid year by his undead mother-in-law. From the depths of his despair, Rod creates "the Regular Guy" fashion look and is magically transformed into the Coco Chanel of the pizza-'n'-poker set. Highlight: at the track, he and Joe Pesci wait behind an interminably slow first-time bettor at the ticket window. "What're ya doin'," Pesci finally bursts out, "buyin' a fuckin' house?" D.W.

FANTASTIC PLANET (1977; Embassy Entertainment). Tiny humanoid Ohms rebel against their zomboid Drog masters in a surreal landscape full of scissor plants, winged monsters and waltzing statues. Smart script, spacy music, Roland Topor's unique graphics triumph decisively over limited animation. D.B.

Richard Crenna tells *Flamingo Kid* Matt Dillon three ways to distinguish knotty pine from beaverboard. (Editors' Archives)

FAT CITY (1972; RCA/Columbia Home Video). John Huston's d-a-r-k screen adapt of Leonard Gardner's novel about Stockton (Calif.) tankers on the ropes. Even if you win, you lose. Wild acting by wild cast: Stacey Keach, Jeff Bridges, Susan Tyrell as stone alky. Last line: "As soon as you're born, your life makes a beeline for the drain." D.B.

FLAMINGO KID (1984; Vestron Home Video). Matt Dillon shleps for seaside swinger Dick Crenna at his Long Island resort, ca. 1963. Beachside, Crenna puffs Panatellas, checks out Janet Jones' one-piece, plays gin with old duffers. The summer wind blows. The sun melts highball ice. The look on duffer Ron McClarty's face says it all: It doesn't get much better than this. B.M., G.S.

HAIRSPRAY (1988; RCA Columbia Home Video). Winner of the accuracy-in-media award for truthfully exposing the secrets of pre-Beatle cool, namely hair and dances. Watch your steps: Madison, Pony, Roach, Bug. Director John Waters outshines an all-star cast (Divine, Jerry Stiller) as psycho shrink Dr. Frederickson. Must-have soundtrack (MCA). B.M.

HEAD (1968; RCA/Columbia Video). After Vic Mature (who plays The Big Victor, a 40-foot matinee idol) read the script, he remarked, "I can't figure it out. All I know is that it makes me laugh." America didn't share Mature's singular sense of humor, and this gobbler bit big at the b.o. But time's been kind to this Jack Nicholson-penned Monkees vehicle. What once could have been dismissed as another wrong-headed youthie might now be dug as an idiosyncratic celluloid curiosity. With Frank Zappa, Tim Carey, Sonny Liston, Annette. R.S.

THE HONEYMOON KILLERS (1964; Vestron Video). Cinematic equivalent of Fifties *True Crime* mag, based on the real life 1949 case of "the Lonely Hearts Killers." Unctuous Raymond Fernandez (Tony LoBianco) cons irritating/funny/sad spinsters & widows out of their bread, but falls in lust with one intended pigeon: fat, obsessive ex-nurse Martha Beck (Shirley Stoller). Posing as his sister, she decides on a "no witnesses" policy, which turns their scam homicidal. Comedy comes no blacker than this. Original director M. Scorsese was replaced by scripter Leonard Kastle who never made another movie. D.B.

JFK (1991). Oliver Stone's three-hour paranoi-epic is so grounded by straight-arrow K. Costner that it permits a whole flock of N'awlins loonybirds to fly around its edges. To wit: Joe Pesci (in sub-Hair Club frightwig and grease pencil eyebrows), Kevin Bacon (a psychopathic racist right-wing male hustler), Tommy Lee Jones (a low-camp Jeff Chandler), and, coolest of all, grand John Candy: a tanned, Ray-banned hipster hedonist spouting the most baroque jive rap this side of N.O. dejays Dr. Daddy-o, Poppa Stoppa and Jack the Cat. As soon as he opens his mouth, you're already miles behind. D.B.

THE KILLERS (1964; MCA Video). Hard to tell who shines brightest here, the star (Dutch Reagan as a mail-robbin' hood in a '59 Ford), or the suits (hitman Lee Marvin in a two-piece aqua-metallic diddybop). Or maybe it's Angie Dickinson, Dutch's moll with eyes for wheelman John Cassavetes. Method head: Marv's pard Clu Gulager sips carrot juice, gargles hooch, and polishes his Raybans on Norman Fell's head. Don Siegel directs.

Let's hear it for Couple Number One! Tone and Shirl, *The Honeymoon Killers*, smooch up big time.
(Hollywood Book & Poster)

The Killers: Norman Fell gets poached by torpedoes Clu and Lee.

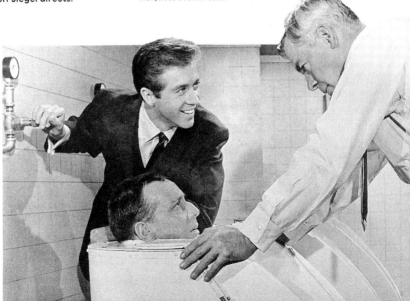

THE KILLING (1956; MGM/UA Home Video). Amid an embarrassment of riches (the imponderable marriage of Elisha Cook and Marie Windsor, Jim Thompson's dialogue), Tim Carey steals the show in Kubrick's tale of a racetrack heist. Approached on his farm by mysterioso hood Sterling Hayden about doing a "job," ex-con sharpshooter T.C. pets his puppy, squints and grits. "What kinda money, pops?" Hayden: "$5000." Carey: "Who do I hafta kill?" Saintly sighting: in the corner of an exterior shot, a club wall advertises "Burlesque. Lenny Bruce." T. H.

THE KILLING OF A CHINESE BOOKIE (1976; no-rent). This small flipped flick stars Ben Gazzara as Cosmo, a Sunset strip- club owner forced to carry out a mob hit. Director John Cassavetes was practically hit by a mob of riled fans for making it. A queasy showbiz freakshow that makes David Lynch look like Disney in short pants. D.W.

KISS ME DEADLY (1955; MGM/U.A.). Mutant Fifties film noir as Mike Hammer (Ralph Meeker) seeks a metal box which contains nothing less than fire stolen from the gods. No one will be admitted during the last five minutes' box-opening scene; the sound alone will give you nightmares. Spillane *hates* this movie—he'd better!—J.T.

"Are you with me, Doctor Wu?" Sterling Hayden, on the set of *The Killing*, wonders what's keeping his chiropractor. (Hollywood Book & Poster)

LES VAMPIRES (1916; no-rent). This eight-hour Louis Feuillade serial from the teens was a

Audience member in 1915's *Les Vampires* suffers migraine trying to follow film's plot.

Martian Crime Wave alien demands location of nearest opthalmologist.

monstro influence on the Surrealists (esp. Magritte). Mystery lady in tights slithers over Parisian rooftops & down chimney with secret message. Poison dart inside glove gives lethal handshake. Library wall slides up, cannon rolls out, fires through open window, destroying watchtower. Almost as boss: Franju's '63 *Judex*, a b & w sound homage shot like a silent (see Sinister Cinema in Shop Around guide). D.B.

MAD MAX (1979; Vestron). Forget *Bladerunner* and its modish image of the future. This is Sid Vicious' version of the by-and-by. Grim, gritty, grease and gas-soaked, a low-budget masterpiece that'll leave rubber all over what little optimism you may foolishly cling to. R.S.

MANDINGO (1975; Paramount). Ultra-lurid, antebellum mellerdrama from the novel by one Kyle Oscott, a pseudonym supposedly hiding the identity of a French Quarter black queen. Everything needed to give any old-line Dixiecrat a massive coronary. Slaves can't hardly work a run-down plantation - they're too busy being whupped, shtupped and pitted 'gainst one another. Owner James Mason uses pickaninnies as footstools to cure his rheumatism. Susannah York swigs sherry and lusts after Ken Norton. Subtle climax involves being pitchforked 'n' boiled alive. Rating: Five juleps. D.B.

MARTIAN CRIME WAVE (1957; no-rent). Super grade-Z laugh-fest from first (and only) time writer-star-director Bill Dennison ("Ace") and his real-life girlfriend Kathy Moran ("Mitzi"). Skull-capped martians, led by Tor Johnson, impersonate a highschool car club in order to pull crimes. Supposedly yanked due to an implied alien-human gangbang in the girls' locker room. Extras: only screen appearance of rockabilly cult-cat Portuguese Joe, who belts his "Teenage Riot," and Nick Adams, almost unrecognizable as the bespectacled, jive-talking gang member "Bebop." - T.H.

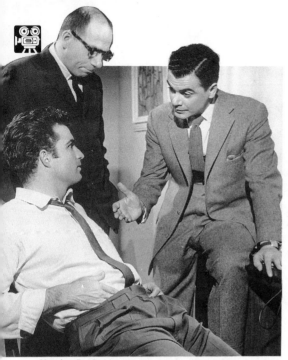

MURDER BY CONTRACT (1958; no-rent). Sort of a Yank version of Jean-Pierre Melville's *Le Samourai*. College student hit-man Vince Edwards waits in hotel rooms, meets his contact (Herschell Bernardi), checks out the target, waits some more, kicks out a hooker, waits, beats up the contact, waits some more. Sometimes he speaks. It isn't pretty. D.B.

MYSTERY TRAIN (1988; Orion Home Video). Jarmusch's trifurcated tribute to Memphis includes a cameo by Rufus Thomas, the plum role of Screamin' Jay Hawkins' career, and more dead space than the great Gobi. Japanese tourists debate Presley vs. Perkins, and decide "Memphis is just like Yokohama with 60% of the buildings gone." B.M.

Murder By Contract: pre-*Casey* Vince Edwards gets counseling on how to work his way through med school. (Hollywood Book & Poster)

NUDE ON THE MOON (1960; Strand VCI). Don't know much about history, but I do know Doris Wishman's lunar probe is the crucial link between late Fifties volleyball voyeurism and Russ Meyer's pioneering softcore. The first sci-fi nudie concerns a young scientist who uses his uncle's inheritance ("He made a fortune in the fur business") to build a rocket and do a Desafinado with his partner, a jump-suited silver fox known only as The Professor. Up there where the air's rare, they uncover a topless-oriented civilization big on collective bathing and Frisbee-tossing. Ralph Young sings the theme "I Lost My Heart To A Moon Doll." T.H.

PENN & TELLER GET KILLED (1989; Warner Home Video). Smart-ass magicians unmask reality as a series of cheap tricks with high-ticket consequences. The sick, sick plot against Penn involves Teller, a Rupert Pupkin type psycho killer, and a lady cop who puts the intended victim into protective custody aboard her houseboat. There, he digs the Velvets' "Femme Fatale" while guzzling diet cola and watching the Three Stooges ("Is this the one where they're plumbers?"). The Bee Gees close the show with "I Started A Joke."

THE PLOT AGAINST HARRY (1969; New Yorker Video 1990). Harry is just out of prison, ready to resume his numbers-running operation. But he's been in stir a long time, and the nabe's changed. There's desertion in his ranks, a gov't rackets inquiry, tough competition. Worse, his doc diagnoses a "swollen heart," compelling him to swear off sex with the bee-hived call girls who might be his only solace. Despondent, Harry hangs a sharkskin-suited spiritual U-turn and tries to reintegrate into his ex-wife's stereotypical Jewish family. Martin Priest's masterly performance as the saturnine Harry Plotkin should have established him as one of the preeminent character actors, but this witty, beautifully photographed masterpiece sat in the can for 20 years. R.S.

And The Heavens Brought Forth The Wonder Of Woman!

A truly different adventure to take you OUT OF THIS WORLD!

ADULTS ONLY

Nude on the Moon

In Beautiful EASTMAN COLOR

Man Discovers A NATURE CAMP On The MOON! Released Thru JER PICTURES INC.

Last known photo of Penn & Teller before fatal accident. Note wobbly front wheel.
(Hollywood Book & Poster)

POINT BLANK (1967). Lee Marvin metamorphoses from the corporeal hitman of *The Killers* into an avenging apparition out to reclaim money owed him by the mob. Great wit and cathartic action, plus the film approaches sci-fi & metaphysics through its skewed time scheme. Marvin has been propelled obliquely through the continuum while everyone else can live only one moment at a time. Finally, it seems as if the cosmos itself is crooked. J.T.

THE PORNOGRAPHERS (1966, Connoisseur Video Collection). Japanese director Shohei Imamura's cool black humor is still too chilled for the chamber. Goofball plot concerns sleazoid small-timer who, lacking yen to make prints, straps five Bolexes together and shoots skinflicks. Somehow he winds up in a boat drifting out to sea with most of the audience. D.B.

Point Blank: Lee Marvin encourages John Vernon to choose between perforation and defenestration.

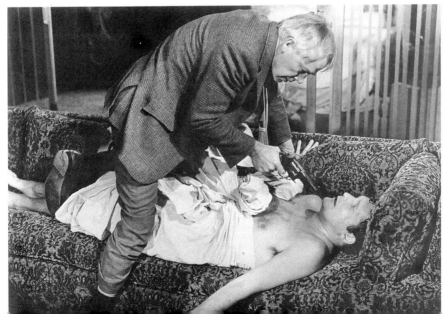

RAT RACE (1960; no rent). Central casts Tony Curtis as a hot sax cat new to the Apple and eager to blow, and Debbie Reynolds as a tiny Beat dancer with a pad to let. The unscrupulous agent: Don Rickles. Playing in the combo that cons Ton' out of his last greenback: Sam Butera. Very sharp title theme by Elmer B.

SERIE NOIRE (1979; no-rent). Alain Corneau just shades Steven Frears' *Grifters* with the best Jim Thompson adaptation. Only Clouzout's *Diaboliques* (from his novel *A Hell Of A Woman*) is as sordid. Fantastic seedy, near-psychotic perf by Patrick Dewaere who kicks shit out of a phonebooth, gets french-kissed by a biker and succumbs to an old whore pimping her niece as rain runs down the window and the Melodians croon "Rivers of Babylon." From the novel *A Hell Of Woman*. D.B.

So Fine: Ryan O'Neal and model Toni Moon (that's her billing) expose the business end of the shmatte trade.

THE SEVENTH CURSE (1986). One of Hong Kong's hippest, this fantasy-horror action-adventure set in the jungles of Southeast Asia is from a novel by Ni Kuang, HK's most popular pulpist. Goodies include flying-killer-alien-baby-monsters, a spinal cord-eating walking skeleton, some startling nudity, and Chow Yun-fat, as the globe-trotting filthy-rich hero Wisley, puffing a pipe and wasting a giant lizard with a bazooka. Also, Hong out with Wong Kar-wei's fiendishly cool DAYS OF BEING WILD (1986). Set in the Sixties and effortlessly evoking the languid, aimless mood of its youthful characters, this is one of the most insinuating and powerful "lost generation" movies ever made. And I mean anywhere.—David Chute. (See Shop Around.)

SO FINE (1981; Warner Home Video). Shmatte freakout! Ryan O'Neal accidentally invents designers jeans with plexiglass bubbles over the ass. Producer Michael Lobell used to work for his dad in Smart-Tee Tee Shirts, and knew whereof he spoke. Cool comedy sunk by its lame trailer. D.B.

STRAIGHT TIME (1978; Warner Home Video). Dustin Hoffman's best, leasty shtiky performance, as ex-con Max Dembo fighting a heavy recidivist jones. Edward Bunker adapted from his tuff novel *No Beast So Fierce*. Bad-ass cast: cool Theresa Russell (her first film), slobnik Gary Busey, and Mr. Nasty himself, E. Emmett Walsh, before he turned into a cartoon. Superscene: wife of ex-crime partner Harry Dean Stanton serving grilled burgers on cramped suburban-hell patio. Wife goes inside. Stanton takes a bite, whispers to Max, "Get me outa here!" He does. All the way. D.B.

STATION SIX SAHARA (1964; no-rent). A bunch of bent character actors including Ian Bannen, Peter Van Eyck and the great Denham Elliott pass the time psychically torturing each other while working an oil rig in the middle of nowhere. Carroll Baker crashes into the carefully controlled b & w photography driving a Caddy convert and the camp comes permanently unglued. Faucet drips sound like bowling balls. Like, super tense. D.B.

TIN MEN (1987; Touchstone Home Video). Barry Levinson's study of Baltimore siding-salesmen reveals scams (the *Life* magazine "photo shoot," "fivespot-on-the-carpet"), and revels in small talk. As Danny DeVito's "closer" Sam, Jackie Gayle explains *Bonanza*'s success: "It's a 50-year old father with three 47-year old sons. You know why they all get along so good? They're all the same age."

WILD IN THE STREETS (Orion Home Video). In '68, it was the squares' most paranoid fantasy about the

"Drink up, gramps!" *Wild In The Streets'* teen Gestapo complete round-up of post-tetragenarians.

impending Baby Boom takeover. In the Nineties, Right revisionists swear this is what the Sixties were really like. Teen star Max Frost runs for prez with a campaign that pushes the vote for 14-year olds and LSD camps for anyone over 30. Dig Dick Pryor as Stanley X, drummer, psychedelic Congressman and cannibal cook. D.W.

THE WORLD'S GREATEST SINNER (1958). Longtime cinema villain Carey was a leering unforgettable presence in many fine films (*East Of Eden, One Eyed Jacks, The Wild One*), but his longest screen appearance was in this hitherto unreleased gem he financed himself. The story, about a man who decides to enter politics using the name God, lurches and turns, peaking when God stars in an unbelievable rock concert. Carey, in a gold-lame suit, with a goatee and a guitar, fronts an out of tune, unrehearsed Mexican band in a show that shames Michael Jackson in a trice. Down on his knees bellowing "please, please, please!" in the best sincerity he can mimic, Carey is the ultimate cracked actor plying his trade. Shot in El Monte and orchestrated by local musician Frank Zappa. The world will never see the likes of it again. (See Shop Around.) A.F.

John Waters' 5 Coolest Porno Titles

Screw The Right Thing
21 Hump Street
Driving Miss Daisy Crazy
The Sperminator
Sperms Of Endearment

Station Six Sahara: Cool Pete Van E and luscious Carroll B wonder what's keeping Bruce Weber.

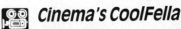

Cinema's CoolFella
SCORSESE

He *is* the greatest. And, like Ali, the cinema champ's a poet, a "scientist" as the rastas would say. Mere greatness alone, though, wouldn't put him in these pages. Style would, and Scorsese's films are flooded with it. Wit, good looks and "outsider" attitude course through them like electrons. Sure, much of this is done in service of realism (he's called *Mean Streets* "anthropological"), but you also get the sense that this director's empathy with his characters goes beyond hitting the historicity nail squarely. Like he knows how sharp his 'fellas feel sporting those scissor collars, that he himself digs the kinetic beauty of their *bing-ba-da-bing!* raps. Pontius Pilate doesn't wear an ID bracelet in *Last Temptation*, but Scorsese wore cuff links to Woodstock.

Film Comment: *Pop music is usually used in films, at least on one level, to cue the audience to what era it is.*

Scorsese: *Oh, no, no, forget that, no.*

The man knows what time it is. He was scoring films to pop before anyone; not with roadsign literalism ("You Are Now Entering 1974"), but with good humor and great records. In 1968's *Who's That Knocking*, the Genies' 1959 doowop title track kicks in as Harvey Keitel's soul-hurt J.R. wanders an empty church, orbing all the ceramic angels & saints. "Boom boom boom, bang bang bang" shout the Genies (quick cuts: Virgin Mary statue; St. Lucy of Sicily proffering her eyeballs on a plate) / "I can't stand this awful pain" (closeup: male saint pointing to the bloodwound on his leg!). The Ronettes' heart-stopping "Be My Baby" is Keitel's wakeup call in *Mean Streets*, and later the Chips' vertiginous "Rubber Biscuit" his accompaniment as he reels, juiced, through pal Tony's place. Louie Prima plays inside Jake LaMotta's Miami dive in *Raging Bull*, and the greatest hits of Robert & Johnny and Johnnie & Joe cycle endlessly in the Terminal Bar that's Griffin Dunne's temp refuge in *After Hours*. Tony Bennett's "Rags To Riches" lights up the start of *GoodFellas* like some mega-volt votive candle, the perfect invocation of the comedy-carnage union that is the film's soul and inspiration.

68

MAMALUCC'! DeNiro's Johnny Boy valiantly tries to hip Harvey keitel's Charlie that "Joey Clams" *is* "Joey Scala." Copyright © Warner Bros. Inc.

Coolness busts out all over, in bits and frames . . . the transcendent cheesiness of Morrie the Wig Man's commercials ("And remember, Morrie's wigs are tested against hurricane winds!") in *GoodFellas*. (Check Morrie actor Chuck Low's sit- and walk-through in *King Of Comedy*, as Rupert Pupkin regales Diahnne Abbot in a Chi-fi eatery . . .

the way "big man" loan shark Michael (Richard Romanus) is revealed as a small-time shmuck in *Mean Streets*; salty over collecting on the coupla K he's lent DeNiro's Johnny Boy, by mid-film he's hustling fireworks to suburban teens and getting burned in the process . . . that momentous first encounter between Jake and Vickie (Cathy Mor-

SALTY SHARK. Richard Romanus' Michael (right) thinks about the K that got away in *Mean Streets*.
Copyright © Warner Bros. Inc.

THE KING OF NAMES
(Seen or heard in MS films)
Billy Batts
Frankie Bones
Frankie the Wop
Freddy No Nose
Jimmy Sparks
Jimmy Two Times
Joey Clams (Joey Scala)
Nickie Eyes
Sally Balls
Sally Ga-ga
Tuddy

NON-SATURNINE WIG MAN. Morrie with DeNiro, *GoodFellas*.

BIG QUESTIONS
"You talkin' a me?" - Travis Bickle
"D'you fuck my wife?" - Jake LaMotta
"Is that cork?" - Rupert Pupkin
"A mook? What's a mook?" - Johnny Boy
"Who do you think you are, Frankie Valli or some kinda big shot?" - Karen Hill
"I amuse you? . . . What do you mean 'funny'? 'Funny' how? How am I funny?" - Tommy
   DeVito
"What am I, a shmuck on wheels?" - Morrie the Wig Man

Vickie LaMotta's wheel-eyes drove Jake wild in
Raging Bull.

iarty). Introduced by his brother (Joe Pesci), Jake stares at her, a tall, cool blond in a bathing suit, the dish of his dreams. "Nice to meet you," he manages. She waits, eyes his wheels, then speaks her first words to the man she'll marry. "Nice caaw." And how about Henry and Karen Hill's fluid glide from curb to ringside Copa seats and the top of the world (*GoodFellas*), a vision of high times so swingin' you can almost see Gleason and Darin rattle their ice, hoist tumblers, and snap for service. Hey, over here, two more Seven-and-Sevens! G.S. & B.M.

After Hours 1985 (Warner Home Video)
GoodFellas 1990 (Warner Home Video)
King Of Comedy 1983 (RCA Columbia Home Video)
Mean Streets 1973 (Warner Home Video)
Raging Bull 1980 (MGM/UA)
Who's That Knocking 1968 (No-rent, but does show on cable)

Preston Sturges: King of Frantic

In a series of faster-than-breathless comedies, director Preston Sturges set a rate for ridiculousness that has never been outcrazed. His Thirties and Forties flicks *Unfaithfully Yours*, *The Palm Beach Story*, *The Lady Eve*, *Miracle of Morgan's Creek*, *Hail The Conquering Hero*, *The Great McGinty* and *Sullivan's Travels* add new meaning to the word "topsy turvy" while maintaining a standard for smart-mouth dialogue and detail that belies the outstanding incoherent unintelligence of the stories themselves. Sturges was always a Grade A weirdo. He first rose to prominence in the Twenties as the inventor of "kiss-proof" lipstick, rocking the cosmetics world and marital fidelity forever. By the time he got to Hollywood, he was really out to lunch.

Forget about plot twists. Sturges had plot pretzels, impossible switcheroos that swindled audiences of all reality while demanding that they follow the most senseless trivialities. In the first ten minutes of *Miracle of Morgan's Creek*, young Miss Crackernacker gets drunk, gets married, gets pregnant, gets into a car crash, and forgets the name of her soldier hubby. Then the story begins. In *Sullivan's Travels*, the director of *Ants In Your Pants of 1929* leaves Bev Hills for Skid Row with ten cents in his pocket to study "real people," is mistaken for a local hobo, convicted of murder, and sentenced to a Mississippi chain gang where he is forced to watch Mickey Mouse cartoons.

Sturges was always willing to take the extra leap into screen insanity, often for no apparent reason. Midway through *The Palm Beach Story*, a group of elderly millionaires (the Ale & Quail Club) board a train, get drunk, shoot out the windows and end up staging a mutiny. In a matter of minutes, the most 'civilized' crew of businessmen is reduced to a pack of howling maniacs, spinning out of control. (All titles MCA Home Video.) D.W.

71

ALL-TIME COOLEST FILM LINES

Local girl to Brando, *The Wild One*: "Hey Johnny, what are you rebeling against?"
Brando: "Whaddaya got?"

Bad-guy to Alan Ladd, *The Badlanders*: "So you're a Mexican-lover, eh?"
Ladd: "Yeah. I even forgot the Alamo."

Jan Sterling to Kirk Douglas, *The Big Carnival*: "I've met some hardboiled eggs in my time, but you—you're 20 minutes."

Music mogul Harry Charms, *Absolute Beginners*: "You know the three most useless things in the world? The Pope's balls, a nun's tits, and a good write-up in the *Record Mirror*."

John Drew Barrymore paraphrasing Queen Isabella's reaction to Columbus, *High School Confidential*: "Christy, what is this jazz you puttin' down 'bout our planet being round? Everybody hip that it's square!"

Mildred Natwick, *The Court Jester*: "The pellet with the poison's in the flagon with the dragon. The chalice from the palace holds the brew that is true."
Danny Kaye: "What about the vessel with the pestle?"

Claude Akins to Clu Gulager, *The Killers:* "You said Johnny North died. How'd he die?"
Gulager: "Questions . . . he asked one too many."

Ralph Meeker, observing a cockroach, *Paths Of Glory*: "Tomorrow morning we'll be dead and that bug'll still be alive."
Tim Carey (smashing the roach): "Now you got the edge!"

Richard Conte to MD reviewing his X-rays, *Oceans 11:* "So tell me, doc. Is it the big casino?"

Whit Bissell, *I Was A Teenage Frankenstein*: "I know you have a civil tongue in your head. I sewed it there myself."

Dennis Farina to henchman, *Midnight Run:* "I want this guy taken out and I want him taken out fast. You and that other dummy better start gettin' more personally involved in your work, or I'm gonna stab you through the heart with a fuckin' pencil. You understand?"
Henchman: "You got it, Jimmy."

Tony Curtis, about to start a hustle, *The Sweet Smell of Success*: "Watch me make a hundred-yard run with no legs."

Ray Liotta, *GoodFellas*: "I'm an average nobody. I get to live the rest of my life like a shnook."

BAD GIRLS DON'T CRY

by Chris Davidson

Bad girls are a blast. This we all know. But it's not all black underwear and fun in dad's Country Squire. Take Tura Satana home to meet the folks and watch the family china approach escape velocity. Bring Mamie, Jayne or even Mimsy to a bar, and throw more punches at ogling drunks than the St. Pauli Girl. Why do we like these wanton women? They swing. So, in this spirit of she-devil appreciation, here are the top of the heathen class, guaranteed straight-F students. Get with it. Only stay-at-homes would date a chick who wears brown leather.

ALAINA CAPRI in *Good Morning . . . and goodbye!* (1967). The classic pick-up line: "You're too much woman for one man" was probably uttered first for Alaina, who rivals a Buick Roadmaster for sheer square footage of chassis. As Angel, she says, "I'm tired of being dirty, easy and bad," then hops in the hay with a construction worker named Stone. Angel's hubby tells her, "We've got to stop running from each other." Her reply: "I'm not running, I'm driving."

PEGGY CUMMINS in *Gun Crazy* (1949). Pulled together by a harmless obsession with shooting everything that moves, Annie Laurie Starr and Bart Tare kill cops and old ladies, while dressing like cowboys and dancing to the big band sound. Annie's eyes beam when her beau gets the killer instinct, and even as the cops are closing in, she's ready to blow lead down their throats. Some people you just can't teach.

SYBIL DANNING in *Chained Heat* (1983). A panzer tank in cut-offs, Danning is a murderous inmate who rebels against a prison staff that hires out the better-looking jailbirds as prostitutes. The carefree fun peaks with a warden who videotapes his smarmy inmate escapades ("Don't call me warden. Call me Fellini") and Sybil slapping five with Tamara Dobson (from *Cleopatra Jones*). One nice thing about this place, the staff cares about hygiene. Everyone takes lots of showers.

JOAN FONTAINE in *Born To Be Bad* (1950). Little tart Christabel Cane gets under people's skin. But she has class, so she's more like a tic dipped in perfume. Robert Ryan has her number, though. "You love only one person," he says, "and it's the love of a lifetime." But who cares about insults? Chris has got a car full of furs to show for ruining everyone's lives. Her motto: Rag and you shall receive.

PATTY McCORMACK in *The Bad Seed* (1956). Who says murder is wasted on the young? Rhoda

Cowboy drag & trigger fingers: Bad Peg Cummins.

So young, so bad: Batty Patty McCormack.

Black Sunday's Barbara Steele stands in for Betty Page at post-Irving Klaw snapshot session.

hasn't hit her teens, and she's got more corpses under her belt than killers twice her age. How a little blond in pigtails could kill is simple: genetics (her grandmother loved to murder, too). But it's crucial to realize that DNA didn't bring mur-

Marcelled Shelley Winters as *Bloody Mama* demands to know which son has hidden her curling iron.

derous habits only—Rhoda's musical talent is considerable. She can trap a man in a burning basement and play the piano even above his piercing screams.

ANN SAVAGE in *Detour* (1945). Why some singers hit it big and others eke it out at the Break O' Dawn Club—and pick up insulting hitchhikers named Vera—is anyone's guess. But our crooner, Al, sure doesn't deserve this broad. Vera bosses him around like a stray dog, hogs the bathroom ("I'm first in the bathtub") and won't give him a civil answer to save her life ("Where'd you hide the butts?" he asks. "On the table, sucker"). Even in death, Vera gives no relief. She dies of natural causes. The poor slob goes up the river for her murder.

BARBARA STEELE in *Black Sunday* (1961). Steele plays both an ancient sorceress and her goody-goody ancestor, so she's running from goblins a lot. But as Asa the witch, Steele dresses in black robes and gets to say, "You too can learn the joy and happiness of hating." Asa eventually burns for thumbing her nose at all that is good, but Steele and her overbite returned in tons of slimy roles. As a crippled warden in *Caged Heat*, she dreams of not only walking again, but of stripping in front of a cheering mob.

SUSAN TYRELL in *Forbidden Zone* (1980). Beneath the Hercules household is a little slice of Hell, a world where bald men sing and box each other and a man-frog in a tux stands guard. This joint's queen wears heels and digs torture chambers. But mostly, she says what's on her mind: "Why does it feel so good to be so bad?" For more Tyrrell, check out *Cry-Baby* ("You're everything a man should be. You're young, stupid and mean"), the rockingest movie of the last 10 years.

SHELLEY WINTERS in *Bloody Mama* (1970). She's no Donna Reed, but Ma Barker cares about her children just the same. Her advice is wise: "I told my boys, you just rob banks and stay out of trouble." And she's always willing to protect her family, especially big dumb Herman who kills an old man during "one of his bad moments." But what's a mother to do when the cops are firing 10,000 rounds into her house? Grab a tommy gun and try to blow their heads off, that's what.

Hard to offend? Need more? Try Susan Cabot in *Machine Gun Kelly*, Carolyn Jones in *King Creole*, Yvonne Lime in *Speed Crazy*, or Sylvia Syms in *Teenage Bad Girl*. Or just round up the local toughs, plenty of fortified wine, and a delinquent drama of your own is but a stretch in reform school away.

SINATRA ONSCREEN: A KING RAT SIX PACK

by Michael Dolan

One word says it all: Frank. He's a legend, an institution, a totally monstered-out guy with legs that won't quit. On record, on film, in person—50 years into his career, and still he's the talk of the town. True, the talk is about did he or did he not shtup the First Broad, but hey! At 75 you should be the topic of such musings.

Frankie went to Hollywood in the Forties, but after a few musicals and *From Here to Eternity* and *The Country Girl*, his career took a turn for the noir. He refined his acting style from hot to cool and from that of an ingratiating boy crooner into a man's man with an edgy on-camera personality that held for years before descending into reptilian self-parody. If Steve McQueen acted with the back of his neck, Frank acted with his forehead—in film after film, the truest part of Sinatra's performance occurs at the confluence of the furrows in the center of his brow. Here with a six-pack of Frank to go:

Suddenly 🦅🦅🦅🦅🦅

The Cold War collides with Mob-fixated paranoia, and the future Chairman of the Board anticipates Lee Harvey Oswald by nearly ten years in a wiggy outing that sees him star as a gunsel being paid $500,000 to assassinate a vacationing President.

Directed by Lewis Allen in the broad strokes of the day, this buried 1954 classic still yanks on the dorsal hairs. Sinatra, portraying a blood-crazed WWII vet who's got a German-made sniper rifle aimed for the presidential skull, says with a dreamy smirk, "I never killed a President before"—rude stuff from a guy who'd wind up singing at one of JFK's inaugural balls.

And all you conspiracy theorists, pipe this: *Suddenly* was put together by an outfit called Libra Productions, as in Oswald's birthsign and the title of Don DeLillo's 1988 novelistic imaging of the assassin's life. Think about it, and check the locks on the back door before you turn out the light, as you will want to do after you've basked in the bughouse glow of Frank's nutty grin.

Von Ryan's Express 🦅🦅🦅🦅🦅

One of the first revisionist WWII films, the 1965 *VRE* stars Frank as a hard-case pilot whose P-38

Lightning—the coolest plane of all time—is shot down in Italy at war's close. Interned in a POW camp full of stiff-upper-lip Britishers, Sinatra outranks everybody else. He irks the Brits but leads the troop in a train-borne race for the Swiss border, along the way jamming a skewer through the happy-band-of-brothers POW camp genre—most notably when he machineguns the only woman in the cast to keep her from blowing the whistle.

As in all his other flicks, Frank runs like a man accustomed to riding in limousines, but *VRE* is worth the ride, if only to see Sinatra, in full Wehrmacht drag, barter wordlessly with a Gestapo weasel over his watch. Made when Frank was in his acting prime, *VRE* even has a score that lays down Nelson Riddle-style chord changes in the middle of a military march theme.

Frank realizes *Von Ryan's Express* doesn't stop at Jilly's.

Frank places drink order in *The Manchurian Candidate*. (Hollywood Book & Poster)

The Man With The Golden Arm 🎩🎩🎩🎩
Okay, okay. So it's a mite hokey, and shot on a backlot Chicago where everybody is white and the glamorama nitery where Kim Novak does something inscrutable is just across the street from her tenement flat. And you can't figure out why Frank, as a recovering junkie just back from a stint in the big house, wouldn't snap to the reality that his ostensibly wheelchairbound wife can walk as well as any and better than most.

And it's tough to believe that a parole officer would recommend that a guy trying to kick the big H go straight by becoming a jazz musician—or that a guy trying this unusual method would find a cure that takes in one dose, as the upbeat ending suggests. But Otto Preminger's 1955 version of Nelson Algren's novel swings hard, thanks to Frank's performance as the cardshark-cum-drummer-cum-addict. Watching him go cold turkey, you'd almost believe he'd had a taste.

Other pluses include an amazingly young Darren McGavin as a Mephistophelean smack dealer with a pencil-thin moustache and the much-mourned Arnold Stang as a Bilkoesque running buddy.

Manchurian Candidate 🎩🎩🎩🎩
Reversing field on the theme of *Suddenly*, this suppressed 1962 outing is positively Zen in some of its interchanges. Frank plays yet another soldier, this time one of the boys in brown brainwashed by the ChiComs during the Korean War. He's assigned to dog Laurence Harvey, a fellow brainwashee, who works his way into sniping range of a presidential candidate but instead eats the barrel himself.

Before he does, the film slithers through some Oedipal scenery chewing between Harvey and Angela Lansbury, as vampy a mom as ever pined for a poofy boy gone off to war, and features Frank in what may have been the first kung fu fight incorporated into a Hollywood film.

The Detective 🎩🎩🎩
With Frank at his Existential Man noirest, this NYPD policer smells like a subway but gets you where you want to go: bumpy ride, lots of grit in the air, occasional flashes of darkness, and a grimly satisfying performance by Sinatra as a man with too much on his mind and a wife whose body won't quit—especially when she's with another guy.

Tony Rome/Lady In Cement 🎩
These two period pieces should be seen as a double feature on the VCR, so you can turn it off. Set in a Miami light years away from resurrection by Don Johnson and Michael Philip Thomas, these private eye procedurals star Frank as a thickbodied wiseass with unbeatable pheromones. At one point Raquel Welch is throwing her considerable self all over him; at another, a gay club manager comes on strong.

Tony and *Cement* both reek of late-Sixties establishment style—there's not a foreign car in any shot, the soundtracks are twelfth-hand Brazil 66, and the mini skirt/faggot jokes are dense and dumb. In tone, the Romes presage *Kojak* and *Rockford Files*, but without the wit. Frank delivers every line intended as funny in a weirdly mannered way, dousing the humor to death and taking his screen presence to a new plateau of dissociation. If you can stay awake through a pair of plots that give new meaning to the term "plodding"—this flick's for you, Jack.

Frankshop: The above films are all available through CBS/Fox Home Video, with the exception of *Suddenly* (Hal Roach, JLT Films & Congress Films).

Lux Interior's 5 Coolest Early Sixties West German Sci-Fi Crime Horror Flicks

Phantom of Soho
Carpet of Horror
1000 Eyes of Dr. Mabuse
Invisible Terror
The Head

SIX FACES OF BAKALYAN

A Countenance Of Cool

Compiled by
Alan Nahigian

Now you see him, now you don't. But he's always been there, in a succession of anti-sosh roles thick with relish. Wiseguy, hard guy, comic meanie. For Dick Bakalyan, the beat goes bossly on.

The Face Today. "You got a problem with that, pal?"

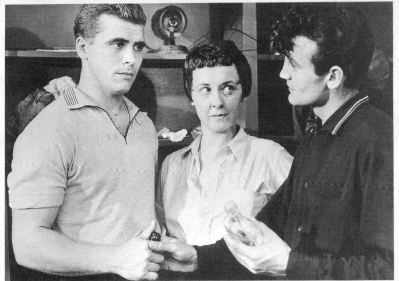

*Bakalyan and female friend cordially suggest Tom Laughlin raise elbows with them in Robert Altman's **The Delinquents**, 1957.*

*Civic-minded Bakalyan thoughtfully examines accident victim's belongings in 1958's **Hot Car Girl**.*

D.B. contemplates Travel & Expenses reimbursement as he takes Richard Conte on a ride and offers him good times in exchange for info vital to the mob. **The Brothers Rico**, 1957.

Dick (second from right) and friends review Der Bingle's application for membership in the Chairman's exclusive club. **Robin and the Seven Hoods**, 1964.

Batman, 1967: As the Joker's henchman "Verdigris," D.B. came on as a martian to convince the citizens of Gotham City they were being invaded by superior beings from another planet.

EIGHT~INCH COLLARS AND A SMORGASBORD OF OVERACTING: THE JOYS OF BLAXPLOITATION

By Chris Davidson

Elvis once sang what could be the motto of every blaxploitation movie hero: "If you're lookin' for trouble, you came to the right place."

And while *Kissin' Cousins* was the closest the King ever came to a blaxploitation flick (lots of gone black-versus-white symbolism with El in a dual role fighting himself sporting a blond wig), the guy knew that a knuckle sandwich beats a conference call as the ultimate tool of negotiation.

From Richard Roundtree to Rudy Ray Moore, every black swinger has done his talking with his fists. That's blaxploitation's greatness: it's long on action, short on smarts and real fruity on clothes (remember, in the early Seventies, when most of this stuff came out, eight-inch shirt collars hanging parallel to the ground were like "In," baby).

Soundsploitation: *Pimps, Players & Private Eyes*, themes from Seventies black movies, incl. *Shaft*, *Foxy Brown*, and *Across 110th Street* (Sire cd).

Yep, these movies are as tough and mean as a pail of Aunt Esther's stick-to-your-ribs hot sauce.

Unfortunately, though, blaxploitation films have pretty much dried up. Not counting Fred "The Hammer" Williamson, dean of the cuff-you-first-ask-questions-later school of film making, who still releases lots of direct-to-video bloodbaths, the bulk of blaxploitation movies came and went around 20 years ago.

The 1970s' blax-batch was the best, no contest. But black action films have been around ever since movies have been moving. You could look back to 1915, I suppose, and say *Birth of a Nation* started it all for black Hollywood, but D.W. Griffith's clunky Klan story uses white actors in blackface, so that's pushing it a bit. Better are the mess of "race films" that came out in the Thirties and Forties, like *The Bronze Buckaroo*, which let black actors tear it up in westerns and crime dramas.

In the Fifties and Sixties, the cat who scratched most in Tinsel Town was Sidney Poitier. He's kinda the grandfather of the whole modern scene, but like granddad, he can be a little too cute sometimes. Not to take away from goodies like *In the Heat of the Night*, *Blackboard Jungle* and *The Defiant Ones*, but Sid's deal was racial tolerance. And that's not what it was all about in the early Seventies. So for the primo product, let's stick to the mushroom-cloud- sized-afro and down-with-whitey years.

One man best captured the feel of this era: Antonio Fargas. You're familiar with him as Huggy Bear from *Starsky and Hutch,* but he rocked bigtime in blax classics like *Shaft* and *Cleopatra Jones*. Sure, his credentials speak for themselves (he was also in *Foxy Brown* and *Across 110th Street*). But as proof of his absolute rightness as the greatest blaxploitation actor, Keenen Ivory Wayans used him in the spoof *I'm Gonna Git You Sucka* as the prototypical, platform-shoe-wearing pimp, Fly Guy.

That particular romp is pretty lame, but it gets a few things right: 1) Fargas, the black Olivier, made blaxploitation movies *real* because he was real. You can't walk around in shoes with aquariums in their heels and fake talent. He lived this stuff; 2) Every blaxploitation movie needs a nightclub scene. Put your characters in a hopping joint like the Blueberry Hill disco in *Avenging Godfather* and watch sparks fly as they sing and swing like it's Arbor Day in a Canuck logging camp; and 3) There is no better weapon against "The Man" (white establishment, chitlin-head) than a loaded pistol and a bad attitude. As Fargas said to white-as-a-white-whale Shelley Winters, "See you around, Super Honky."

Now before you get scared away, and rent *Rebecca of Sunnybrook Farm* tonight, march yourself to the nearest neighborhood video store/pawn shop/check-cashing center and pick up a copy of *Coffy* or *Hell Up in Harlem*. Steer clear of the major video chains for most of this stuff, lest you be coerced into renting a Bill Cosby movie and thinking the job done. You've been warned.

Below, we've gathered together the best in blaxploitation. Sort of a blacklist of where to find the most far-out flicks. Dig the way cats like Jim Brown would rather rap you upside the head than look at you. Dig, too, how a lot of the racial tension message is still lingering around today. But dig most importantly, that these movies are for everyone, no matter what color you were dipped in upstairs.

Avenging Disco Godfather (1979, Active Home Video): Kinda late in the game for this stuff, but Rudy Ray Moore doesn't even notice. From his disco headquarters, Rudy's fighting an angel dust epidemic, but he's a little too nice to kids and dogs, and comes off like Roy Rogers in double-knits. Still, this monument to bad acting, bad dialogue and bad music has a final 15 minutes where Rudy gets a taste of drugs and goes loco in his green sweatsuit. He defies all comparison as he screams bloody murder at a hallucination of his Aunt Betty.

Blacula (1972, HBO/Cannon): Count Dracula bit a black prince in 1780, and cursed him to eternal sleep inside a coffin.

William Marshall (Blacula) startles intended victim by sporting only known Afro-widow's peak in existence.

Pam Grier as *Coffy* applies Vicks Vapo-Rub to paddy shut-in. (Davidson Archives)

Who cares? No one, really, until the prince wakes up as an ultra-smooth vampire who talks like King Lear, terrorizes cabbies and orders Bloody Marys in a bar. Starring William Marshall (who popped up as the King of Cartoons on *Pee Wee's Playhouse*), this spawned a sequel, *Scream, Blacula, Scream*, which firmed up Marshall as the black vampire of choice. Just once, how much would you have given to see Blacula take a piece out of Pee Wee's hide?

Black Belt Jones (1974, Warner Home Video): For sheer buffoonery, Jim Kelly should get his own series. Straight from his role in Bruce Lee's *Enter the Dragon*, Kelly proves again that his acting skills deserve a karate kick out the door. On the other hand, as an action hero Kelly romps, dicing and slicing some bloated Italian hoods who're about as ethnic as frozen lasagne. This flick is another jewel in the crown of Scatman Crothers, who's Kelly's karate teacher (as well as the voice of cartoon dog Hong Kong Fooey).

Black Caesar (1973, Filmways Home Video): Blaxploitation's busiest actor, Fred "The Hammer" Williamson, sees a lot of his films dive straight into the bargain-bin. But this violent feature is his best. His character, Tommy Gibbs, grows from street punk to a combination Public Enemy/Soul Brother No. 1, and then confronts a white cop who had harassed him as a child. It's no ordinary

beating, though. Tommy pulverizes the cop with a shoeshine box, paints his face with black shoe polish, and tells him to sing "Mammy." Tommy came back for *Hell Up in Harlem*. The cop didn't.

Cleopatra Jones (1973, Warner Home Video): Super-beautiful Cleo (Tamara Dobson) is a Bond-like special agent, kind of like a taller Roger Moore without the bra. She's after Mommy (Shelley Winters, in a smorgasbord of over-acting), a drug queenpin who presides over underboss Doodlebug Simpkins (Fargas). Cool cars (Cleo's black Corvette has hidden gun compartments in the door) and funny minor characters (Doodlebug has a henchman who only says "That's right") can't steal the gusto from Fargas. With his ruffled shirt and walking stick, he even gets to say, "Hair is like a woman. Treat it good and it'll treat you good." Give this guy a theme park.

Coffy (1973, Filmways Home Video): Pam Grier pulls the ultimate grooming gaff, and puts razor blades in her hair before a catfight with some hookers. Later, she jams a needle in the great Sid Haig's neck. Coffy wraps up her policy of nonviolence by killing almost every man in the script. Luckily, she never loses her cool, although her shirt isn't quite so lucky. With Allan Arbus (the hypnotist who uses Shakespeare to make Oscar neat in *The Odd Couple*!) as single-serving-sized mob boss Vitroni. Fargas stars in the follow-up, *Foxy Brown*.

Shaft (1971, MGM/UA): One of the first (and maybe the classiest) 1970s blaxploitation movies, this dumps Richard Roundtree in the middle of a Mafia-vs.-Harlem gang war. Almost better than the action, though, are the little touches: John Shaft's crazy leather-trenchcoat-and-turtle neck ensemble, his reel-to-reel tape player, the espresso he drinks, and the way he cracks a bottle of booze over a mobster's head with the finesse of a jackhammer. Two poor sequels followed.

Super Fly (1972, Warner Home Video): Not exactly a guy you want to bring to see *The Sound of Music*, Priest (Ron O'Neal as the title cat) makes up for his lack of good humor with a mean right cross and a wailin' Fu Manchu. He's quitting the drug game (Priest looks like who The Velvet Undergound is singing about in "I'm Waitin' For The Man"), but he's got one final deal to pull off. Don't call him "white looking," by the way. The last guy who did got his clock cleaned.

Superfly Ron O'Neal contemplates dividing his lapels into time zones. (Davidson Archives)

Richard Roundtree as *Shaft* dispatches offscreen evil-doer before Duracell failure.

The Mack (1973): Talk about ambition: John "Goldie" Mickens, the world's greatest mack (that's a pimp, son), thinks he's the ebony Wizard of Oz. He performs wiggy brain-washing speeches on his ladies in a planetarium while blasting space music and telling them to obey his commands through a loudspeaker. Played by Max Julien (who wrote *Cleopatra Jones*), Goldie locks his enemies in the trunks of cars with a bagful of rats to keep things amusing. *The Mack*, also with Richard Pryor, is so realistic, you'd swear you mistakingly rented a documentary called *How to Sell Women and Inject Battery Acid Into Your Enemies*.

Penitentiary III (1987, Warner Home Video): The *Penitentiary* series swings. But No. 3 has midget wrestler/thespian giant The Haiti Kid, and a prison kingpin who's like Brando's Godfather crossed with an even wispier Warhol. Haiti goes from being a slobbering missing link to a boxing coach who's overdosed on Zen, and helps Leon Isaac Kennedy fight his way out of the can. At one point, the warden asks, "You know what your trouble is? You've seen too many bad prison pictures." Exactly.

SHOP AROUND

Back when we published the *Catalog of Cool*, fewer than 10% of the coolflicks we touted were available on video. Thankfully, the picture has since improved. Many of our *Screen* entries turn up in the pages of the following catalogs. So will a number of abundantly sharper, and sillier, cinematic ventures. Print quality varies, so be sure to inquire about condition of each title before ordering. The first three are our top choices for quality and selection.

The Fang video catalog; P.O. Box 804, Flushing, N.Y. 11375.
   Specialties: vintage horror and JD films.

Sinister Cinema; P.O. Box 4369, Medford ORE 97501-0168.
   Phone: 503 773-6860. Specialties: sci-fi, horror, mystery.

Something Weird Video; P.O. Box 33664, Seattle, WA 98133.
   Specialties: sexploitation and cult.

Critics' Choice Video; 800 Morse Ave., Elk Grove Village, IL
   60007. Phone: 1-800 367-7765.

Moore Video; P.O. Box 5703, Richmond, VA 23220. Fax: 804
   745-9785.

S.F. Rush Video; 1576 Fell St., #1, San Francisco, CA 94117.
   Phone: 415 921-TAPE.

Shock-toon Video; Brian Archibald, RD #4 Box 136-A Rockaway
   Valley Rd., Boonton, N.J. 07005. Phone: 201 625-4389.

Video Search of Miami; P.O. Box 16-1917, Miami, FLA
   33116-1917. Phone: 305 387-6807.

For information on *Nude on the Moon* & other exploito titles, write Strand VCI; 3350 Ocean
   Park Bl, Suite 205, Santa Monica, CA 90405.

To order *The World's Greatest Sinner*, write Absolute Films, P.O. Box 1254, Temple City,
   CA 91780.

Like most Hong Kong movies, the two we've listed are subtitled in English and Chinese.
   Videos are available in most Chinatowns in North America. Issue #4 of the mag *Naked!
   Screaming! Terror!* featured an overview of HK cinema. Write Kronos Productions, MPO
   Box 67, Oberlin, OH 44074-0067.

For the best coverage of specialist, cult and all-around weird movies, pick up on
   Psychotronic Video (see the magazine section of our *Ink* chapter.)

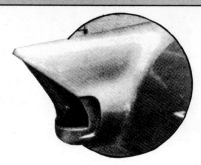

Paul Bartel's 5 Coolest Cartoons

Clock Cleaners (Walt Disney)
Concerto For Sub-machine Gun (Zagreb)
Rootie Toot Toot (UPA)
King Size Canary (Tex Avery)
Mickey's Trailer (Walt Disney)

John calls it the beginning;
To Trashmen it's the Bird.
You give yours on the witness stand,
And get it when you've heard.
Even future-shocking cyberpunks
Can't do without the Word.
To sample some truly gelid ones,
Scroll up the following blurbs.

Bound for Glory:

30 Boss Books

A BEAR FOR THE FBI—Melvin Van Peebles (Pocket 1968).Mario's dad didn't just conquer Broadway (*Ain't Supposed to Die a Natural Death*), bust moves on Hollywood (directing Godfrey Cambridge in *Watermelon Man*, writing and starring in 1971's *Sweet Sweetback's Baadasssss Song*), and cut the outrageously hip *Br'er Soul* lp (A&M,1969). MVP wrote one sharp little gem of a growing-up novel, now sadly out of print. Dig the wicked "dozens," sex mentor Sammy, the throat club and more.

BORDER RADIO—Gene Fowler & Bill Crawford, with foreward by Wolfman Jack (Texas Monthly Press 1987). They sold baldness cures and death-bed remedies, pushed bibles and baby chicks and raw blues. They were the the million-watt mad daddies of Cal-Tex-Mex radio, in the crackling nights before the dawn of formats and faceless jocks. This is their story.

COLLECTED POEMS 1947-1980—Allen Ginsberg (Harper & Row Perennial Library; paper, 1984). In his heyday, Ginsberg was like nothing that had

ever shot out of the canon of American poetry: a high-strung, certifiably flipped word machine flashing on the impending mania. Remember, when Big Al dropped such electric Highway Poesy as "Howl," "Kaddish" and "Reality Sandwiches," most of America was bowling. D.W.

COMING THROUGH SLAUGHTER—Michael Ondaatje (W.W. Norton 1977). Wildly hallucinogenic account of the saga of Buddy Bolden, the schizoid "inventor" of New Orleans jazz who blew so hard blood once came out of his cornet. Storyville seen through a cockeyed kaleidoscope. Unforgettable set piece: the fiery death of Bellocq, the hydrocephalic dwarf who photographed whores. D.B.

THE COMMITMENTS—Roddy Doyle (Random House 1990). Tough, funny, no-shit-whatsoever account of an Irish green-eyed soul band's rise & fall. Mostly dialogue and simple sentences. James Brown's "Night Train" gets a local re-do: "Startin' off in Connolly / Movin' on ou' to Killester/Harmonstown Raheny/ an' don't forget Kilbarrack the home o' the blues!" Tight and all right! D.B.

Dancers in the Scalp House
A novel by William Eastlake

DANCERS IN THE SCALPHOUSE—William Eastlake (Viking 1975). Something's gone positively batshit in Indian Country. The water is rising rapidly at the new dam, threatening to engulf Checkerboard Mesa and annihilate the Navajos. Developers are bulldozing the once pristine landscape and throwing up The Back To God Estates. Out by Route 44 an FBI man is playing with himself beneath a 60-foot, lasso-twirling naked neon lady. And some nutcase has a scheme to transport the Caspian Sea to New Mexico as a tourist trap.

Are the noble redmen PO'ed? You bet your sweet, leather burned tuchas. But there won't be any flaming arrows this time out, no staking the palefaces to anthills or impaling them on the nearest teddy bear cholla. This time, you see, the Indians have an atomic bomb! R.S.

DEADWOOD—Pete Dexter (Random House 1986; Penguin paper). *Paris Trout* author's second and best. A fantastic, poetically compressed western. Begins with Wild Bill Hickok, cursed with gallstones, needing half an hour to take a leak, and just gets better. Almost as good: Ron Hansen's retelling of a cool blizzard in his collection *Nebraska* (Atlantic Monthly Press 1989). D.B.

DELIBERATE SPEED: THE ORIGINS OF A CULTURAL STYLE IN THE AMERICAN 1950'S—W.T. Lhamon, Jr. (Smithsonian Institution Press 1990). "You should have been there," Lennon said, but not everyone could make the gig. This perceptive study of the decade won't take you there, but it makes a strong case that much subsequent American culture—from the vaunted Sixties to the vacuous Eightiesnineties—is one long aftershock from the shook-up epoch. Looks book: **POPULUXE**—Thomas Hine (Knopf 1986), a solid-state overview of the designs of the times (1954-1964).

THE DUBLINERS—James Joyce (orig. 1916; Penguin paper). The original Jimbo had the word right from the start with this amazingly clear-eyed study of a world that remains in the psyche of many of us. Social problems that would be treated in turgid TV movies today are painted with chill lucidity in prose that is the definition of "deceptive simplicity." J.T.

GO—John Clellon Holmes (1952; 1988 Thunder's Mouth Press). Before Jack hit the road, Holmes sleuthed for truth in the crash pads of Forties N.Y. bohemia. Many of the same cast tread the boards in both books (here, Neal Cassady's "Hart Kennedy"), but they play under different lights. More "conventionally" written than Kerouac's account, Holmes' somehow manages to tune in more acutely. Like Seymour Krim says, "His radar dishes were up."

THE GREAT ROOB REVOLUTION—Roger Price (Random House 1970). The former *Mad* humorist didn't live to see Desert Storm trading cards or last week's Big Hair band, but his treatise on the vulgarization of American culture still drops savage science. Why are good movies, books and music in such short supply? Price's First Law: "If everybody doesn't want it, nobody gets it."

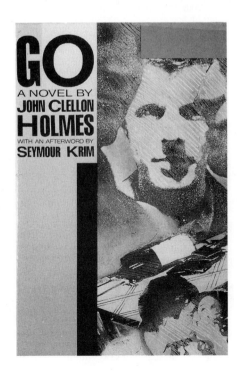

HIGH TIMES, HARD TIMES—Anita O'Day (Putnam's 1981). As Krupa and Kenton's canary, she got hooked on jazz and sang a storm. As a bop Boswell, she tells well of scenes and swingers. On her first hubby, drummer Don Carter: "He had a thing about water. When it rained in the middle of the night, he'd get dressed and go for a walk. When he'd come back, he'd write down the rhythm of the raindrops on the umbrella."

S.E. Hinton by permission,
Bantam/Doubleday/Dell
Publishing Group

S.E. HINTON

Tulsa native wrote her first book (*The Outsiders*, Viking 1967) at age 17. Rumor has it the androgynous tag was suggested by a publisher who thought the masses would have a hard time buying gritty gang dramas from a teenage girl. Her books, including *Rumblefish* (Delacorte 1975) and *That Was Then, This Is Now* (Viking 1971), create a blue collar world filled with dysfunctional or out-of-the-way parental units, kids who are either socs (madras shirts, new wheels) or greasers (denim jackets, cool wheels) and teen angst for days. If for no other reason than she named the female soc in *Outsiders* Cherry Valance, these books are recommended. Coppola made a series of art films for pizza-faces outta them, the best being *Rumblefish* which has Matt Dillon, Dennis Hopper and Mickey Rourke as kin. A literary breath of Marlboro-stoked air for future sluts and JD's. A.L.

HOMEBOY—Seth Morgan (Vintage Contemporaries 1990). A tossup. Some find it a "trust kid's stab at *nostalgia de la boue*." Others dig it as a crazed scumbag cartoon slangfest. Whichever, this tour of S.F.'s Tenderloin freaks and pornomakers is the last we'll get from Morgan. In 1990, he drove into a wall and out of this life. D.B.

HUNTER—J.A. Hunter (Harpers 1952). Ultimate Brit white hunter *sangfroid*. Unfazed by the stickiest wicket, the author faces down every bad-ass beast in the African bush, then rates 'em on a danger scale. Find out what the baroness was

after when she stripped in front of our hero during the lion hunt. D.B.

I JAN CREMER—(Shorewood hardcover 1965; Signet paper). An autobiographical (we'll have to take his word for it) novel by post-Beat, Kerouac-influenced Dutch "action painter." Cremer might very well have lived the life credited to Jagger. Art, Harleys, hardcore sex and an anarchist's jaundiced eye make the book an encapsulation of proto-Europunk. B.M.

INTO THE HEART OF BORNEO—Redmond O'Hanlon (Random House). In 1983, British naturalist O'Hanlon and his poet-journalist buddy James Fenton took off for the world's third-largest island to contend with rivers, tropical jungles, and mountains no Westerners had tackled in 50 years. *Into The Heart Of Borneo*—one of the hippest travel books ever—is O'Hanlon's half-surreal, mostly hilarious report on their crack-brained expedition. Armed with books, medications and liquors and daily doused with anti-fungus powder until their "erogenous zones looked like meat chunks rolled in flour," the pair and their three antic Iban guides meet with nations of pests (leeches, wild-boar ticks, inch-long ants) and dazzlingly rare creatures (fish-eagles, pig-tailed macques, dinosaurlike water monitors) alike. They see 800 weird kinds of trees and have almost as many bizarre jungle-inspired dreams. Though the rumored blowpipe-toting Bornean cannibals never materialize, the explorers are obliged to teach the natives they do encounter the seven-step disco and to improvise war dances for them in raucous—and bibulous—tribal jam sessions. The Iban tribesmen, O'Hanlon writes, always lay down when they "know that they are going to laugh for a long time." Definitely the sort of book to take lying down. P.F.

I PAID MY DUES . . . GOOD TIMES, NO BREAD—Babs Gonzales (Expubidence Publishing). The bop bard ("Oop-Pop-A-Da," "Be-Bop Santa") and raconteur spills all in this 1967 autobio. Daddy G's a king word-head (upon hitting the Apple, he gets a gig and "enough bread to burn a wet mule") who had his priorities in place from the start ("With my paper route, my gambling in school and my other hustles, I was able to acquire a radio and two new drape suits"). In '61, Babs participated in an anti-segregation "wade-in" in Tampa Bay, and opened his own N.Y. nightclub, the Insane Asylum. The waiters and bartenders dressed in strait-jackets.

JUKE JOINT—Birney Imes (University Press of Mississippi 1990). His funny, funky-exotic photos of a culture both strange and familiar prove Imes is not just some whiteboy shutterbug slummin' through the Delta. These trip pix show he's got a great eye, and a great heart too. D.B.

KING BLOOD—Jim Thompson (Korgi 1989). Judged too psycho-sadistic for U.S. publication, it's only available as a Brit paperback. A "western" unlike any other, written by the king of *roman noir*. D.B.

LES CHANTS DU MALDOROR—Comte De Lautreamont (Isidore Ducasse) (Originally published 1879; available now in Penguin, New Directions paper). In the mid-Nineteenth, Izzy laid these pages—the first Surrealist prose wig-out—on a publisher, then split. Narrator raps with toads, hermaphrodites, and a gigantic hair inside a whorehouse before balling a shark. D.B.

LIBRA—Don DeLillo (Viking 1988). The unofficial, hence coolest, version of one of contemporary history's darkest chapters, with prose so heady you expect side effects. Says as much about the haunted here & now (converging vectors of fate and politics, small men swept up in big events) as it does about 11/22/63.

LOST IN THE COSMOS: THE LAST SELF-HELP BOOK—Walker Percy (Washington Square Press, 1983). The late Louisianan pulls the rug out from under the cult of mediocrity in this self-help book which argues that there may be no self, and no way to help "it." D.W.

THE MAMBO KINGS PLAY SONGS OF LOVE—Oscar Hijuelos (paper; Harper & Row Perennial Library, 1989). Don't let the fact that this was a national best-seller, copped a Pulitzer, and has been turned into a big-time H'wood flick make you take a left. The saga of Cuban musician brothers Cesar and Nestor Castillo, who come to New York in 1949, ride the Latin music-craze wave, and bend to the pleasures and perils of semi-fame (after a tune of Nestor's hits the charts), is hands-down cool. Writing with equal parts soul and chops, Hijuelos quickly has us not only seeing, hearing and smelling but also thinking right inside the Castillos' world. You have the opulent food, drink, sex, and streetlife; the packed and jumping nightclubs; and the cheesy small-time recording studios, yes. But the main richness is in the penetrating psych portaits of brooding, bedeviled Nestor and of

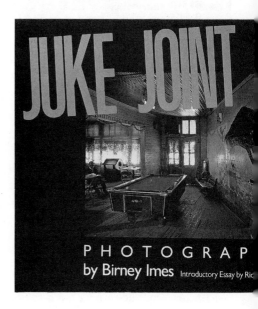

STONE CITY—Mitchell Smith (Signet paper 1991). Ancient history prof convicted of manslaughter is forced to solve a murder in a place where everybody's a killer: state prison. Portraits of different gangs and rich introspection of the main character add depth to this disturbing chiller. J.T.

SUMMER OF NIGHT—Dan Simmons (Putnam's 1991). The dinosaurs aren't dead; get a load of the bloated monstrosities snorting and farting in the horror section of your local bookstore. But, if you *are* in the market for a chillin' read you can stretch out with, here's one long horror novel that earns its length—in uncanny fashion, actually, since someone (or some *thing*) has cunningly arranged the hardcover edition to come out to exactly 555 pages-111 short of 666, the number of the apocalyptic Beast—while the story itself relates how a bestial Advent was forestalled in rural Illinois in 1960 by a bunch of kids who could have been you or me. Simmons lovingly evokes the time and place and the dreamy pastoral of summer vacation, giving life to characters who rub you this way and that like your real friends do. Standing on the last edge of childhood, these young folks take on a virtual invasion from the land of the dead—one which emanates from the slimiest aspects of adult authority—and it's a real heart punch what happens to the best and the brightest. And if the plethora of *things* snaking through the cornfield or smirking in the sump pump makes the book feel a little like the Mormon Tabernacle Choir is singing "Monster Mash," hell, I'd love to hear it. A graveyard smash. J.T.

VIEWS FROM A WINDOW: CONVERSATIONS WITH GORE VIDAL—(Lyle Stuart 1980). Vidal hits above and below the belt in what could serve as an excellent intro to the prejudices, criticisms and unique observations of America's greatest living essayist.

On American gullibility: "Television and newspapers are all part of the con game. Revolution will begin when people find they haven't got the money to buy what they need, and when this happens they'll get angry, and since a fair percentage own Saturday-night specials, the consumer society will fall apart."

On American men: "To hear two American men congratulating each other on being heterosexual is one of the most chilling experiences—and unique to the United States. You don't hear two Italians sitting around complimenting each other because they actually like to go to bed with women. The American is hysterical about his manhood." R.S.

nonstop hedonist Cesar. In the novel's especially powerful second half, Cesar ruminates on Nestor's untimely death and slowly rots because of it and his addiction to carnal delights. The insides of a helpless sensualist have rarely been so deftly plumbed. All this and Desi Arnaz as a fully realized character, too. P.F.

THE MONKEY WRENCH GANG—Edward Abbey, with illos by R. Crumb (Tenth Anniversary Edition by Dream Garden Press, 1985). An eccentric physician, a sexy feminist, a river-running Mormon polygamist and a supremely self-sufficient, violently unpredictable Vietnam vet decide to actually *do* something about the environment. Their ultimate goal? Blow up the despised Glen Canyon Dam. Warning: *Not* for Sting-oriented armchair environmentalists. R.S.

SAME BED, DIFFERENT DREAMS—Hugh Gross (Midlist Press 1991). Japanese adman Toshio Matsuzaka is an irreverent wise-ass whose bullet-train-paced banter and sardonic brain, like his nightly business "entertaining" amid the "snacks" and "pink salons" of Tokyo, compensate him somewhat for his entrapment in a workaholic culture. Toshio also does a mean *karaoke* version of "My Way"—"The Salaryman's Anthem." Gray flannel suit, Rising Sun style. J.T.

WANDERER—Sterling Hayden (Knopf 1963). "I wonder whether there has ever before been a man who bought a schooner and joined the Communist party on the same day? I smiled in spite of myself as I poured from a tall green bottle." Precious fluids had Hayden's head long before he obsessed about them as *Strangelove*'s Commander Jack D. Ripper. Here's his outspoken account of, among many things, his affair with the sea—to which he took after he walked out on Hollywood, marriage and mortgage one velvet morning.

WISEGUY—Nicholas Pileggi (Simon & Schuster 1985; Pocket Books 1987). The true story of *Good-Fellas'* Henry and Karen Hill, the Lufthansa heist, Sonny Bamboo, Charlie Flip, etc. Reality check: read back-to-back with the *GoodFellas* screenplay (Scorsese & Pileggi; Faber and Faber paper 1990).

YOU CAN'T WIN—Jack Black (Macmillan 1926). Crusty old "Bull Lee" Burroughs copped a lotta style offa this hobo/ yegg's memoir from the aughts and 'teens. Falls somewhere between *Huckleberry Finn* and *On The Road*, but with jewel thieves and opium dens. Second edition boasts intro by Mr. B himself, cover by Joe Coleman, one of the scariest artists alive. D.B.

Sterling Hayden: smiling but sea-bound.

INTO THE PAPER UNIVERSE by Jim Trombetta

The Last Word
In Hyper-real Reads

There are those who love deconstruction, who dig more than anything else the feeling of being *wised up*. Others, however, would rather believe the puppets are real than tear the theater apart to reveal . . . a nondescript or even shabby person crouching and waving his mitts around. We latter folks love to be fooled: give us a world which is so truly strange, so hypnotically convincing, that when our visit is over we're not exactly sure what *is* real . . . a world like that of A.A. Attansio's *Radix* (Bantam, 1981), a fever dream of Earth bathed in the radiations of a rotating black hole. Here sometime fatso Sumner Kagan improves his muscle tone considerably as he confronts the killer android Nefandi (created to look like Clint Eastwood in *A Fistful of Dollars*), the eerie voors (aliens in human bodies who have taken vodoun to new heights), and, in a bizarre continent that used to be South America, the artificial intelligence Rubeus, the nastiest sorcerer's apprentice in history, past or future . . .

A Vegas of the Soul,
A New Orleans of the Mind

"To those who remember starlight, the spring sky over Charn is one of the most desolate sights in the universe," writes Paul Park in *Soldiers Of Paradise* (Avon, 1987). Take the elevator to the mountaintop and check out Charn . . . a Vegas of the soul whose blazing neon signs advertise not gambling but *religion* . . . a belief so extreme it provides prisons for babies astrologically judged to have done bad things in their previous incarnations . . . yet now that the years-long winter is ending, even some of those blessed with the sacred Starbridge tattoo are losing their faith . . .

What makes Park's world creation here and in *Soldiers'* sequel *Sugar Rain* (Avon, 1987) truly fabulous is, paradoxically, the way it includes the mundane: people are driving battered trucks, toting bolt-action rifles, hanging out by the railroad yards . . . smoking reefer. For more such funky strangeness, look no further than the recently reissued *Man in the High Castle* (Ace, 1962), by alternate-reality maestro Philip K. Dick. The recent prevalence of the (former) Axis powers gives new bite to this classic about a world in which they won WW II, especially that moment when Mr. Tagomi, the Japanese administrator of San Francisco, falls through a hole in the text into our world . . . which he experiences as a vision from hell from the Tibetan Book of the Dead . . . a vision which inspires some courageous acts on his part.

Post-industrial Sex
& Galactic George Smiley

One reason to read Michael Swanwick's *Stations of the Tide* (Avon, 1991) is a theory of why TV will still be addictive even after more powerful media have been invented. Another reason is the planet Miranda's Tidewater region, a Louisiana bayou/New Orleans of the mind . . . where the genius mindfucker Gregorian is hiding out from his pursuer—the nameless "Bureaucrat." This off-kilter hero is a kind of galactic George Smiley whose wits have been honed by office politics conducted through the last word in "virtual reality." The Bureaucrat's deadline is strict—the Tidewater region will shortly be drowned by tidal waves from the melting polar icecaps. He learns finally that the secrets of Order are more bizarre than those of Chaos —and, along the way, gets to sample some pretty hot post-industrial sex.

Which brings us at last to *Stars in My Pocket Like Grains of Sand* (Bantam, 1984) by Samuel R. Delany—if it isn't the most "politically correct" object in the universe, the light from the others hasn't reached us yet. In a galaxy-wide future of many complex human societies linked through an instantaneous communications "Web," even the pronouns "he" and "she" don't mean what they used to; they don't describe a speaker's sex but his or her *perceptual stance* . . . I think. Then there's this one planet where "normal" sex is a *menage a trois* between humans and certain native. . .creatures.

Delany sets not only gender but eroticism at a distance so we experience them not as facts but as creations of imagination. The mental stretch is worth it because it draws us into the suspenseful tale of one "Rat" Korga, the sole surviuvor of an entire world whose atmosphere has been ignited by the aliens known only as Xlv . . . who *don't* communicate . . . who have who-knows-what kind of intentions . . . and who seem to be following Korga around . . . Delany doesn't play with your head to give you a lecture or even to *tell* you about the future—he wants you to *be there*.

UNSCIENTIFIC FICTION:
Philip K. Dick's Outsider Classics

by Alan Karp

It's a familiar story, sad but true. Talented artist struggles in obscurity, gains limited measure of recognition, but dies or goes crazy before he gets his due.

Things were just starting to pop for Philip K. Dick when he bid the world adieu in 1982. *Blade Runner*, which was based on his novel *Do Androids Dream Of Electric Sheep?*, was about to be released and the establishment of Dick's reputation as one of the finest science fiction writers this side of Alpha Centuri was a virtual fait accompli.

With the success of *Blade Runner*, a whole new generation of readers became acquainted with his luminous SF, the most famous examples of which include *The Man In The High Castle*, *Ubiq*, *Martian Time Slip*, and *Do Androids . . .*

Zoro's Electric Sleep

More recently, the public has also been regaled with a cornucopia of personal revelations that are every bit as mind-boggling as Dick's fictive speculations. The seminal text is *The Selected Letters Of Philip K. Dick, 1974* (Underwood-Miller 1991), which blends some heady hypotheses on the meaning of the cosmic visions he experienced in March of that year (that he was visited by a super-

intelligence variously interpreted as being Zoroaster, the Delphic Oracle, and Bishop James Pike, among others) with paranoid delusions (?) about KGB plots to sequester him behind the Iron Curtain and his ouster from Marin County at the behest of the FBI and/or CIA.

And so the legend grows. But wait, there's more. Because for those who only know Dick as a cultish SF author, the biggest revelation of all may very well be that he also wrote at least one "mainstream" novel that has no peer in terms of the penetrating way it combines loopy humor with an intensely paranoid vision of middle American life in the Fifties.

PKD 1973, Fullerton, California.

Photo by Tessa Dick.
Courtesy of the Estate of PKD.

A must read for aficionados of the era, *Confessions Of A Crap Artist*, which was written in 1959, is ostensibly a "Chronicle of Verified Scientific Fact, 1945-1959" penned by Jack Isadore, a character who reappears in slightly altered form in *Do Androids Dream Of Electric Sleep?* Although he is initially portrayed as an imbecile par excellence (according to PKD, Jack was modeled after Isadore of Seville, a medieval scribe who wrote the world's shortest encyclopedia), Jack Isadore is also the penultimate survivor and Dick clearly loves him for it.

Regrooving Frisco

Like many of Dick's sad-sack heroes, Jack's entire existence begs the question of what is real or sane and what constitutes artificiality or madness, concerns that haunted the author until his death. It makes perfect sense then that, as the novel opens, Jack Isadore is toiling away in San Francisco as a "tire regroover," a typically Dickian paradigm of useless (and flagrantly fraudulent) labor, in which the "trained technician" paints a groove on worn down tires to give them the appearance of being new.

The two other major characters, both of whom also serve as first-person narrators, are Fay Hume, Jack's upwardly mobile sister, and Charlie Hume, her oafishly complacent husband. In many ways Jack's polar opposite, Fay is essentially defined by her fiercely self-centered quest to become the ultimate suburban matriarch, a position she seems to accept as her birthright. As for poor doting Charlie, he really has no place else to go but around the bend after he provides Fay with the suburban dream house that completes her fief.

Although many of the key incidents in *Crap Artist*—from the resentment that Charlie feels when Fay coerces him into buying her Tampax to the hilariously lurid account of Fay's extra-marital tryst that Jack writes up (to make it seem more "real") for the hospital-ridden Charlie—are played for laughs, what finally emerges is a nightmarish vision of the fabulous Fifties that turns *Father Knows Best* upside down. And in the final accounting, it is th eeerie starkness of this vision (the "reality" of it, if you will) as refracted through the comic innocence of Jack Isadore's perceptions that make *Confessions Of A Crap Artist* required reading.

Looking For The Little Green Men

While most of Dick's other mainstream novels (he wrote about 13) tend to be far less satisfying than *Crap Artist*, the hybrid *Time Out Of Joint*, which is generally considered to be SF, is a special case in the Dickian oeuvre and the book that those with an aversion to SF and an affinity for the Fifties would do well to turn to next after *Confessions*. Ironically, although Dick's publisher asked him to trash the first two-thirds of *Time*, presumably because it was too mainstream, it is precisely those first two-thirds that are most rewarding, due to the brilliance of Dick's serio-comic meditations on life in the Fifties.

Time Out Of Joint, which Dick claimed Martin Scorsese had optioned in 1974, was eventually sold (for $750) as a "novel of menace," a crude but not all that inaccurate description of a novel about a man who believes that his entire world is a fake. In retrospect, it almost seems as if Dick were saying that American life at the time had become so overbearingly weird and conformist that it could not possibly have been real. Maybe he was right.

Like Jack Isadore, *Time*'s protagonist is a grown man who lives with his sister, only in this case, instead of regrooving tires, Ragle Gumm's daily routine revolves around solving the nationally syndicated newspaper puzzle "Where Will The Little Green Man Be Next?" Ragle's problems begin when his physical reality begins drifting away, only to be replaced by slips of paper that signify what has previously seemed to exist—like "soft drink stand" or "toilet bowl." Can this really be happening? Has Ragle gone nuts?

As with *Invasion Of The Body Snatchers* and a host of other films and novels of the era, it is easy to read political messages into *Time Out Of Joint*'s paranoid underpinnings. And yet, what resonates most strongly in this book is the sense that for Dick, time really is out of whack. That is, although Ragle Gumm has created a bogus reality, circa 1959, in order to escape from a cataclysmic future, it is the stultifying complacency of the Fifties that the author seems to be trying the hardest to dismiss.

Unfortunately, the last third of the book, with its obligatory reliance on some all too familiar sci-fi conventions, fails to bring the book to a fully satisfying conclusion. Nevertheless, *Time* still ranks as a classic of outsider fiction whose wonderfully wry and twisted observations on madness and sanity create a remarkably engaging portrait of life in the Fifties as envisioned by one of that decade's most underappreciated writers.

Goods: *Confessions Of A Crap Artist* (Entwhistle Books 1975; paperback 1977); *Time Out Of Joint* (Lippincott 1959; paper, Dell 1979).

MAG BAG

Cadwallader J. Cadd

It's more than their publishing schedules that make the following publications highly irregular. Each one gives attitude and gets right to the point of view . . .

DUMB ANGEL GAZETTE. Domenic Priore's book-length periodicals resemble a pop-cultural car crash at rush hour. Your eyes collide with bits and remnants of cool 'n' curious scenes half recalled and here clarified with lotsa love. DAG's a good place to go for everything you ever wanted to know about Big Daddy Roth, the TAMI Show, the *Smile* album, Mr. Gasser or Delvy McNort. Moon-equipped, and not afraid of dissing its gods (an especially dumb photo of Mike Love is slugged "The Shmoe From Kokomo"). P.O. Box 4131, Carlsbad, CA 92018.

CAD. Sweaty-palmed, beady-eyed sexism returns at full gallop in this book-mag pastiche of Fifties/early Sixties male skin mags, e.g. *Dude, Nugget, Rogue, Escapade*. Get those flashlights under the covers again. D.B.
Feral House Publishing, P.O. Box 861893, Los Angeles CA 90086-1893).

THE REALIST

Paul Krassner's venerable magazine/newsletter, founded in 1958, isn't for everyone, but neither are John Sununu or lethal injection. Real and imagined events are reported, but never differentiated, in *The Realist*. Does the sour Tom Wolfe-Spike Lee transcript come from a real interview? Does coverage of the grand opening of Hawaii's Aloha Bar (a death-themed Hard Rock decorated with car parts from the crashes of the rich and famous) come from Waikiki or some place less accessible? *The Realist*'s editorials rock in no uncertain terms: "Why Andrew Dice Clay Is No Lenny Bruce."
Write P.O. Box 1230, Venice, CA 90294.

PSYCHOTRONIC VIDEO

PV is assuredly non-fiction, though its content frequently bests pure fantasy. Its cult-soaked pages regularly hip acolytes to the sacred cornerstones of filmic flotsam—everything from Fifties monsterdrama (*Zontar*) and teenbeat (*Rock, You Sinners*, starring Jackie Collins) to Seventies softcore (*Dagmar's Hot Pants*) and beyond (a trenchant treatise on "Christopher Plummer In Canadian Drug Movies"). No lie: Its obit column "Never To Be Forgotten" consistently salutes the best & the baddest (Gene Clark, Slim Gaillard, Mike Mazursky, Doc Pomus). If you don't swing, don't ring. Otherwise, 151 First Ave., Dept. PV, New York, N.Y. 10003.

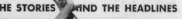
RENT A WIFE FOR A MONT

ROBERT HARRISON The High Priest of Sleaze

by Nick Tosches

PDC **WHISPER**
THE STORIES BEHIND THE HEADLINES   JUL

SIN WITH A MAMBO BEAT

BABES ARE BOOBY TRAPS

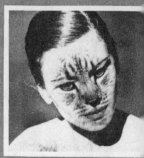
INSIDE NIGHTMARE ALLEY

Robert Harrison, of whom little is known and less remembered, began publishing *Beauty Parade*, the first of the girlie magazines, in 1941. Amid advertisements that were often stranger than fiction ("Girls Can't Resist the KISS ME NECKTIE as it GLOWS in the DARK!"), *Beauty Parade* offered everything from hair fetishism ("Titian Tresses") to catfighting ("Battling Babes"). "Dramatizing Lingerie" (February 1942) and "Ankles Aweigh" (May 1952) were representative of a decade of purposeful editorial thinking. Early issues included color centerfolds by Bruno of Hollywood.

Beauty Parade was five years old and going strong when Harrison began putting out *Whisper* in early 1947. This new bimonthly featured even hotter fetish photos. Every cover featured a dame in

hosiery. It was almost as if a dame without hose was no dame at all. But *Whisper* featured something else as well: scandal exposes and true-crime stories. *Whisper* took its readers to a "Benzedrine Thrill Party," where "kids become hopped up." (Of course, all the gals at the thrill party were pictured wearing high heels and stockings.) In July 1948, *Whisper* gave the lowdown on "Dope: Our Secret Sin": "Soft lights . . . the plink of the guitar . . . the moan of the saxophone . . . And in the faces of a few in every youthful gaping group in Hipsters Heaven—52nd Street, New York—one can see the glazed eyes that signify this or that poor youth has joined the big tea and witch hazel mob (marijuana and heroin if you're not hep to jive)." There was also practical advice. "Don't go around figuring you're the smartest bucko since Ein-

98

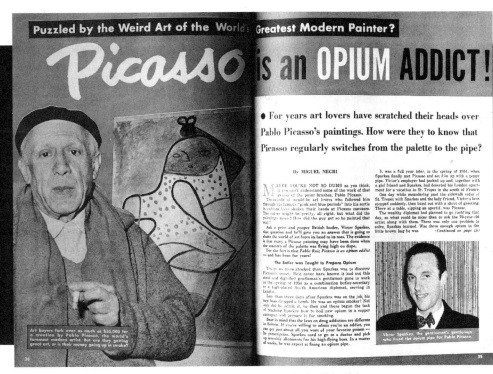

Harrison dredged up Pablo's slip from the straight and narrow in *Confidential.*

stein," *Whisper* warned in "How the Shakedown Sweeties of the Big Town Ply Their Nefarious Trades" (March 1948), "because there's a racket for you, and a smart gal who'll make you throw caution to the winds."

Whisper's blend of flying saucers, garterbelts, bondage, and hardboiled hepcat journalism was as successful as it was sublime. There was no stopping Harrison now. Late in 1952 came *Confidential*, the ultimate distillation of Harrison's vision of a sleazo-centric universe.

Though *Whisper* was by far the most intriguing and outrageous of Harrison's publications, *Confidential* was the crown of his ascendance. As a prosecutor later put it, *Confidential* "maliciously dredged up from the gutters a slip from the straight and narrow path by a prominent individual and depicted it as the individual's way of life," i.,rerring "by innuendo the lewdest sort of situations." *Confidential* was *The Scarlet Letter* for real, *Time* magazine for the salt and scum of the earth, the confirmer of every vicious suspicion;

the *logos* of America's cheap, meaningless mythology. By 1957 *Confidential*'s newsstand circulation, estimated at four million, was the largest of any magazine in the country.

The beginning of the end came in June of that year, when Harrison and his associates were arraigned in Los Angeles on charges of conspiring to commit criminal libel. Under a court agreement that autumn, Harrison relented: *Confidential* and *Whisper* would revise their editorial policies in exchange for the dismissal of criminal charges. The magazines lingered, wraiths of their former glory, through 1973. Harrison's end passed un-noted. But his legacy, while still unhonored, imbues every breath America takes. Many have spoken of America in search of herself. Robert Harrison found her, posed the way men like 'em.

SLEAZO-CENTRIC INK: *Unseen America: The Greatest Cult Exploitation Magazines, 1955-66, The Illustrated Price Guide And Index To Scandal Magazines: 1952-1966*; both from Shake Books, 449 12th St., # 2R, Brooklyn, N.Y. 11215.

COMIC COOL

by Danny Weizmann

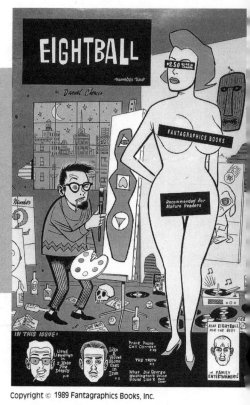

Pop art, shmop art. Most of today's so-called "underground" or "alternative" culture klatches are actually run by vicious shmucko soda-pop corps who'd sell their souls to a three-headed dog faster'n you can say "dross." There is, though, one medium that still encourages the individual *artiste* to fly solo, from idea through execution, free from the party line: the underground comic. Let's just come right out and say it: they're better than ever. Today's u'ground comic cat is practically a walking relic, a single person with a single vision, and very little to lose. The new comic underground is full of men and women with funny, crazy, truthful things to say, right here in 1992.

Not that these graphic auteurs don't have history. *Mad, Panic, Krazy Kat, American Splendor, Raw, Weirdo,* and the genius of R. Crumb preceded them. And that cultural luggage is just the point. The new artists are part of a long tradition of breaking tradition.

The following is a hand-picked what's what of currently publishing cool-coms. Cop & orb.

EIGHTBALL. A razor-tongued meanster with an eye for the graphically hep, Daniel Clowes first made waves by creating the fridged-out P.I. *Lloyd Llewellyn.* In *Eightball,* Clowes serializes "Like A Velvet Glove Cast In Iron," the mod pilgrim's

100

Copyright © 1990 Fantagraphics Books, Inc.

journey through a far outer limit that includes New Age weirdie concentration camps and face-less dogs and dandruff with eyeballs. Issue 4 also features "I Predict The Future," a prophecy which posts Armageddon shortly following the invention of hi-fi pizza. From Fantagraphics, 7563 Lake City Way NE, Seattle WA 98115.

HATE. Superman flies, Plastic Man stretches. Peter Bagge's Buddy Bradley scowls, in all his paranoid, disgusted, proto- slobular glory. Buddy, who first appeared in Bagge's *The Bradleys*, also slouches — through lo-rent bohemia, ducking dumb jobs,

crazed ex-girlfriends and fascist siblings like they were ten tons of kryptonite. Wildest is Bud's bud Stinky, world's greatest skateboarding mohican boho confidence man, who woos ladies with a "Secret Love Formula: LSD + TORN FISHNETS + A FIRMLY ENTRENCHED CAPITALIST PATRIARCHAL SOCIAL STRUCTURE = GREAT SEX." Throwing blows over the last can of cheap beer in the fridge, Buddy and Stinky make for a portrait of the last vestiges of disenfranchised youth culture that is alternately moving and ridiculous. Issue 5 shows real-life winners of the international Win A Date With Stinky contest. Heroic. (Fantagraphics)

JIMBO. *Adventures in Paradise.* Gary Panter's proto-punk finds trouble under every trash heap, saves his receipts from Burger King, has a nervous breakdown collecting recyclable cans, and grooves on out with "The Walking Cremated." Less like a comic book, more like the lost hieroglyphic scrolls of a post-nuke maniac, *Adventures in Paradise* is hard to follow but bears big fruit, not the least of which is a 29-page scrawl-map of Jimbo's Final Days adventure, "running barefoot on fire with his clothes melted off." Blechhh! (Raw/Pantheon/Random House)

LOVE AND ROCKETS. Gilbert and Jaime Hernandez' tales of survival in both the urban sweatbox and the fictional Mexican village of Palomar are staggering in their sophistication. The comic-book form has seldom been the stage for so much dramatic interplay, subtle characterization and gripping realism. In another era, *Love And Rockets* might've surfaced as hi-brow lit. We're glad it's comics: the Hernandez bros. know how to draw some dynamite-looking women. (Fantagraphics)

STICKBOY. In various alternate universes, Dennis Worden's Stickboy has a round head, a square head, an oval head, and a marshmallow-shaped head. The "All Filosofy Issue" peaks when the oval-headed Stickboy discusses existentialism with an intellectual fly that has crawled up a dog's rear end. "You can see these pages," the fly says, "as a prison or as the space which allows you to exist." Also pick up on Worden's *Pedestrian Vulgarity* (both Fantagraphics).

WARTS AND ALL. No show-biz celeb is safe from the picture-perfect graphic replications of Drew and Josh Alan Friedman. The Friedmans transport

has-beens and never-weres into a flippant mismatch world that lies somewhere between the realm of *National Enquirer* cut-and-paste sensationalism and the cut-the-throat gag-ism of early *Mad*. *Warts And All* features the rise & fall of Joey Heatherton, "Dick Clark Models Rock Hairstyles," and an unbearably surreal snap-draw of Milton Berle giving Lee Harvey Oswald a noogie. See also *Any Similarity to Persons Living or Dead is Purely Coincidental*. (Penguin Books).

WHY I HATE SATURN. Kyle Baker's sharpest heroine is a beer columnist named Anne who writes for *Daddy-O*, the mag that promises "Fashions you don't have the body for . . . Black people: Their music, Their art, their hats . . . plus We Mock People We Thought Were Cool Last Month . . . Continue Our Morbid Fascination With The Lower Classes." Like, it's not sci-fi. Anne's sis Laura just *thinks* she's from Saturn. (Piranha Press, 666 Fifth Ave., New York City 10103.)

(Recent work by many of the comic artists cited above is collected in Fantagraphics' two volumes, *The Best Comics of the Decade*.)

DOOM PATROL. New series by Grant Morrison, Richard Case, Mark McKenna, John Nyberg, et. al. Down among the quarks, where the waves and particles meet, there could be as many as *thirteen* dimensions; to scope some of the extra ones, check out any issue of this DC monthly—no special glasses needed. Just when you think you get it, the book mutates in your face. The style of art may even change from page to page, to suit stories as convoluted as the brain itself; indeed, one of the best sequences had our heroes exploring an infinitely-regressive modernist painting. Actually, the Patrollers can barely keep their own changing bodies or personalities sorted out—especially schizo Crazy Jane who's got at least one new self per issue (and whose manifestation as Scarlot the Harlot could resurrect a cemetary full of Frederic Werthams and send them screaming for Jesse Helms). As for the storyline, well, they were evidently composed by Gnostic theologians at a communion breakfast—with something funny in the wafers. Learn to fear the Cult of the Unwritten Book (and its Unholy Ghost), not to mention the Men from N.O.W.H.E.R.E. and their Tearoom of Despair; get out your hankies for the tender romance between the mercenary super-gorilla Mallah and the disembodied brain in his care. Wonder what finally happened to the sand-kicking victim in the Charles Atlas ad? Why the Pentagon is shaped like that? Answers offered here. J.T.

Locked in galleys, doing life terms on pages, they may well possess the power to move worlds. But words heard publicly — pouring from radios, stumbling in the funny lagoons of stage and disc — cast a spell all their own. Test these speakers.

BOB & RAY. If they were a martini, they'd be five parts gin to one of vermouth. But this duo-jet's radio humor is more than wickedly dry and flat. They discovered the hysterical planes of Non-phenomena—in public service announcements for the Office Of Fluctuation Control And Ceiling Repairs and industrial ads for the Monongahela Metal Foundry ("Having unexpected guests see your dull steel ingots is an embarrassing prospect for everyone"), and plumbed the norms of Odd (the priceless "Slow Talkers Of America" interview). There's much more, on five volumes of *The Classic Bob & Ray*, available through RadioArt, P.O. Box 2000 GPO, New York, N.Y. 10116.

STAN FREBERG. The Weird Al of the Fifties, and the Golden Gate between old-style Forties comics and the new "sick" comedians. Best remembered for his savage parodies of Presley ("Heartbreak Hotel"), Johnny Ray ("Cry"), and Lawrence Welk ("W'unnerful W'unnerful"), the mild-mannered adman also scored fastbuck teen stardom in "Old Payola Roll Blues," which exposes the true source of retardo warbler Clyde Ankle's falsetto (he's goosed by a stick). Stan's strangest: his Gleason satire, the "Honeyearthers," which casts Ralph, Ed & co. as sitcom moonmen. More recently, Freberg's the voice-dad in "The Family Dog" episode of Spielberg's *Amazing Stories*, and the star of National Public Radio's "The Stan Freberg Radio Show" (1991).
Capitol Collectors cd *Stan Freberg, Stan Freberg Presents the United States of America* (Capitol lp).
D.B.

Illustration: Peter Bagge

(Courtesy Capitol Records)

107

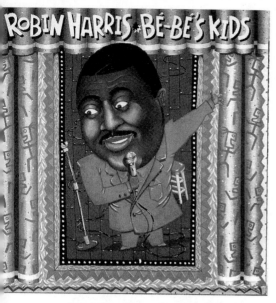

THE BEST OF WORD JAZZ, VOL. 1

'Man, how do I get to Carnegie Hall?' So I said, 'Practice, mother, practice.' Little later, this other cat come up and he said, 'Meeow . . .' He was a real *cat*!" Delivered in a rusty, pre-Waits rasp, Graham's routine includes a parody of Slim Gaillard's "Cement Mixer," an impression of Harry The Hipster officiating at a bop school commencement, and a lecture on the proper way to puff "left-wing Luckies" and "progressive Pall Malls" that almost redeems dope humor. "Of all the instruments, the furnace is the hippest. It's got a draft . . ." This long out-of-print LP also features Louie Nye's tri-martini salute to Mad Ave., "Thimk, Scheme and Plan Ahead," and an excerpt from Pete U's racy riffing (see below).

DICK GREGORY. How about Dick Gregory, stand-up comedian, civil rights activist, writer, and nutritionist? On latenight television, Rev. Jesse Jackson and the Washington D.C. cop commissioner are debating what makes the youth of today want to break the law. Uninvited, some guy stands up in the audience and points the finger: "You two keep talking about family, family this, family that. Family's got nothin' to do with it. The Nazis had family. The Mob has family. It ain't about family! It's about self-respect!" Was that Dick Gregory? The first black comedian to work the white night clubs? The same Dick Gregory who delivered a two-hour speech (1963) in Selma, Alabama, surrounded by police, a move which political historian Howard Zinn has described as "a cultural turning point for the whole South"? The same guy who appeared in *People* under the head "NUTRITION COMEDIAN HELPS THE EXTREMELY OVERWEIGHT WITH INTENSIVE DIET PLAN"? Talk about your American originals! Dick'll lecture the Reverend and the police commissioner, crack some jokes, fight on the frontline for civil rights, then mix up a tropical fruit smoothie so everyone can keep the pounds off!
Books by Dick Gregory: *Nigger: An Autobiography* (Dutton 1964), *No More Lies* (Harper 1971). D.W.

ROBIN HARRIS, *Be Be's Kids* (Polygram). Fat, black and 36, the "sepia Jackie Gleason" (Sweet Dick Willie in *Do The Right Thing*) cut but one cd before he died in 1990. Still, it's a marvel of hit-and-run humor, Harris zinging household names and anonymous hecklers alike with savage speed. Recalling 'Pops,' who constantly reminded him "When I was your age, I walked 20 miles to school," Harris quips "That why you didn't graduate, you was *tired*?"

KEROUAC. The bard's the word on the three-cd box *The Jack Kerouac Collection* (Rhino Wordbeat). Blues and haikus for days. Dig the Railroad Earth.

RONNIE GRAHAM. On the late-Fifties Riverside comedy sampler *How To Be Terribly Terribly Funny*, Graham "was walkin' up the beach the other day, lookin' for some ashtrays in their natural state. This cat came up to me and said,

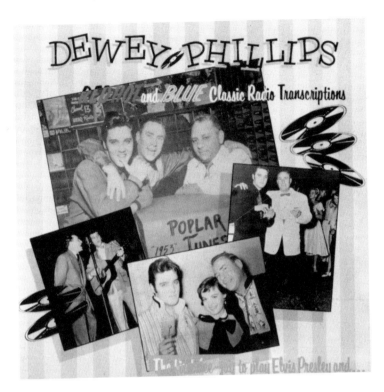

KEN NORDINE. Tom Waits calls him "the guy with the pitch fork in your head saying 'Go ahead and jump.'" The truth is, you've heard him. He's the pipes behind hundreds of radio and TV commercials. What you may not know is that this voice is attached to one of the coolest brains in history. When he isn't hipping the world to Murine or Motorola, Nord takes the time to talk groovy on a series of unparalleled "word jazz" goof discs. Nordine's short-short unpoems carry the listener down a twsting word-road where puns sway and far-out concepts bloom. His mellow, straightfro-ward manner (usually backed by an uptight jazz quartet) is deceiving. Even the squares have been known to experience "IT" — that shimmering plateau of psychedelic knowingness — while digging such Kennord classics as "My Baby," "Reaching Into In," and "The Sound Museum." Essential: *The Best of Word Jazz, Vol. 1* (Rhino/ Word· Beat). *Devout Catalyst* (Grateful Dead Merchandising) D.W.

DEWEY PHILLIPS. For folks brainwashed into the "more music, less talk" stalag of the last two decades, it may seem incomprehensible that a crazed-cat deejay could enhance the records he spins, goose them to greatness with sanctified shouts & spieling. If, as Dyl claimed, Smokey was a poet, then Memphis motormouth Dewey—the first jock to play Presley (1954)—was, like Murray and Wolfman and the Real Don Steele, a shaman-saint, trash-talkin' the word jazz of the spheres into a new nation of ears. Be there now. Try *Red Hot And Blue: Classic Radio Transcriptions* (Zu-Zazz Records). That'll flat git it.

PETER USTINOV (Riverside lp 12-833 *Peter Ustinov*). "During the first Grand Prix du Roc in nineteen hundred and six . . . Roger Knute was disqualified for soliciting aid in pushing his thousand-horse-power Navajomobile, built incidentally in Tucson, after his engine stalled as he swerved to avoid a monkey which had strayed from the rock to watch the race." In the late Fifties, wheelman Ustinov, armed only with a set of notes, faced a live mike and winged an entire Grand Prix race on the Rock of Gibraltar, sending up every nationality and producing an eccentric comedy classic. The French try to demoralize the Germans by bringing girls into the pit, the German driver sneezes on schedule to decrease weight, and the American's car is so heavy that its rear wheels are up in the air, etc. As freshly funny today as when first cut. Vrrrooom. D.B.

Buckley, Nichols & May and Theodore Get With It Without An Audience

By Dr. Demento

LORD BUCKLEY (1906-60) became far better known posthumously than he ever was during his colorful lifetime. Most of his fame sprang from three live albums, two of which were released only after his death.

Much harder to find are his first three albums, all cut *sans* audience. His 1955 ten-inch LP *Hipsters, Flipsters and Finger Poppin' Daddies Knock Me Your Lobes* (RCA Victor) is worth a spot on any Cool Wall just for the title (and cover art) . . . but the best early Buckley is on *Euphoria* and *Euphoria Vol. II*, both on the impossibly obscure Vaya label. Recorded in 1951, these were among the earliest spoken comedy LP's by *anybody*. I'm sure the gregarious Lord would have preferred a live audience, but live recordings were rarely attempted in those days, and the undaunted Buckley filled the empty studio with lively, ebullient renditions of his finest material, including "The Naz," "The Gasser," and "Jonah and the Whale." Did you know ol' Jonah not only enjoyed a toke on the killer weed, but it also helped him escape his Biblical predicament? Here Buckley was, on the very threshold of the McCarthy era, doing stuff that still seemed highly liberated in the late 1960s. No wonder these babies are rare . . . even the 1960s single-LP compilation of these recordings on Crestview (*The Best of Lord Buckley*) is pretty scarce. (Just a couple of years after *Euphoria*, Steve Allen and Al "Jazzbo" Collins hit commercially with much tamer offerings in Buckley's favorite comic genre—retellings of familiar old stories in contemporary hipster slang.)

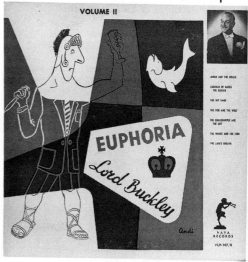

Before Hollywood beckoned the future directors of *The Graduate* and *The Heartbreak Kid*, MIKE NICHOLS AND ELAINE MAY worked together in improv comedy for a decade, making quite a name for themselves in theatres and nightclubs, and making three highly successful and entertaining albums. I'm especially partial to *Mike Nichols and Elaine May Examine Doctors* (Mercury, 1962), the last of the three, and among the very last big-name comedy albums of any kind to be recorded without a live audience (until Firesign Theatre revived the art under very different circumstances in 1969).

At least two of the tracks on *Doctors* are all-time comedy classics. In "A Little More Gauze," physician Nichols cunningly blackmails nurse May in the midst of an operation. In "Physical" May is the doctor, Nichols the bashful, circumspect patient obliged to disrobe in a lady's presence. Most of the others are of similar high quality, with the two artists playing a variety of doctors and patients, exploiting devilishly designed comic situations for all they're worth. Several of the doctors are psychiatrists, in keeping with the runaway #1 comedy topic of the late Fifties and early Sixties.

Not to knock Nichols & May's live act (captured on another strong Mercury LP), but the studio setting allows for subtle and delicious shadings of interplay that just wouldn't have been the same in live performance. We're right there in that operating room, delightedly eavesdropping, rather than out in a noisy audience. We still get intimate comedy like that in the movies, now and then, but it's a shame that more comedians weren't motivated to try that sort of thing on records during the comedy boom of the mid-Sixties.

Coral Records, the Decca Records subsidiary that gave us the Burnette brothers and Buddy Holly, also produced quite a few good comedy records between 1954 and 1959 — singles mostly, with and without music, nearly all of them recorded in studios without live audiences. Coral's stars included Eddie Lawrence ("The Old Philosopher"), Buddy Hackett ("The Chinese Waiter") and, briefly, Bob and Ray, among many others.

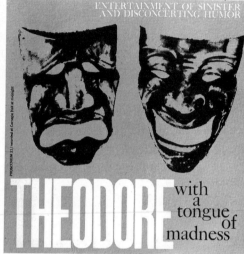

One of Coral's last studio comedy projects was a 1959 album called *Presenting Theodore*. The artist is Austrian-born Theodore Gottlieb; you might have seen him in the Eighties on TV with David Letterman or Billy Crystal. Suffice to say they sure don't make entertainers like Theodore anymore. *Presenting Theodore* is not a comedy album per se, but a program of four monologues (with occasional brief musical coloring) which entertain the listener in a wide variety of ways. "The Willow Landscape," an Oriental meditation on beauty and mortality, is quietly heartbreaking. "The Curse of the Toad," a tragic little fable with a Beat Generation twist, is stretched out to nine eventful minutes as Theodore calls forth his ample skills as a theatrical raft-ringer. With his accent, Theodore the tragedian may well remind you of Peter Lorre — which doesn't hurt him a bit on the macabre curtain-raiser "Berenice." Most comic of the four is a discourse on the desirability of humans reverting to walking on all fours, which fills all of Side Two. This wouldn't look like much at all printed on paper, I'm sure, but give Theodore your full attention (this *is* a record to listen to with the lights out and the phone off the hook) and you'll be amply rewarded.

(Also highly recommended, if you can find it: Theodore's 1955 live album, *With a Tongue of Madness* (Proscenium), a manic performance concentrating on the artist's sinister and macabre side.)

SHEP'S TRIP: A MIND AND A MIKE

By Ronn Spencer

Unlike 32° fahrenheit, the Lowest Common Denominator is not a fixed physical point. We have
seen it lowered year after tiresome year by the
cynical panderers and glorified accountants who
dominate most of the culture. Everywhere there
is a terrible sameness, a monotonous and punish-
ing uniformity where every drum beats the identical rhythm, each voice has a similar timbre, and
nearly every citizen has comparable tastes and
opinions limited and dictated by the status quo.

But once, back in the Fifties and Sixties, a uniquely
gifted voice filled the evening air in New York City.
WOR radio gave humorist Jean Shepherd a microphone, a certain amount of freedom and the cat,
well, he just plain...*wailed.* Shep reminisced,
told masterly stories and made incredibly hep,
dead-on observations about the American scene.
And, unlike today's self-consciously world weary
Po-mo's, Shep wasted no time slouching in front
of a mirror practicing being bored, bloodless and
neutered. Instead, he was vocally robust and
emotional, charming and persuasive—a voice
that could make you *feel* the sweetness, frustra-
tions, ironies and absurdities of everyday American life. Listening back to shows 25 or 30 years old,
they sound every bit as incisive and bright as they
did when first broadcast.

We haven't heard Shep on the radio in years.
Maybe he isn't interested. Maybe no one in radio
is adventurous enough to nick him a slot. Maybe
it's enough that in another America, not so long
ago, it was night and the radio waves buzzed and
sang with wit and imagination and Jean Shepherd
made us pause, reflect and laugh.

(Radio show collectors or SPERDVAC might help
you score Shepherd's old shows. Comb the collectors' stores for a copy of his excellent 1960 Elektra
lp *Will Failure Spoil Jean Shepherd?* His 1983 movie
A Christmas Story is available on video. Barnes &
Noble regularly carries a cassette collection of
him reading his short stories. Or check out his
books, *In God We Trust...All Others Pay Cash, A
Fistful of Fig Newtons, Wanda Hickey's Night of
Golden Memoirs,* and *The Ferrari in the Bedroom.*)

DIRTY COMEDIANS I HAVE KNOWN

by Rube Ruben

114

In the hip *boîtes* and watering holes of Hollywood 1993, a wild new Young Man With A Gag is cracking 'em up nightly. His name is Rube Ruben. Rube's not the king of comedy yet, nor even the prince. Plumber-custodian is closer to his current status in the horselaugh hierarchy. We asked Rube to pull our coat to some of the prime sources that pushed him over the top . . .

OK, lemme see. You wanna know who influenced me as a comedian. I'd like to say nobody. Zip. Zilch. Zed. Like, I'm a unique individual human being, y'know. Before I was a comic, I was an M.C., y'know, a real Massacre of Ceremonies. But that job went over like a pregnant gal doing the pole vault. So I decided to become a comic. I listened to the old pros and stole as much as possible. That's what made me the star I am today. Personally, I've been less inspired by the Borscht Belt and more by the just-plain-hit-you-in-the- guts-and-pull-down-your-pants funny. Truth is, they ALL influenced me. From the crummiest fifth-rate "zanies" of burlesque to the wise-cracking high-rollers of Vegas, they all taught me something: stay out of show business!

Top o' the list, I'd have to say the great Hap Happy. Never met the man myself, and have had a lot of trouble getting much solid on him. I ran across a battered copy of Hap's brilliant *Cruising Time* lp (Comic-kaze) while combing through used-record bins in Chinatown wid me pal Danny d'Louse. When we saw that cover we laughed and started bawling like babes for half an hour. I even peed my pants. Hap's Floridian, nasal twang and drunken slurring delivery won us over instantly. Here was a well of inspiration to drink from. I'll never forget Hap's clever ditty, "I got a girl and her name is Nance / She's got a moustache but it's in her pants."

There was Bert Henry, night-club celebrity, FAX recording star and all around creep. His salty ribaldry and smoker stories were truly ear-scorch-ing for their time. Bert's high-pitched, rapid-fire delivery of adult humor enthralled thousands of spice enthusiasts. I haven't talked to Bert in over a decade. He probably wouldn't even remember me. But then, who does? Check out *The Uncensored Humor of Bert Henry* and *Bert Henry at the Hungry Thigh* (FAX Personality series) to get acquainted with this neglected comic phenomenon.

Woody Woodbury let the gags roll out with a casual ease that took years to master. His great "keyhole" album cover (*Woody Woodbury Looks at Love and Life*, Stereoddities) can still be found in used comedy record sections. It's a gasser!

THE shocking HUMOR OF

WILD BITS OF SEX, SIN AND RIBALD WIT

FAX RECORDS

FAXLP 1012N

Woodbury branched into merchandising with his "Booze Is The Only Answer" club. Membership included a card, pin, diploma and charter to start your own branch.

Way back when, a trip to Hollywood wasn't complete without a visit to Ray Bourbon's Hollywood Rendezvous at 1841 Cahuenga. Ray was host and resident jokester, Jack was the barchief, and you gave your hats to Tilly. Bourbon was the first great cross-dressing comic who openly displayed his limp-wrist problem, if you catch my drift. The later it got, the dirtier Bourbon got. He sold his records at the club, causing one wag to quip, "Take home an anti-wimpus disc . . . a la Bourbon . . . to play on your pornograph." Bourbon made many records (on UTC). It's funny, queer stuff, sorta like Anna Russell squeezed through a lavender keyhole. He died in prison, accused of murder. The titles say all: *Don't Call Me Madam, You're Stepping On My Eyelashes, Bourbon: 100 Proof, Let Me Tell You About My Operation.*

I'll never forget Max Asnas, proprietor of N.Y.'s Stage Deli at Seventh Ave. and 54th St. We called him "the Corned Beef Confucius." Max had a punning Russian Jewish wisdom that rivaled his food in attracting customers. Earl Wilson called him "the beloved baron of bagels, blintzes and borscht," and once recorded the following exchange.

"What do you think of La Vie En Rose?" Harry Kurnitz asked Max.

"Levine & Rosen I never heard of, and I thought I knew every company in the garment district," Max answered.

Asnas even put out an album, an impromptu deli-side of "gag sessions" (Kimberly), with Jack E. Leonard, Morey Amsterdam and other comics making funny. The back of the platter bears the legend: "IF YOU DON'T LIKE THE CONTENTS OF THIS ALBUM, SPREAD WITH CHICKEN SCHMALTZ AND TRY EATING IT!"

There are so many more. Like gravel-voiced B.S. Pully, master of "venereal material and single entendre." Pully once worked a Miami burlecue house with his partner, a midget named H.S. Gump. Do I have to tell you what the B.S. and the H.S. stood for? Go out of your way to find his great disc *B.S. Pully: Fairy Tales* (Surprise).

And the rest. Terri "Cupcake" O'Mason, Bub Thomas, Belle Barth, Pearl Williams, Mickey Katz doing "Borscht Riders In The Sky." The list goes on and on. Hard searching will turn these nuggets up, like arrowheads in a tractor maw.

It's my hope that we might resurrect these neglected artists. And perhaps a few, such as myself, might further the cause of lowbrow terlit humor. For man is never closer to his own soul than when he's on the can. Kids these days are taking themselves too damn seriously. We "funnymen" must rebel against these conservative eunuchs. I figger, so what if the joke is a little offensive — it's FUNNNNNY! Ya made that oil painting laugh! That's what counts in my book, a book that I shall now close until next time.

(Rube Ruben's single, "Shmendrick"/"Ballad of the Terlit," is available from Sympathy For The Record Industry Records, 4901 Virginia St., Long Beach, CA 90805.)

FRINGE RADIO

Trigger-happy and bifurcated, it shreds at the edges.

By Davin Seay

With the possible exception of home shopping channels, infomercials and those popcorn-and-soda trailers they run between coming attractions and the main feature, there is simply no blander, more homogenized, or just plain dull form of entertainment than modern radio. Formatted, segmented and demographed to within an inch of its life, mainstream radio often reaches beyond the Lowest Common Denominator to create a whole new species of inert mass audience, programmed to believe that freedom of choice is the ability to pick between Classic Rock and Quiet Storm.

But even in the sonic Sahara of the airwaves, there still lurks the occasional oasis of perverse personality, lunatic dynamism and sheer broadcast bravura that's always been the hallmark of real radio. While it's pointless to spin the dial looking for FM's formerly free-freaking extravagances or the manic word salads of yesterday's AM screamers, the dedicated seeker may still find thrills to the far right, and left, of the radio band.

Those are, we hasten to add, political points of reference. Nowadays, the weirdest, most frenzied and fullest court loonies on radio are being heard at the far ends of the body politic. True believers, left and right, routinely use, and abuse, the airwaves in a manner ruled verboten by the vast middle's dogged insistence on the inoffensive. Put aside your own political persuasions for the moment, and come along for a wild ride on the far sides of radio.

Support the Troops And Shrimp Louie

Notwithstanding the recent popularity of rotund gadfly Rush Limbaugh (broadcasting on the ominously named Excellence In Broadcasting network), the most enduring examples of radio's right-thinking crypto-fascists can be found on innumerable local broadcasts, sandwiched in between the Farm Report and the Hour of Power. And first among fractured equals has to be Los Angeles' own George Putnam, heard daily over KIEV AM. Broadcasting from a glass booth deep in the basement of a downtown L.A. shopping mall, Putnam and his sonorous, booming baritone have been Southern California institutions for going on 40 years.

A good portion of that time is given over to an unrequited nostalgia for yesterday, specifically the reign of Mayor Sam Yorty (1961-73), who once threatened to erect scaffolds at the airport to hang incoming drug offenders on the spot. It's just the sort of brass-balled approach to social ills favored by Putnam and his myriad of gun-toting geriatric listeners, who regularly call in to voice hearty approval of George's hardheaded, no-nonsense agenda.

In one recent flurry of frenetic chest-pounding, listeners—most of whom sounded like veterans of the Spanish American War—beseeched George to explain why, in God's name, couldn't the Neutron Bomb just be dropped on evil Iraq, thereby saving invaluable oil drilling equipment and the lives of American boys. An anguished George was at a loss to explain this shocking lapse of horse sense.

On another occasion, a moribund eatery named the Smokehouse, another Southland institution and one of Putnam's longest running sponsors, came under attack from a local upstart food critic. Jowls aquiver, George spent the better part of a week spewing invective at those who, from ignorance or sheer malevolence, could not appreciate the sumptuous virtues of the Smokehouse's special garlic bread and Shrimp Louie.

Backward Masking & Birkenstocks

While George Putnam may speak, in *basso absurdo* tones, for an entire legion of crackpot extremists, the left has no such monolithic radio voice spreading political rectitiude.

Quite the opposite: the liberal insistence on equal time for each and every bore-sighted clique, klatch and coven under the sun has resulted in programming so bifurcated as to give harrowing new meaning to the term special interest.

The best example of this post-logical evenhandedness can be heard on any one of the listener-sponsored Pacifica radio stations currently begging for money across the nation. Earnest gays and lesbians promoting equity-waiver musicals about AIDS; rheumatic Wobblies evoking the ghost of Joe Hill; Birkenstock-shod folkies interviewing the interpreter for a visiting Abyssinian lute player; strident prison activists advocating statehood for San Quentin; utopian eco-feminists waxing eloquent on the virtues of life without electricity . . . all jostle for their paper-thin piece of the programming pie.

All this political correctness might well prove mind-numbing were it not for the rank amateur status of most listener-sponsored radio regulars. Tapes played backwards or at the wrong speed, coughing fits, deafening paper shuffles, unbroken stretches of dead air, impromptu conversations with the engineer or pizza delivery boy, and voices that alternate between nails-on-a-chalkboard nasality and phlegm-choked death rattles bring welcome relief from the litany of doctrinaire diatribes.

The next time a glistening spokesmodel invites you to a lifetime of easy listening or some smarmy yup extolls the pleasures of your local New Age outlet . . . remember, there's real radio to be had on the fringe. Better make that the lunatic fringe.

WISEGUYS, TIN MEN & TABLE SHPRITZERS:
In praise of the tongues that slay
by Danny Weizmann

"I'd like to kill myself on television. It would be a real first. Of course, the producer would be nervous: 'You're not gonna say anything dirty, are you?' . . . No, it's my cleanest act. I just take four pills and die."
—Lenny Bruce

"You heckled me 20 years ago. I never forget a suit."
—Milton Berle

"The big companies, the way they project an image! The banks! No more 'banks'! Now, you've got a 'friend.' If the banks are so friendly, how come they chain down the pens?"
—Alan King

"I played a horse so slow the other day, the jockey kept a diary of the trip."
—Henny Youngman

Happiness is being shingled: Tin-man Jackie Gayle (white suit) with peers.

Bam! The wiseguys are waiting for no one. Swift and rhythmic, they drop lines that fly like graceful left hooks. They swing on-the-spot commentary that plows through 80 layers of balony and conjecture, grabbing truth by the nuts.

They are the sharp progenitors of a talking style that cuts quick . . . but, real quick, to the essence of coolspeak: *wising off.*

> "At my age, what's to look forward to? If I'm good and I eat real healthy, then I can get sick and die."
> — Rodney Dangerfield
>
> "Hey, hey, somebody please put somethin' in his mouth, 'cause my zipper's stuck."
> — Robin Harris to club heckler

Shakespeare dug that brevity was the soul of wit, but it took a whole lot of aluminum siding salesmen to prove it. Like seltzer bottles and clip-on ties, wising off was born of practical necessity. It's no accident that stand-up swingers like Dangerfield and Jackie Gayle got their start selling tin shingles. In both comedy and sales, if you shlep you're sunk. A smart sales pitch explodes on a hotbed of 60 seconds of wheedling, hustling, cajoling and shpritzing. You need guts of steel, crazy chutzpah, and the ability to economize words in order to Make Believe before twelve heartbeats are up. Henny Youngman's *Giant Book of Jokes* (Citadel Press 1963) contains 400 traveling salesman jokes! Among Hen's dot-dash definitions — "Race track: A place where windows clean

people . . . Ecstasy: something that happens between the scotch & soda and the bacon-and-eggs . . . Herbie, you drive. You're too drunk to sing."

You can just picture deadbeat road merchants trading these corn pearls at motel diners across the country, like secret members of a smart-aleck society. By the mid-Fifties, every shlubnik shikker nightclub worth its protection budget or strippers' wardrobe featured full-blown standup wisenheimers, plenty of them named Jackie: Fat Jack Leonard, Jackie Gayle, Jack Carter, Jackie Mason, Jackie Vernon, Jackie Lord, Jack Roy (later Rodney Dangerfield). (On the *Steve Allen Show*, comic John Byner even parodied the rimshot rappers with a character named Lenny Jackie.) These guys weren't strictly conventional comedians. They didn't slip on banana peels or lean to limericks. As emcee's, they were paid to provide interstitial programming between dancers, and their workspace had all the elapsed time of a dragster popping its chute after a quick quarter. Their humor hit 'n' split, and you never knew what'd come out next.

> "If Jesus Christ came back and was electrocuted, you'd all be walking around with electric chairs around your neck."
> — Dick Gregory
>
> "We were married by a Reform rabbi. A very Reform rabbi. A Nazi." — Woody Allen
>
> Don Rickles to Sinatra: "Make yourself at home, Frank. Slug somebody."

To a lot of onlookers in the later Fifties and early Sixties, these comics seemed "sick" or "cynical," but they weren't haters. They blasted each other's misgivings, often with the same candor—and underlying compassion and outraged sense of ethics—that they used to blast the corruption and hypocrisy of society at large.

> "I can't get worked up about politics, man. I grew up in New York, and I was hip as a kid that I was corrupt and that the mayor was corrupt . . . You believe politicians, what they say? If you were to follow [Fifties liberal Democratic Presidential candidate, Adlai] Stevenson from New York to Alabama, you would shit from the changes."
> —Lenny Bruce

They came in all shapes and sizes. Some of 'em, like sadsack Jackie Vernon and *arch-paesano* Pat Cooper, were just funny, funny guys. Some were brutally honest, like Dick Gregory and Lenny Bruce. Some were just honest, like Mort Sahl and George Carlin. Don Rickles was just brutal. But what they all had in common was *talking cool*: a way of honing in quick and making a play.

Standup is really only one accountable form of wising off. Today, "wiseguy" is often taken to mean "gangster," and, to be sure, plenty of these guys broke bread with other guys who broke heads. But you have to dig that the Shpritzkrieg is everwhere! Wentworth and Flexner's *Dictionary of American Slang* defines "wiseguy" as "one who is aware of contemporary happenings" and "a person who says he knows everything, a smart aleck; one who gives advice and criticism freely; a troublemaker." Wiseblood flows in Jay Leno, but it also courses through the characters of novelist/ screenwriter Richard Price. Teller's unsilent partner Penn Gillette's a wiseguy, and there's a wise-gal sensibility under the shtik in Joan Rivers too.

Their breed's made of thinner stock today, but AM deejays have always posted high wise-cell counts. Behind the scenes, payola greased the wheels. On mike, boss jocks word-danced like hell, shoving syllables into the space around three-minute singles, hardselling everything from tapered slacks and Hawaiian getaways to used auto parts and records nobody on earth would care about a month later. What's the dif? It's all hep talk to them. On cable's Home Shopping Club network, sales-crazed hucksters move mock ice with mock enthusiasm ("Are you crazy? We've already sold *a hundred and fifty* of the cubic zirconiums *just this morning*! Comin' home to ya!") and zero eye contact. In low budget television spots for suits, hair care, weight loss and tech schools, modified coolspeak is the lingo of choice.

And it isn't stupid. Because, for all its velocity, wiseguy fast-talk embraces knowledge: far-out facts, bet-you-didn't-know-this arcana, nutball anecdotes and wild metaphors, out and out b.s. . . . anything so you get the picture *just right*. The shpritz surfs along the twilight edge of a free jazz solo and a rugged blast of rock 'n' roll energy. Check out Billy Batts (Frank Vincent) and Tommy D (Joe Pesci) spraying and slaying each other in a game of high-stakes insult pingpong during their barroom scene in *GoodFellas*. Or step into the deli and eavesdrop as the table heavies celebrate hardluck vaudeville manager *Broadway Danny Rose* over hot pastrami. Like Dyl's Howard says in "Highway 61": "Tell me quick, man, I got to run."

True shpritzing runs on freedom and fluidity, the uncanny ability to both accelerate and stop on a dime and respond to the moment. A great many king shpritzers started out in the Forties and Fifties as Catskills resort court jesters, where they were expected to be FUNNY everywhere all the time. Bruce worked the Catskills. As did Mel Brooks. As did Phil Silvers:

"I was the emcee. It was a frenetic business. The comedian had to work with the social director as the hotel buffoon, the *tummeler*, the noisemaker who would do anything to keep the guests from checking out. Potato races, "Roll the peanut." "A Night in Tahiti." The hotel owner gave me strict orders: "I don't want ever a dull moment." . . . The work onstage loosened me up. I tried everything. I didn't have time to think of failure."

Guys
who are wise
know
that smart dolls
have eyes
for guys
who wear

HOLLYWOOD CLOTHES

Tummeling, pummeling Phil Silvers

Dig it: "Professional" comedians stuck in repetitive "routines" only approximate what is coolest about wising off: namely, that undefinable drive that makes some wiseacres talk the talk because they just can't help but react, publicly, to the moment. For example, both Albert Goldman's *Ladies and Gentlemen, Lenny Bruce* and Phil Berger's study of standups *The Last Laugh* sing the praises of Joe Ancis, notorious Marquis de-Sphritz. Ancis was a tin man with a bachelor's degree in accounting who lived in his mother's apartment till he was 35, and had no aspirations of ever being a professional comic. Afternoons in the late Forties and early Fifties, he made the

---

WISEBUYS

Today, there's a glut of vertical jokers on the circuit, most of whom couldn't crack wise to save their lives (A.D. Clay's X-rated juvie act has all the wit and spontaneity of a horse race re-creation). If you want to swing, give these a ring . . .

Sounds:
The Lenny Bruce Originals (Fantasy Records)
Rodney Dangerfield: No Respect (PolyGram)
Richard Pryor: 'CRAPS' After Hours, Live at Red Foxx Club — (Laff Records lp)

Woody Allen: Standup Comic (Casablanca double-lp)

Screen:
The Great Standup Comics, feat. Jack Carter,
    Jackie Vernon, Joan Rivers, Alan King and more.

A Toast To Lenny, with Steve Allen, Jackie Gayle, etc. (Fox Hills Video)

Ink:
Why A Duck? - Richard Anobile (Avon 1972): a book of verbal and visual gems from Marx Bros. films.

The Last Laugh- Phil Berger (Ballantine 1971).
The Essential Lenny Bruce- ed. John Cohen (Ballantine 1957).
How to Talk Dirty and Influence People-Lenny Bruce (Playboy Press 1963).

This Laugh Is On Me — Phil Silvers (Prentice Hall 1973).
Mad's Al Jaffee Spews Out More 'Snappy Answers To Stupid Questions (Signet 1972).

Richard Price
The Breaks (Simon & Schuster 1983)

Wiseguys in Uniform:
Sgt. Ernie Bilko (*Phil Silvers Show*; CBS TV 1955-59), Ensign Lester Gruber (Carl Ballantine, *McHale's Navy*; ABC TV 1962-66)

scene at Hansen's Cafeteria (1650 Broadway, Manhattan), where pro yucks-cats such as Dangerfield, Buddy Hackett, Bruce and the rest would be killing time, waiting for the big break. For the sheer pleasure of it, Ancis would burst into bull's eye insults, spontaneous monologues and surreal riffing that "crippled" the whole damn deli. "You shmuck," Joe would howl, "you look like a fuckin' fire sale at Sears and Roebuck!"

While most of his genius has gone unrecorded, you can tell from rumors and reminiscences that Joe Ancis is a great example of the type of *everyshmuck* anyone in a big city will come across sooner or later: the fast-thinking nudnick who lives to make you die laughing. These free-range smart alecks raid the sandwich shops, streetcorners, the subways and elevators and block parties and backrooms, daily waging a full-scale war on the doldrums. They celebrate life in language,

relying on what are probably age-old, maybe even instinctive, equations of speed and knowledge and insight into the human condition.

On a recent trip home to Philly, a legendary L.A. bossjock runs into an old crony, a PA king swinger: " . . . We go down to the bar. As soon as we walk in Jerry's buyin' drinks for everybody. 'Hey, one for my man over there! This one's on me! Set 'em up!' I look at him, I say, 'Jerry, are you nuts? You're gonna go broke, you're buyin' drinks for people you don't even fuckin' know, man.' He stops, looks at me, he says, 'Hey, you never know who's gonna be on the jury, man . . . '"

GOOD LOOKS

"All the eyeballs flickin'
when she walks by
She's a stone upsetter
and I'm tellin' you no lie"

— "(She's A)
Homicide Dresser,"
Billy Harner

If looks could kill, jails would be jammed with them. Arresting objects. Sometimes they've got records as long as your arm (Gaudi's gobby architectural desserts), sometimes they're just-booked (Martin's sleeves, the Martians' cards). They're here to hold us up, and get away with it. Just watch 'em now ..

JACK COLE. He's best known for his fantabulous Plastic Man of the late Forties/early Fifties (see *The Catalog of Cool*). But dig the Eclipse reissues of his two *True Crime* books. One story, "Murder, Morphine And Me," not only has one of the all-time gonzo-lurid splash panels, but it so pissed off anti-comic crusader Dr. Wertham that the Doc used a panel of it to illustrate his favorite hangup, the "injury-to-the- eye" motif, in his classic tome *Seduction of the Innocent.* This is as close as comics get to rock 'n' roll. Crazed, nonstop ballsy locomotion. It'll leave you ahh breathless-uh. D.B.

JIVE 5

Billy Gibbons' 5 Coolest Cars

"The California" Kid '34 Ford coupe
'64 Dodge Dart
Ed Roth's "Beatnik Bandit"
Lamborghini LM002
'66 AMC Marlin

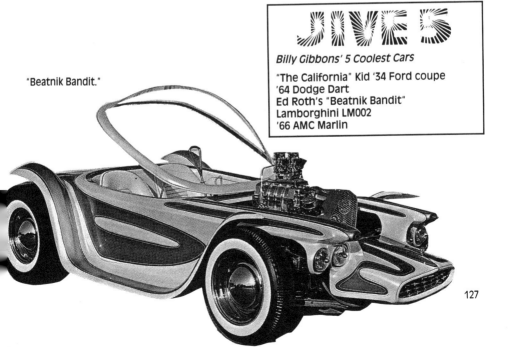

"Beatnik Bandit."

FLAT-EFFECT RAGTOPS

When it comes to car design, nothing is so powerful as an idea whose time has come and gone and come again.

One example of this phenomenon is what might be called the "flat effect" convertible—a no-nonsense machine with a lean, long profile barely interrupted by anything so gauche as a bump or a fin. Some of them are as level as the Bonneville Salt Flats, some of them barely curve, but except for the windshield frame, these babies run straight back from snout to stern.

It's a cool look, an understated look, one that says, "Save the swirls and whatchamajigs for the rubes. I'm gonna slip into a pair of Ray-bans and hit the roadhouse, then maybe make it by the DQ." What with auto designers' obsessive emphasis on zero drag coefficient, the minimalist mode is all the rage in new cars, but older examples of the genre have been showing up in cinematic hommages, to wit:

* Susan Sarandon's turquoise T-bird in *Thelma and Louise*
* Kevin Bacon's retrosaurean Nash Metropolitan in *The Big Picture*
* The Galaxie 500 in which Pam Tillis tools through the music video for "Don't Tell Me What To Do"

One set of flat-affect wheels practically had star billing in a short-lived TV series of the mid-Eighties. In *Kaz*, Ron Liebman played a frazzly ex-con turned criminal attorney whose career found its supreme metaphor in the protagonist's battered but indomitable Chevy II ragtop, a granny-white edition known to aficionados as the "box Nova."

The coolest ragtop flatliner is also the saddest: the 1963 Lincoln Continental, a convertible so long it could accomodate four doors, the rear pair hinged at the back. Lyndon Johnson had one that he kept down on the ranch. For a hood ornament, he affixed a set of bull's horns. The King of the Pedernales liked to load that slab-sided behemoth up with a bunch of sissy Eastern reporters and chase cattle, weaving among the salt licks and mesquite bushes at 70 mph and whooping like a cow-hand, go-cup balanced between his thighs and a pack of terrified scribblers frozen to the leather seats of the creamy-white Lincoln.

Another president is inextricably linked with the same model Lincoln, albeit of a different hue. John F. Kennedy breathed his last in the back seat of a shiny black suicide-door '63 Lincoln, which sometimes must give pause to the surviving members of the K clan when they summer on the Cape. One of the cars the family uses to shuttle between the beachfront compound and the local airport is a Lincoln ragtop, identical to the one in which JFK died except for its steel-blue finish. At dusk of a summer's day on the Hyannisport airfield, that big, long Lincoln shimmers in the heat like a persistent memory, cool and powerful and evocative of times long gone but still just a shot away.
- M. D.

Level best: Slab-sided Linc Connie.

Not Toad Hall: Gaudi's ceramic amphib scales wall of Parc Guell, Barcelona.
Courtesy National tourist Office of Spain

GAUDI ARCHITECTURE

Do the high-ticket public buildings erupting around you today seem closer to "architorture" than architecture? If so, you'll find an antidote in the work of Antonio Gaudi (no relation to "gaudy"), one of bizarre Barcelona's most-shook sons. Here's a guy who got his architecture degree from the U of Dreamland. Born in 1852, Gaudi hit his stride while the sweet delirium of Art Nouveau was seeping through Europe—but he took this early brand of modernism more than one step beyond. Backed by deep-pocketed industrial barons, he created an office building that looks like a dragon, an apartment house resembling a precision-gouged stone quarry, and a ceramic shard-surfaced park bench that undulates around a big plaza (Parc Guell) like some multicolored primordial serpent. The lobby of his Casa Batllo office building sways, bulges, and melts with the loony logic of a painting by fellow unhinged Spaniard Salvador Dali. And the roof terrace of his Casa Mila apartments is an abstract-surrealist playland of buckling walkways, disorienting arches, and enigmatic chimneys shaped like hooded medieval figures.

Despite these and many other shrink-tickling delights, virtually all of them built in and around Barcelona, Gaudi's niche in architecture's hall of fame is assured by a gig he never finished—the vast Sagrada Familia (Holy Family) church. This many-towered mud-colored structure, often tagged "the sandcastle cathedral," was begun in ultra-square neo-Gothic style by another architect in 1881. Gaudi took over the next year and worked on it desultorily until 1914; after WWI he dug in obsessively for the rest of his life. "Sandcastle" is one way of putting it, because the stone of the four towers soaring up from the front porch, where the Nativity is depicted, seems to drip just like that. But the stone framing the scene is scalloped and toothed and punctuated by assorted seashells, making the setting of Jesus' birth feel more like a grotto than a manger. The insides of the towers provide another jolt to the expectations, spiraling up eerily like something out of H.G. Wells. How such strange juxtapositions were to add up to a whole isn't clear: Gaudi died in 1926, struck down by a streetcar, with the church nowhere near done. He left but the haziest of sketches and no master plan. Evidently, it was all jazz to him—figure it out as you play.

Sagrada Familia
cathedral epitomizes
AG's aspiring
architecture.

The church-in-progress fell on hard times after Gaudi checked out. At the start of the civil war in 1936, Spanish Republican zealots, blind with rage at Catholicism, pillaged the place and tried to burn it down. George Orwell, who got many things right, called the Sagrada Familia "one of the most hideous buildings in the world." Despite his knocks, and those of other critics who seemed embarrassed by Gaudi's eccentricities, the church managed to hang on until the tide shifted and construction resumed in 1952. Building continues to this day, funded meagerly by random donations and ticket sales. It might be completed within our lifetimes—and then again, it might not.
-Phil Freshman.

Where the Gaudis Are: The Parc Guell, on Carrer de Larrad (just northwest of the center of Barcelona) . . . Casa Batllo and Casa Mila, on Passeig de Gracia (northwest of the Placa de Catalunya) . . . Sagrada Familia church, at the corner of Mallorca and Sardenya, also near the Catalunya square.

FRANK LLOYD'S FILL 'ER UP

We all know that Frank Lloyd Wright, architect and self-promoter nonpareil, designed scores of astonishingly original buildings—the Guggenheim Museum, Tokyo's Imperial Hotel, Racine's Johnson's Wax Building, dozens of houses, etc. But how many of us are hip to the fact that, in the late 1950's, Mr. Wright gave us a gas station, in the little log-oriented northern Minnesota ville of Cloquet?

What made FLW, then nearing 90 and at the peak of his fame, take on such a seemingly humble gig? An unsnuffable utopianism. During the Thirties he had inked grandiose, never-realized plans for a burg called Broadacre City, a rational, decentralized zone sans the usual urban yuck, where everyone would own land and sculpt his or her own destiny. In Broadacre, mobility would equal freedom—so cars and gas stations were key. Wright went so far as to sketch a standardized, prefab model he reckoned would make Shell or Texaco (and himself and his backers) a bundle.

Breaking with the conventional, space-wasting pump-island scenario, the design had gas stored above the driveway in a cantilevered structure, from which hoses dangled down that motorists would simply reach up for. When Wright pushed the notion on his backers, they took a left.

Cut to 1956. Minnesota bulk oil entrepeneur Ray Lindholm, for whom Mr. Wrightstuff had lately crafted a house, asked him to design a Phillips 66 station in Cloquet of his that he wanted rebuilt. Wright jumped in, and on Halloween 1958 Dick's Master Service had its grand opening; among the souvenirs were playing cards "engraved" with an architectural rendering of the joint.

Driving up today, the first thing you catch from the road is the stylized, 60-foot-tall tower imprinted with Wright's elongated take on the Phillips 66 logo. Nearby rises a taller billboard pole with a *real* Phillips sign atop it—don't monkey with brand-name psychology! Pulling in, you see that Frank didn't get his overhead gas hoses (not

Courtesy Minnesota Historical Society

You used to ride on a chrome horse with your diplomat…

kosher per the Cloquet fire code). But the ho-hum pump island is overspread by a vast 32-foot copper canopy, held up by neither pillar nor post. An odd ten-sided, glass-walled office faces the driveway. Next to the office are three parallel, skylighted service bays, with a fourth tucked away in back for don't-breathe-down-my-neck repairs. Above the office, under the canopy and gabled copper roof, is an angular glass-enclosed observation deck that juts up and forward like the prow of a space-age ship. You climb a likewise futuristic angled exterior staircase to reach it. Wright, who envisioned the gas station as a "meeting place," thought customers would wait and relax on the deck while repairs were being done, taking in the bustle below. (Like maybe young Bob Dylan, Duluth-bound from Hibbing a hundred miles north, might tool in and talk Rimbaud with Cloquet's bohos while gassing up.) In modern American fact, no one waits around: the observation deck is unused and kept locked.

For Wright biographer Brendan Gill, it all adds up to "an exceptionally disheveled-looking structure." Amen to that. But how could you be near the intersection of State Hwy 33 and Cloquet Ave., just north of Interstate 35, and resist a look? P.F.

"MARS ATTACKS" TRADING CARDS
They're back. Withdrawn after a six-month shelf life in 1962, the controversial series of 55 pulp-lurid cards depicting an alien invasion of Earth has been reissued by Topps. Cool and collectable, especially numbers 21 ("Prize Captive"), 36 ("Killing A Dog"), and 13 ("Watching From Mars," in which Mars-heads orb the Big E's destruction on a widescreen while toasting their victory with Martian gimlets!). Check your local comics shop.

THE SLEEVES OF DAVID STONE MARTIN

With the possible exception of his mentor Ben Shahn, no one dominated illustration of the postwar-to-early-Sixties period as thoroughly as Chicago-born Martin. With the exception of Rick Griffin, whose vivid colorblasts vibrated in perfect synchronicity with California acid-rock, no other commercial illustrator so effectively expressed music on paper. Martin's countless mag, book and album covers mixed trad and modernist styles and utilized an array of techniques (most notably a "sensitive" line) to go where few pen-and-inkers had gone before. His early Fifties lp sleeves for Verve grab the elusive, shape-shifting jazz spirit and bring it back in two cool dimensions. -J.D. King.

"SUCCESSIVE LAYERS OF EYEBALL PLEASERS":
JOHN SOANE'S MUSEUM

The classic tourist blitz of London consists mainly of bigtime museums and pubs. But few visitors trip upon the tiny Sir John Soane's Museum, which looks, at first glance, like it was created by someone grinning under the sway of one too many pub crawls. This is the townhouse *cum* museum of the guy who designed the Bank of England back in the early nineteenth century and whose work has lit the bulbs of many a postmodern architect. You've probably noticed that postmods love to throw disparate riffs together in a single structure—a note of classical Greece here, a "quotation" from Bauhaus modernism there. Soane, who was born in 1753, was a great one for departing from the architectural norms of his time by blending classical themes. Nowhere does this show up more than in his pad, which he worked on from 1808 to 1824. He used the place to play and mingle some of these themes. But one of the main fascinations for the postmods, and for everyone else who walks through, is Soane's ingenious fiddling with light. He had spent some of his malleable years in Italy and came back to dreary old London with a love of light that never left him. So when he built his dream house, he manipulated light by mixing its various states—from the direct and indirect to the refractive and dispersed. Light pours in from mysterious sources, and ceilings and domes seem to float, partly due to the mirrors and mirrored panels he used to multiply and heighten his effects. He was especially gone for convex mirrors, which change the way something looks completely just by shifting your viewpoint a bit. Altogether, the real and the reflected interact with a daft but unknockable logic.

Besides designing the house to reflect his assorted ideas, Soane built it to hold his antic collections of archaeological finds (including a sarcophagus that supposedly held the bones of Paraoh Seti I); paintings by Hogarth, Canaletto, and Turner; architectural drawings by Piranesi and Adam; his own models and drawings, a group of cork architectural models; and plenty more. All of this glorious stuff is jam-pack juxtaposed, in ways that seem calculated to raise a smile.

To wit: Soane had so many paintings that he concocted the 12 x 13-foot Picture Room, in which the canvases are mounted on giant hinged doors that swing open to show successive layers of eyeball pleasers. The last set of doors opens to reveal an elegant statue of a woman, backlit by a garden window. Elsewhere, beneath a glass dome, is a room burgeoning with rows and ranks of Greek and Roman urns, ancient buildings' cornices, capitals, and ornaments, statuary hands and feet, busts, and plaster angels. In the basement, near the sarcophagus, is the Monk's Parlour, a little stained glass-lit shrine containing

Art swings
in Soane's
Picture Room.

Sir John's pad: bustin' moves & disparate riffs.

questionable archaeological bits and pieces that satirize the antiquarianism that was the rage in the early nineteenth century. There's also a book-lined breakfast room, dining room, library, and sitting room, each riddled with little visual tricks and treats.

The sum of these far-flung parts is a building that marches to the beat of a very unusual drummer but that nonetheless swings with a terrific rhythm. Nos. 12 and 13 Lincoln's Inn Fields, near the Holborn Underground station. Open Tues-Sat, 10 AM-5 PM. P.F.

BASIL WOLVERTON. In the early Fifties, cartoonist Al Capp ("L'il Abner") had a contest to see which of his readers could come up with a picture of Lena the Hyena, "The Ugliest Girl In Lower Slobovia." Basil's entry won in a walk. God knows his funny stuff is a blast (you can find it in the odd *Mad* or *Panic*). But the Wolv's real genius lies in the (as yet uncollected) early sci-fi "Spacehawk" stories he did for Target Comics, and subsequent horror tales like "Brain Bats Of Venus." Not to mention the illustrated Bible he drew for evangelist Garner Ted Armstrong. Sequestered up in the Northwest, Big Bad Bas, a *sui generis* case *par excellence*, communicated with Gotham City only by mail. If anyone influenced him up there, it must have been the brain bats. D.B.

Clap for the Wolv-man·
Basil's sci-fi stuff.

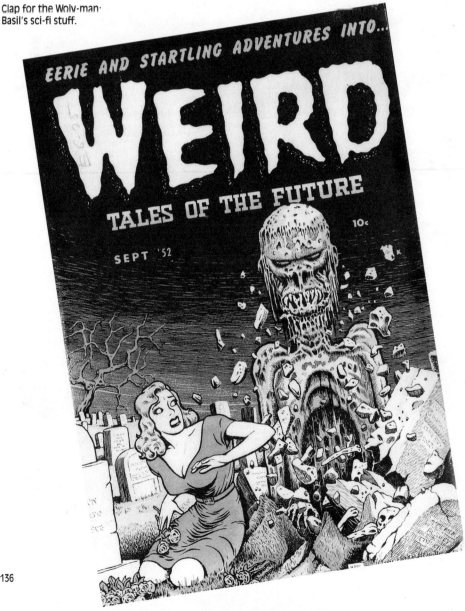

CERTIFIABLE ART:
Some Palette-pushers Got Real Gone

by Dick Blackburn

The image of the mad artist is forever set in the old pop consciousness, thanks to such wild-eyed perfs as Robert Newton's in *Odd Man Out*, Alec Guinness in *The Horse's Mouth*, and beatnik sculptor Dick Miller (pouring plaster-of-paris over his just-felled victims) in *Bucket of Blood*. Personal fave: Kirk Douglas as Van Gogh in *Lust for Life*. Who could forget intense Kirk, eyes aglitter, teeth clenched, exhorting a pissed-off Tony Quinn (as Gaugin) during a windstorm to "Nail your easel down!"

Actually, the number of famous nutso daubers is quite low. The majority who turn to painting after a psychotic breakdown are said to produce work that is more interesting medically than artistically.

137

Ah, but if they were artists *before* their trolleys left the track, the story is often quite different. Witness the aptly named patricide Richard Dadd, a skillful British mid-nineteenth century painter/illustrator of Shakespearian scenes. When a lord took him on a Middle Eastern trip to make sketches—much as one might take a pocket camera today—mad Dadd began limning tiny figures in a vast expanse. According to nut docs of the day, such drawing denoted the kind of acute alienation that precedes a big crack-up.

Richard Dadd,
ca. 1856.
Courtesy Bethlem Royal Hospital
Archives and Museum.

138

Your Move: Dadd's painting *The Child's Problem*.
Tate Gallery, London/Art Resource, N.Y.

The Vast Detail

Sure enough, Dadd returned to London in the throes of what was then diagnosed as *monomania* (being in the grip of an all-consuming delusion, viz: that the devil was inhabiting his father). Dadd mortally stabbed his pater on a trip to Kent, fled to France, was apprehended and tossed into the State Criminal Lunatic Asylum attached to Bedlam Hospital where, continuing to paint, his art became . . . different. He spent nine years working maniacal detail into what is often acknowledged as his fantasy opus, *The Fairy Feller's Master Stroke*, in which misshapen little folk stand about as one of their brethren raises an axe to split the smooth surface of a hazel nut that resembles the polished pate of one intently staring elfin oldster .

Other canvases were equally bizarre. The heads of two mean-looking eighteenth century officers are at the bottom of *Patriotism*, a watercolor largely given over to crabbed writing and chimerical geography. Or dig *The Child's Problem* (1857), which features a hyperthyroidal urchin trying desperately to suss out a chess move on the lap of a sleeping crone. On the wall: a framed picture of a shackled slave.

Weird & Wired:
cats of Louis Wain.

Louis Wain.
National Portrait Gallery, London.

Pussy Paranoia

Up to the time Louis Wain started selling his
treacly, late nineteenth century drawings of
kitties gamboling at the beach, in the parlor and
around the dining table, cats were largely re-
garded solely as mousers for farmers. Wain's
candybox fantasies helped popularize them as
house pets well into the 1920's. After his wife
kicked three years into their marriage, he either
came suddenly unstuck or the event sped up a
process that was well under way. Oh-so-cutesy
felines developed the large staring eyes of
paranoia. Colors and expressions turned so fierce
they broke through the outlines, exploding Indian
rug-like into pure abstraction. Wain went to the
laughing academy while middle-class legions,
ignorant of his way locomotion, continued to coo
over the cat scans.

140

Wain's corkscrew cats on a cup.
Available from Bethlem Hospital.

Years later, psychiatrists arranged eight of Wain's drawings in a chronology of their own devise, to chart what they thought was his *progressive* flipout. This simplistic stunt, never questioned, was taken for gospel and often reprinted. Subsequent shrinkwork suggests that the cat-man was wacko from the start, and may have deliberately intended many of his weirder works for textile design.

For years, famed cartoonist/crossbow collector Chas Addams was considered a key link in the art-insanity chain. Rumor held that Chas, the *New Yorker* legend and creator of Fester, Lurch and Pugsley, would tip *his* shrinks when he was ready to wig—by drawing the same cartoon over and over (allegedy a sketch of a vampire accepting a newborn from a maternity nurse, with the caption "Don't bother to wrap it, I'll eat it right here." *New Yorker* associates have branded the tale a fabrication. Yet, a collection of morbid memorabilia (old photos and engravings of elephant electrocutions, torture instruments and rat hunts), *Dear Dead Days* (Putnam's, 1959), shows the Family's patriarch to have been *somewhat* unhinged. Nail your easel down, Chas.

SHOP AROUND.

Raw Vision magazine covers the art of the "outsider," including visionaries and nut cases. Dept. 193, 1202 Lexington Ave., New York City 10028.

Postcards, a mug and a catalog of Wain felixiana *(Cats)* are available from Art & History Collections, Bethlem Royal Hospital and The Maudsley Hospital, Monks Orchard Road, Beckenham, Kent BR3 3BX, England. Fax: 081-777-1668.

FERD'S ROCK DREAMS

In 1879 Ferdinand Cheval, a rural postman outside Lyon, picked up a weirdly shaped stone, nearly chucked it, saved it, examined it, dug it, began picking up more stones/fossils/shells, got a basket when they started tearing his pockets, graduated to a wheelbarrow, and then, possessed by a vision and with zip building experience, spent 33 years creating a staggeringly unique frozen dream palace. Gaze upon his Palais Ideal and glide back into the collective unconscious.

— D.B.

Say it with BULLETS
RICHARD POWELL
Complete and unabridged
35¢

LURID LOOKS: COVERS THAT SIZZLE!

ECSTASY NOVEL

PAULA HAS A PRICE!

PROUDLY ILLUSTRATED

JAN 35¢

Kitty Couldn't Stay Away From The Barn

STABLE BOY
by Adam Rebel
35¢

HOT DAMES on COLD SLABS

10¢ DELL BOOK

WILLIAM IRISH
A cheap and evil girl sets a hopped-up killer against a city.

MARIHUANA

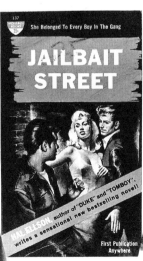

137

She Belonged To Every Boy In The Gang

JAILBAIT STREET

HAL ELLSON, author of "DUKE" and "TOMBOY", writes a sensational new bestselling novel!

First Publication Anywhere

"THE HARDEST-BOILED YARN OF A DECADE"
—Saturday Review of Literature
"A NOVEL FULL OF FIRE AND FEVER"
—Philadelphia Ledger

25¢ AVON 496

FAST ONE

He didn't know whether to kiss her or slug her. So he did both.

PAUL CAIN

AN AVON BOOK—COMPLETE AND UNABRIDGED

LOVE WAS CHEAP AND LIFE WAS HIGH IN THE TORRID ZONE OF "LITTLE OLD" NEW YORK!

HOME TO HARLEM
CLAUDE McKAY

COMPLETE AND UNABRIDGED

143

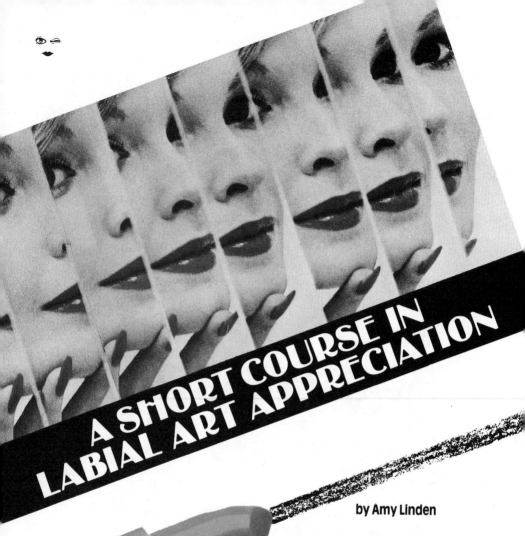

A SHORT COURSE IN LABIAL ART APPRECIATION

by Amy Linden

All shiny and glossy and, despite a vaguely naturalistic look, there was never any doubt you had something chemical on your mouth.

More than any other form of femme apparel or apparatus, lipstick separates the girls from the sluts. The first time mom allowed you to don a fetching shade of lipstick deeper than the color of your naked lips was a major milestone. It's lipstick that you shoplift. It's lipstick that's left on cocktail napkins, cigarette butts, zippers. Lipsticks have cool names, like Naughty Iridescent Violette. Do they even give blushes names? Singers sing about lipstick traces, poets go on about ruby lips. The ultimate height of tack/cool (depending on your p.o.v.) is whipping out that tube at the dinner table and reapplying a fresh coat of allure. One clue that lipstick is slightly dangerous and there-fore beyond hip is that men hate it. Granted, they claim to hate make-up in general, but they hate lipstick the most. It's more than a desire for untainted womanhood that fuels men's hatred; the first telltale sign of an extracurricular love thang is the old lipstick on the collar. Notice we're talking about lipstick, not lip gloss, not lip shine.

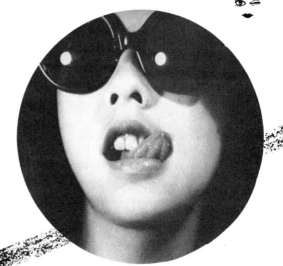

All that is merely Chapstick with some food dye tossed in. The credo must be: No stain, no gain. Natural lipsticks, the ones that barely blush your perky lips, are for the birds. Natural make-up is an oxymoron. If you wanted to look natural, why put the stuff on? The idea is to look painted, enhanced, stained. Lipstick defines and delineates just what type of dame you are. Lipstick is the art of artifice.

Each generation has shades that are its own. Dig some tube titles from the swingin' Sixties: Great Granny Red . . . Carnaby Coral . . . Pink Paisley. They just scream out *happening*, don't they? The same decade offered Yardley Slickers—all shiny and glossy and, despite a vaguely naturalistic look, there was never any doubt you had something chemical on your mouth. The best thing

Cut up, cut out, cut loose with Max Factor's

CALIFORNIA PINK-A-PADES

Two pink escapades for lips and fingertips.
Two sheer...two shimmering...too tempting!

It's the great new color adventure for summer.
Say it Pink-A-Pale (soft, feminine, fragile)
or Pink-A-Fling (lively, zingy, daring).
Wear it either super-sheer or super-frosted.
Any way you play it, have a wild
pink Pink-A-Pade!

California Pink-A-Pades by Max Factor

As one matures, and finally learns how to correctly apply the stuff, lipstick becomes a lot less trendy and more classic. There will never be a time when a good pair of red lips is not a welcome sight. Be you tramp or glamourpuss, or just unable to accessorize, a true sign of style is the tried and true lips of eternity. The lips that'll endure are the ones that (lord knows) our mothers probably wore (if their mothers let them wear lipstick, or if they were sort of loose). To this end, here's a highly subjective list of shades that are timeless and quintessentially cool . . .

TRUE CLASSICS FOR EVER AND EVER

**Revlon's
Love That Red
Cherries in the Snow
Fire and Ice**

(All intro'd by Revlon in the early Fifties, and still hot. Also worth noting: the late lamented Orange Flip and Uptown Tangerine; the discontinuation of a fave shade is a pain no man will ever dig.)

about Slickers was their spokesmodel, Jean Shrimpton, whose sister Chrissie went out with Jagger, thereby ensuring her place in the Cool Looks hall of fame. The white lips to match the white boots spelled out the essence of groovy fashion.

The Seventies saw the rise of the women's movement which, unfortunately, brought about anti-lipstick hysteria. While the reaction may have been justified at the time, in hindsight it was misguided, since all it did was drive a wedge between those who did and did not paint their faces. In retrospect, we all know that a little lip color can't do as much damage as the Supreme Court. The end result of all this anti-make-up fervor was that the natural look became more prevalent and that lines like Clinique, with their antiseptic, good-for-you vibe, took over. Rule of thumb: if it's dermatologist-recommended, it ain't cool.

Punk rock saw a rise in the application of lipstick, the more garish the better. Again, history has shown us that walking around with OD blue lips may not be all that agreeable, but it made its point back then. Since punk was an excuse to look as ugly as possible, green lips seemed to be quite appropriate.

Coty 24. These available-in-drugstores (i.e., cheap) matte shades stay on, as the tag suggests, for 24 hours.

Artamatic Black Orchid. The ghoul-girl choice. At last look it was a buck a tube (in its heyday, 69 cents).

Bruccis Paula's Pink. Cheap brands have the best names, and Paula's is so pink it'll make you puke.

Chanel Star Red. An endurable classic. French. Very expensive, but lasts and has a hip case (as do all pricey brands).

MUSTS TO AVOID

Estée Lauder (Republican) Natural Wonder
(natural, ha!)

Most Clinique, or any product tested on animals (you can be cool and PC at the same time).

TUBE

"There are days when any electrical appliance in the
house, including the vacuum cleaner, seems to offer
more entertainment possibilities than the TV set."
—Harriet Van Horne,
New York World-Telegram, June 7, 1957

True enough. But not even the new Hoover Elite II Upright with attached caddy can compete with some of these...

WAY GONE SHOWS

THE AVENGERS (U.K.; 1966-68, ABC). Leads Patrick Macnee ("John Steed") and Diana Rigg ("Emma Peel") were a two-mod style council (wit and bumbershoot for him, wit and karate chops for her), and the scenes were downright kicky: disappearing towns, relentless Cybernauts, and a wheelchair-bound fat man named Mother commanding the show from atop a London bus. Sixty-five episodes are available for sale from E.M.G. Video.

THE BEAT GENERATION. Way wigged episode from Brit series *The Comic Strip* which ran occasionally on MTV (late Eighties). Guy 'n' gal coolniks, along with an Angry Young Man, fall by a rich, aspiring hipster's country house where Kicks, wildman poet, uses the toaster for a skeet shoot. Endless monologues, sexual misfires and proclamations: "I want to marry a Ne-gro, be really poor and eat ice cream!" D.B.

COCAINE: ONE MAN'S SEDUCTION (1983). Dennis Weaver stars as a one-man midlife crisis center in this mega-camp made-for-TV movie. One toot and mild daddy Den's a house-rockin' papa in a leather coat, cruisin' with the windows down and the volume up. Just say yes to this one. Often rerun. T.V.

THE CONTINENTAL (1952 CBS, 1953 ABC). Bogue-sophisto Eurotrash that anticipated Bryan Ferry by 20 years. For 15 minutes, an ascotted geek looked squarely into the camera, purring in an Ezio Pinza accent, inspiring every tired hausfrau to fantasize that she was on a date with him. He poured your wine, leaned forward to light your smoke. Lampooned in *Mad* #14: "Hallo dar-r-ling! Here I am, all alone, waiting with a glass of shamponya for-r-r you!" D.B.

Diana, in full Sixties rig, refuses to re-expose choppers until further bonding.

Illustration: Drew Friedman

149

CRIME STORY (1986-88, NBC). "What decade did you drop out of?" a Fed asks Lt. Mike Torello, and we might wonder.

One of the best Sixties cop shows didn't debut until the late Eighties. When it did, *Crime Story* copped prizes for the coolest casting, art direction and music use (Al Kooper and Four Seasons arranger Charlie Calello utilized everything from Chuck Jackson and Bobby Bland to Dean Martin and Jimmy Smith; in one episode, a psycho-punk shoots up a beauty salon to the —suddenly sinister—tune of Kenny Dino's 1961 redundo-rock hit "Your Ma Said You Cried in Your Sleep Last Night").

First set in Chicago and later Vegas, the series was a virtual meditation on Coolstyle, as the decidedly un-glam Torello (Dennis Farina) battled dapper Ray Luca (Anthony Denison, who picked his peacock-shocking wardrobe from an endless vine-yard of periwinkle shirts and cobalt ties). Putty-faced John Santucci resembled a rummy Louie Prima as Luca's wildcard go-fer Paulie. Luca's other boy was goofball rockabilly cat Frank Holman (Ted Levine, *Silence of the Lambs*' Jame Crumb), while A.D. Clay did the only decent work of his career as Miami thug Max Goldman. Criminally underused: sexy Darlanne Fluegel and Patricia Charbonneau as Torello's wife and galfriend.

Hearing that *Crime Story* has been cancelled, former felon John Santucci gets ready for new day job.

Gamma radiation from *Crime Story*'s A-bomb episode didn't even part Ray Luca's hair.

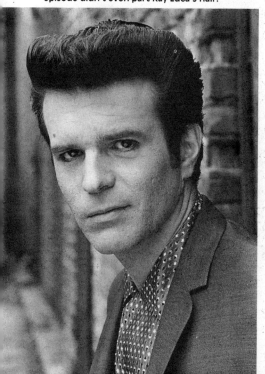

Unfortunately, no amount of style could compensate *Crime Story* for its often disorderly plots. But sometimes, sheer spectacle could. In the first-season closer, "Ground Zero," Luca busts up a motel-room B & D session to off a rival, flees downtown where he and Big Mike wage a neon-lit *Wild Bunch* firefight (maximum firing, minimum reloading), then escapes to an abandoned pad in the desert. The next bright, Ray wakes to learn that his safe place sits in the center of an A-bomb test site. Scared shitless, he and Paulie peel out across the sand in their Eldo just as a huge mushroom engulfs the pad and the Jive Bombers burble the tremelodious doowop "(I'm Just A) Bad Boy" ("I'm taking the trouble/ To blow my bubbles away"). The kicker: Luca survives, like some chem-resistant hood roach, to torment Torello the following season.

Crime Story has recently rerun on USA Cable. The series' two-hour pilot is rentable (Starmakers Video). It climaxes with a marathon shootout in a Chi-town dept. store between mobsters and Torello's squad. In big hats and dark overcoats, they look like dueling rabbis.

DUKES OF HAZZARD: Belt buckles 'n' bulgin' baskets flank Barbara Bach.

DUKES OF HAZZARD (1979-85 CBS; syndicated). Eeeehahh! The major stoopid goof of the late Seventies/early Eighties is serial art that burns rubber all over Warhol's *16 Jackies*. Every week for six years, the same plot: two city slickers hit town with an evil plan and the Duke boys foil 'em. Narrator Waylon Jennings plugs plot holes with homily grits while sheriff Boss Hogg (Sorrell Booke) makes like Vesuvius.
Further study: *Ernest Goes To Jail* (1990; Touchstone). B.M., G.S.

GET A LIFE (Fox 1991-). If full-strength silly is your cup of tea, pour yourself a potful with this highly inane show starring Chris Elliott as a 30-year old paperboy who still lives at home (with Mom and Dad—Bob Elliott of & Ray). Check the acclaimed "Walletboy" episode (where our anti-hero loses his billfold in the Big City) or "Tool Belt Fight" (Chris befriends a slovenly crew of construction workers, engages them in a belt fight, then learns they're ripping off his dad). While not for everyone (as Nielsens indicate; it's consistently in the Bottom Ten and could be gone by the time you read this), nice lo-cal dementia for those on a dumb-conscious diet. T.V.

HUNTER (1984-90, NBC). That's right—perhaps the draggiest traditional cop drama of all time *in its maturity.* But when it first came on, when it was shamelessly trolling for an audience, it achieved, if not quality, an abandoned sleaziness almost as good. Each week Hunter turned over a rock to see what would crawl out. A rubber-suited freak who torched warehouses with his very own flame-thrower—to the tune, no less, of the Stones'"Play With Fire"? A National Guard sniper who got his jollies plinking newlyweds in the park? A filbert so obsessed with a fast-draw video game that he started playing it with real cops? Or—oh yeah—the late John Matuszek as an especially tall spike-haired safety-pinned *punk rock hitman?* And let's not forget fabulous Dennis Franz, who had created the bent cop De Benedetto for *Hill St. Blues*—the guy who tweaked the loan shark's nose with pliers—and who reprised the character in all but name for a rip-roaring *Hunter* two-parter . . . in which he cornered seven or eight people who "knew too much" at gunpoint . . . and had them line up and *file* offscreen to be killed . . . as if he was going to make them take numbers! Yes, here were perps worthy of the misanthropic Fred Dryer when he still wore polyester shirts, drove a primer-blotched domestic clunker and was, along with Bruce Willis, the first proto-baldy tube hero. Kudos as well to sidekick Stepfanie Kramer as the "Brass Cupcake," who could also take down a scrote faster than you could say "Miranda decision," when she wasn't complaining about her lack of dates. And she even worked as a lounge singer in one episode! (Shoulda sung "You Can't Get A Man With A Gun"!) J.T.

IT'S HAPPENING. A Boss City of the Mind, this lo-budget, high-impact R & R show was launched on SoCal cable three years ago. Real teens dance, contemp combos cook (Hoods, Head Coats, Black Diamonds). At press time, it was playing on public-access in Austin, Tucson, L.A., N.Y., S.F. Catch it if you can. (See Shop Around.)

MIAMI VICE (NBC) : "Definitely Miami" episode (1986). The Wasteland-grail quest was never so hip as when Ted Nugent baited fools with Arielle Dombasil, then buried their cars in the salt flats with a steam shovel. But the modern day Round Table (Vice boys) is just one beat faster. Combines mythic weight with a total lack of redeeming social comment. J.T.

Hunter : A disillusioned Fred Dryer opens up on the guy who stepped on his minoxidil. (Hollywood Book & Poster)

Kids frug as combos cook on *It's Happening.*

Blow Up: Public Access' Balloon Man, *Mr. Morrison.*

MR. MORRISON (1982-). He started "working his act" in the comedy clubs and folk rooms of the early Sixties. He's done time as a lieutenant navigator in the Air Force, a car salesman, a guide to stars' homes. Now, on L.A. public access, in a yarn cap and silver hair, Bill Morrison spews co(s)mic truth in tangents and rants while plucking balloons from his vest, blowing them up, and letting them fly around the studio. Unrehearsed monologues soar like Buckley, expand to mock-pomp vocalizing, collapse like souffles. Spaulding Gray couldn't carry his latex. D.W. (See Shop Around.)

QUANTUM LEAP (NBC 1990-). The worst episodes match high concept (time travel, bodyswitching) with "relevant" issues. The best leap for sheer hep entertainment value. In one, QL cat Scott Bakula falls in with a NorCal biker gang and bumps into Kerouac spouting Beat jive. Another, an hommage to *Spinal Tap*, time-jumps Bak into a metal band. Check the listings; if it looks good, sit down and dig. T.V.

missed link between Victor Borge and Revere's Raiders) did it all, weekly, on network TV. Creaming candelabra, fish-spurting saxophones, "Twelfth Street Rag" in drag. Dali beamed. *Best of Spike Jones Vols. 1-2* (Paramount Video).

THE TWILIGHT ZONE (1959-65; various episodes available on CBS/Fox Home Video). A long time ago, in a galaxy far away, the empire decided the universe had been completely mapped and that an accurate representation of it should easily fit into a *small glass box* . . . I know I'm not fooling

SHINDIG (ABC 1964-66). Despite hokey set-ups and guest hosts (Zsa Zsa Gabor), American TV's first full-length rock 'n' roll series left lasting impressions: peak perfs from Sam Cooke, Jackie Wilson, Beach Boys, and the Stones introducing a mean-looking H. Wolf. Video active: *Shindig Presents*, a multi-volume set from Rhino Home Video. Diggin'-est: the Jackie Wilson and *Frat Party* volumes (the latter featuring an electrifying clip of Roy Head doing "Treat Her Right").

THE STREET (1988 Universal syndication). Super-minimal copshow done for $1.98 an episode. Sometimes a suspect was questioned. Sometimes linoleum was put down on a basement floor. DP Rob Draper often used a single flashlight beam as the sole light source. Hip to the vanishing point: every week it was rescheduled to a later and later time slot. D.B., J.T.

SPIKE JONES SHOW (1952-61; NBC, CBS). Back in the days when there were still (musical) conventions to assault, the godfather of Zappa's Mothers (and

"Vinnie who?" *Wiseguy* villains Steelgrave (Ray Sharkey) and the Profitt siblings (Spacey and Severance).

anybody with this two-bit allegory, all you have to do is turn on your TV to see what I mean: a seamless version of the world which swallows the alleged distinctions between comedy, drama, news and commercials, a cosmos which is middle-class from sea to shining sea, safe, intelligible and above all *consumable*. But deep down, everybody knows that "reality" has some hole in its act; if you don't watch out—or even if you do—you could fall through one. Weirdly enough, it was TV itself, back when it was younger, that gave a brand-name to such experiences with Rod Serling's *Twilight Zone*. "Get the Raid," we think when we see those creepy little men scaring that poor old lady—until we read NASA on the side of their tiny metal ship. A kid's imagination runs wild and a man's head pops out of a jack-in-the-box. What's waiting outside that fallout shelter? Which side of that zoo cage are you really on? If the moralizing was often pat, you could always trust the goosebumps. Even the anthology format (now unsalable to network development) expressed a basic truth: you can't step in the same universe twice. And somewhere there's one where Mr. Serling is still typing like crazy. J.T.

WISEGUY (1987-90 CBS). For the bad guys. Ray Sharkey's mob don Sonny Steelgrave chewed scenery like a chow-starved pit bull. Joan Severance's Susan Profitt sashayed, seduced, had a curious relationship with brother Mel (Kevin Spacey), whom she'd shoot up between his toes with a special "elixir." "Ah," the becalmed Mel would coo, "the toes knows."

YANCY DERRINGER (1958-59 CBS). Urbane western (N'awlins) starred Jock Mahoney as unflappable gambler accompanied by Indian mute Pahoo (actor: X. Brands). A 19th century Pete Gunn, suave Yance was celebrated in the title song: "He had ruffles at his wrist / But iron in his fist." D.B.

ALL TOUGH, ALL BUSINESS:

Honey, Peel, 99, and that Darned Catwoman

by Amy Linden

Happening role models, femme division, were not easy to come by on the tube until recently. In the Sixties, for instance, choices were limited. You could either aspire to be a mom or a Jeannie. Since most of us were fated to be some variation on the Carol Brady theme, why did we have to Stepford out so young? I mean, making healthy meals for your family may be satisfying, but is it cool? Did boys play dad, wherein they went to work, stressed out, and had heart attacks at age 45? No, they got to be James Bond or the Man From U.N.C.L.E., while we gals got stuck being Mrs. U.N.C.L.E. or secretary or made snacks for the villains. That's until the swingin' sisters of the serials burst out of the Zenith. Honey West, Emma Peel, Agent 99, Catwoman: all tough, all business, and all any aspiring sociopath could hope for in a goddess. Twenty odd years later, their roles still hold up, if for no other reason than that the fashions (primarily all-black, skintight unitards and cool dark shades) are what most of us tend to wear. But it's more than sartorial daring that makes these babes once and future queens of my day. It's attitude, and attitude, like black stretch pants, is something you can never have enough of.

Honey West (from the '65-'66 series of the same name), as played to icy perfection by the sultry Anne Francis, mole in place, takes her blond flip and pony-skin car coat into one risky situation after another. Like most hip hers of the Sixties, Honey is some sort of spy or cop; something where she is making the world safe for democracy and getting to shoot bad guys. Honey has a pet ocelot named Bruce, drives a cherry sports car (these are chicks who would rather blow up a station wagon than be caught dead behind the

Anne Francis: ocelots over guys. (Editors' Archives)

wheel of one), and has a male partner ("Sam Bolt") who may or may not be her beau. But she's so busy keeping her hair from mussing up, she probably doesn't have time for some dopey man! With Foster Grants on her face and bongos playing in the background, Honey lived dangerously and looked really boss doing it.

> Best of all, Emma kicked guys, a lot, down there.

Emma Peel, from *The Avengers*, set standards for avant female attire and behavior. Diana Rigg, the ever-so-Brit actress who was the more widely viewed Emma (Honor Blackmon of Pussy Galore fame was the other Ms. Peel), had cheekbones to die for, a knowing smirk on her lips, that flip (note that on these girls it's a wild wig, while on *That Girl* or Marilyn Quayle it's L7), those clothes (including the racy leather ensembles, making her the first

S & M mistress of the airwaves) ... and she had a unique relationship with both her partner John Steed and that umbrella. Best of all, Emma kicked guys, a lot, down there. She was probably the only TV character that both dad and daughter could lust after. Sleek, well versed in karate, and clad head to toe in hides, Emma Peel was the antidote to suburban life.

Batman's Catwoman, as portrayed by Julie Newmar (not Eartha Kitt! Too exotic to be truly cool), is the first great space cadet / evil temptress. The curvy Circe of Gotham City seemed somewhat out of it, as though she was dipping into the catnip. Newmar was a wonder. On a show filled with sexless nerdy superheroes, she slinked and lapped milk like a vamp, tossing her long fall back with authority. She wore a catsuit like white on rice and got to boss around her posse of hapless henchmen, teaching all of us girls the valuable lesson: get some guy to do the shit work. Is it any wonder we rooted for her to triumph over Batman and Robin? Truly good bad, and she had cute little kitty kat ears.

Julie Newmar receives a Felix for her purr-fect role as Catwoman.
(Golden Apple Archives)

> It's attitude, and attitude, like black stretch pants, is something you can never have enough of.

Agent 99 suffers Smart attack

Get Smart's Agent 99 was the only nonincompe-
tent on the show. Barbara Feldon did not get as
tough a wardrobe as the other gals. She doffed
Carnaby Street duds, but was no bombshell. This
was due, no doubt, to the fact that she was seeing
Maxwell Smart, and couldn't look too sexy. (In fact,
they finally did her in by giving her twins, for
chrissakes.) But she had Cool Chick coursing
through her veins—since she was a secret agent,
had a flip, saved the day a lot, and had the best way
of rolling her eyes back whenever Max would
screw up, which was all the time. The "Oh Max' riff
would be yet another invaluable lesson for all
future gal pals out there, since most of us would
wind up spending our lives apologizing and
standing by the unfortunate choices we made,
mate-wise. Each roll of the corneas was an unspo-
ken signal that said, "We all know I'm the only one
with half a brain, it's a man's world, and at least
the writers don't make me look like a jackass."

Women may have more options today, although,
due to *glasnost*, spy ain't one of them. Yet, despite
all the Armani-clad supergals cluttering up the
screen with their six-figure CAREERS and their
quality-time children, none will ever be as inspiring, memorable or important as the cool chicks of
the boob tube who gave us little girls hope and
lifetime fashion tips.

© 1992 Amy Linden

(As of this writing, *Honey West* and *Get Smart* are
running on Nick At Nite. *Batman* continues to be
syndicated in various markets. E.M.G. Video offers
65 episodes of *The Avengers* for sale on VHS. For
info: 202 Camino Cortina, Camarillo, CA 93010.)

158

"Can I Get A Witness?" Televangelism's Holy Hit Parade

by Davin Seay

Any cultural anthropologist worth his Coke-bottle
glasses will tell you: rock 'n' roll was born in the
church. From Little Richard's lascivious glossolalia
to Presley's mordant pieties, the style and substance of the devil's music was cradled in
the House of God.

But it wasn't just the rhymes and rhythms and
raucous testifying of the music that sprung,
sweat-soaked and signifying, from the snake-
handling Pentecostal sects infesting Dixie like
sanctifying swamp fever. In keeping with the
hallucinogenic revival fires that had been sweeping the nation since a former slave by the name of
William Joseph Seymour set the spark in Los
Angeles in 1906 with the infamous Azusa Street
Revival, a whole new kind of preacher began
hogging the limelight from the Holy Ghost in the
late Twenties: strutting, preening, boasting and
beseeching, the Pentacostal preacher was the
prototype for the modern rock superstar.

And, while the style might fit Axl, Alice or any
number of professional bad boys, it was the new
breed of savvy, smarmy sermonizers who wore it
best. Disdaining the hidebound religious trap-
pings and tiresome theological training of established denominations, these glitzy pulpit-pound-
ers used the sheer force of their personalities to
gather the meek and mild unto their silk-clad
bosoms. "This morning I intend to explain the
unexplainable," claimed one high-stepping Holy
Roller, "find out the undefinable, ponder over the
imponderable, and unscrew the unscrutable."
Another Bible belter commanded the faithful to
petition God for "the blood that cleans up, the
Spirit that fills up, the fire that burns up, and the
dynamite that blows up."

A half century later, the heirs of this Pentacostal
personality are still at it, thanks to the magic of
the electronic altar. And, while Swaggart's
glycerine tears and Bakker's overreactive hor-
mones might have besmirched the profession's
already unsavory reputation, there are still a few
preachers, prophets and shameless hucksters
berating their flocks from earth-orbiting satel-
lites, with the authentically addled fervor of their
forebears.

Among the most celebrated, if not the most flamboyantly apostate, would have to be the Rev. Dr. Frederick J. Eikerenkoetter II, better known to his covetous minions as Reverend Ike. The Godfather of pulpit pitchmen, Ike works from a homespun theology that can be summed up by his simple mantra, oft-quoted in his ministry's glossy broadsheet *Action!*: "Don't be a hypocrite about money. Admit openly and inwardly that you like money. Say: 'I like money. I need money. I want money. Money is good: I bless the idea of money in my mind.'" During the late Sixties and early Seventies, Ike's trailblazing thesis of obscene-wealth-as-divine-right plowed the ground for the convoluted creed known as Mustard Seed Faith. Perfected by the dour paranoid Oral Roberts, the notion of having it all by giving till it hurts has served as the cornerstone for evangelistic fund-raising ever since.

Ike likewise set the pace for the Nielsen-conscious preacher's penchant for snappy, stylish, or simply outrageous wardrobes. Given to floral patterned blazers, flared pastel slacks and patent leather jodhpurs, Ike found his most zealous fashion convert in Akron, Ohio's Rev. Ernest Ainsley. God's own Liberace, Ainsley delivers his mellifluous homilies beneath a hi-rise toupée, perched in an ethereal, Greek-columned portico and sheathed in three-piece suits ranging in color from iridescent apricot to bilious aquamarine. Strategic lighting reflects the glint of his pinky rings and goiter-sized diamond stick pin, anchoring jumbo paisley neckware. A self-professed healer, Ainsley found his finest moment recently when curing a woman afflicted by a "partial sense of smell." A cologne-drenched handkerchief, shoved under the reeling supplicant's nose, proved the miracle-working power of the pudgy clothes horse.

Healing, of course, has been the crowd-pleasing main attraction since the days of Billy Sunday's

Ikie: Get with the gelt and it's gonna work out fine.

massive tent revivals. And little of the divine physician's barnstorming ballyhoo has changed, as exemplified by the frenzied ministrations of Peter Popov.

In a loose, flapping tie, with shirt sleeves rolled to the elbows and drenched at the armpit, the Texas-based evangelist's laying on of hands is accompanied by a restless roaming of aisles, the better to ferret out the infirm. The Lord's ostensible healing power flows through Popov's massive frame with alarming jolts and shudders and the healing touch, when it comes, is delivered with a numbing impact on the forehead of the lame, blind, or partially-scented. Prospects of rampant charlatanism fade to insignificance in the face of Popov's heroic, hair-raising performances.

Curing the crippled may be an inherently theatrical occupation. But TV's gifted men of God can eke drama from the most mundane of pursuits. On-the-air Bible studies can, in the hands of a spirited practitioner such as Dr. Gene Scott, become wrenching revelations into the viewer's simpering spiritual state as well as the Pasadena, California-based preacher's own towering hubris.

Scott, a wildly eccentric curmudgeon given to wearing a variety of whimsical headgear (from English bobby helmets to ten-gallon Stetsons) illustrates his biblical theorems by erratic scribbles on a large slab of mounted plexiglass. Insight into the Levitical offerings may be capriciously interrupted by a shameless demand for call-in pledges. If an equally arbitrary goal is not met, Scott will promise to stare silently into the camera until his followers pony up. Making good on his threat, Scott at once perfects a new fund-raising technique and explores the outer reaches of interactive television much in the manner of Ernie Kovacs.

The ranks of TV's oddball avatars is endless, from Dr. E. Howard Estep's tirelessly extrapolated mathematical proofs of the Second Coming, to O.L. Jaggers' eerie evocation of God's gilded throne, lovingly recreated with tin foil and dashboard saints. While rock 'n' roll may have stolen its best licks from gospel, the biggest stars are still the true believers.

JIVE 5

Joey Ramone's 5 Coolest TV Shows

Addams Family	Hullabaloo
The Simpsons	Shindig
Ed Sullivan	

In 1968, TV Guide cited social historian Arnold Toynbee, on a trip to Haight-Ashbury, as saying that if hippies hadn't materialized when & where they did, America would have invented them. Or TV would have. When it comes to covering the unsquare "fringe," the medium is widely known to "get it late and get it wrong." Which is often what makes TV's efforts such gone goofs. Witness what happens when . . .

TV Meets the
Beats, Punks & Hippies

By the late Fifties/early Sixties, jargon-pushing jazzmen and hipsters had logged plenty of tube time. Peter Gunn hung at a dive called Mothers, Johnny Staccato (John Cassavetes) tinkled tusk at "Waldo's" on MacDougal, and Phil Harris is said to have laid down a bop rap that would not stop, portraying a hopped up horn man on *Burke's Law* (1963). (In the *Phil Silvers Show* episode "Bilko's Bopster," comic Ronnie Graham played a drummer drafted into Bilko's motor pool.) But *beatniks*, the jazzers' scruffy younger cousins, were never that big a noise. *Dobie Gillis'* Maynard Krebs (1959-63) was the most prominent exception; beating his bongos and eschewing "work!?!" at all costs, Bob Denver's MGK was a real role model for ne'er-do-wells.

The bossest beat treat, though, may well be the *Beverly Hillbillies'* 1965 two-parter, "Big Daddy Jed" (!) and "Cool School Is Out." In the former, bearded guru Shelley Epps ("May the saxophone of life blow you nothin' but cool notes") hits Jed Clampett up for rent money for his coffee house.

When Mr. Drysdale insists the beat-crib vacate its current location in his bank's basement, Shel wails that he may "move to a new pad on Peel Street" (relocate to Sunset Strip). In the companion episode, Jethro (renamed "Clyde" by the beat groovers), Elly May and Granny all 'nik out, under the tutelage of Shelley and his pals Wiggy and Horace (a comatose poet who periodically wakes to bestow "major hipness" on deserving candidates by snapping his digits). High points: Granny, demonstrating how they uproot tubers back in Bug Tussle, Ark., accidentally starts a dance craze, the Tater Digger, and addles Jed with her lingo ("I'm splittin' for the kitchen. Eyeball you later!").

Smokin' Crawdads, Boostin' Lilacs

Timing and technology allowed the hippies to best the beats when it came to TV access. They were simply in the right place when the voracious eye was hungriest for sex and color. The long running *Dragnet* probably weighed in with more hippie tales than any other show. Gary Crosby's a commune cat whose "lady" has a bad-check habit in "Forgery," while "Narcotics" (both 1969) unleashes pot-sniffing canines. Unquestionably the coolest, though, is 68's infamous "The Big Prophet." Friday and Gannon confront "Bentley," a Leary type who nonchalantly proselytizes LSD for everybody, including kids. Much of the episode consists of the trio debating hotly, seated in lotus positions on the floor of Bent's pad.

In the *Hillbillies'* "Robin Hood And The Sheriff" (1967), Jethro, playing Robin Hood in Griffith Park, is hailed as a guru by a band of roving hippies. When their leader, Sir Guy of Gisborn (Alan Reed, Jr., who also swung as beat cat Shelley), hears that Jethro "smokes" crawdads, he begs J-man to catch a batch. Ready to trip, Sir Guy verily swoons when Jethro presents him with a bag of fresh crawdads ("Grab me, baby! Sir Guy will be the first to set sail up Moon River!"). As he reaches into the bag, a bad 'dad practically chomps off his hand.

Illustration: Alex Jones

For high concepts, it's hard to beat *Batman*'s "Louie the Lilac" episode (1967). Pinstriped mobster/florist Louie (Milton Berle, devouring scenery with an appetite only a couple of calories shy of Frank Gorshin's Riddler) plans to corner the flower market in Gotham City. His strategy: induce petal scarcity by stealing every plant in town. When Louie picks all the posies in Gotham Park, the flower kids (led by Princess Primrose) are deprived of the mums 'n' daffs they need for their love-in, thus bringing Batty to the scene. A wig-kick from stem to stamen, this episode and a followup, "Louie's Lethal Lilac Time," boast the ubiquitous Bakalyan as Lou's flunkie "Arbutus," and rugged dialogue. Hippie to Princess: "You've tripped out, Primrose. Groovy, but in the wrong groove!"

Pretty Vacant

The last (and probably final) time the kids got all shook up—the punk era—continues to be square-TV fodder. On the sitcoms, the spike-hairs come and go, as if such cliches, popping up in prime time more than a decade after their introduction, could raise anyone's hackles. And yet, when TV first tried to p-rock (early Eighties) . . . Don Rickles pogo'ed with the Dickies on his short-lived *C.P.O. Sharkey*, and Jack Klugman's Quincy, in the episode "Next Stop Nowhere," investigated the death of a kid ice-picked in a slam pit. Onstage, a Fear clone ("Mayhem") howls ("Saw a blind man the other day/Took his pencils and ran away"). On the floor, a punkette asks Q, "You work here?" Quincy: "No. I'm with the Coroner's Office." Punkette: "Oh sure, I've heard you guys play. You got a great band."

But the absolute best-worst of the tele-Vicious incidents occurred on C.H.I.P.S. Heroic hog-straddlers Ponch (Erik Estrada) and John (the one who's not Estrada) are called in when *another* Fear rip ("Pain") is suspected of stealing other bands' equipment. Pain's singer Potato Head slings stolen guitars off a Venice rooftop, causing a three-car pileup. Doug McClure, owner of a renamed P.J.'s nightclub, is threatened by a switchblade-toting Painster: "Talk to me, earth dog!" Having vanquished the punks, Estrada closes the show by giving the misguided kids what they really wanted all along: him, belting sub-disco in glitter togs and strutting across the stage like the cool guy he's sure he is. Exquisite.

Watch for the *C.H.I.P.S.*, *Batman*, *Dragnet* and *Quincy* episodes wherever reruns run. The CBS Video Library has packaged the three *Hillbillies* eps cited here onto one rentable cassette, *Groovin' With The Clampetts*.

New Rose Hips: Ponch's deft moves trash punks in *C.H.I.P.S.*

Route 66

A new culture got its existential kicks on TV's hippest roadshow

By Davin Seay

In the late Fifties, during the robust adolescence of American television, most popular, family-oriented programs seemed to have been situated within a few blocks of each other. The Cleavers, Donna Reed's brood, the Father who Knows Best and Ozzie's offspring all occupied the same psychic and geographic neighborhood—in one of those newly minted suburban tracts that were fast becoming the locus of the American Dream. While Kramden and Norton, by virtue of *The Honeymooners'* blue collar context, were forever consigned to their dreary tenement walk-ups, even Lucy and Ricky had up and moved to Connecticut to be closer to their viewers' aspirations.

Yet, by the early Sixties, a faint malaise was beginning to make itself felt all along those broad, elm-lined avenues. It would be a few years, of course, before the heirs of America's post-war plenty would flee their bland environs in search of themselves, but in 1960 the signposts of cultural disintegration had already been clearly posted . . . along *Route 66*.

Created by producer Herbert B. Leonard and TV's Silver Age *uber-scribe* Stirling Silliphant, *Route 66* posited a whole new, tremendously appealing and popular American archetype—rootless, vaguely disaffected, searching for meaning and hungry for life. That such existential concerns could stand as character motivation in television's complaisant milieu was in itself remarkable. That, during its four year run, *Route 66* dealt honestly, sometimes brilliantly, with the fraying fabric of the American consensus, is an enduring testament to TV's occasional ability to transcend its mandate.

The show's premise was simple, inspired . . . and subversive: Tod Styles (Martin Milner) and Buz Murdock (George Maharis) plied the legendary interstate in a Corvette convertible encountering people and situations that, as one critic put it, "challenged their values."

Maybe, but the truly intriguing subtext of the series was that Buz and Tod's values were themselves in flux. Why else would two able young men, who should have been thinking about corporate careers and the requisite wife and 2.3 children, be roaming the country, living in motels and financing their travels with low-paying day labor?

Spirit of 66: Buz, Vette, Tod.

The show never confronted the question directly, but, in a series of highly charged, fearlessly didactic scenarios, most often bearing the stamp of Silliphant's overheated aesthetic, Tod and Buz embodied, all unknowing, the growing conviction that the American way of life had become a grey-flannel straitjacket.

Not a particularly stunning revelation for those who had already heard the call around the bend in Jack Kerouac's *On The Road* and elsewhere. But this was, after all, primetime television, and the show's success could only be attributed to the collective yearning of a nation suddenly disenchanted with its split-level sophistry.

The liberating possibilities of wanderlust were underlined even in the casting and backstories of *Route 66*. Notwithstanding his character's wholesome handle, Maharis' non-specific yet conspicuous ethnicity was in sharp contrast to Milner's corn-fed and freckled Midwestern pudge (later to harden into immobile rectitude on *Adam 12*). The very best of their adventures took place in the wide open spaces of the Southwest, with appropriate Western themes of freedom, individuality and outlaw nobility. This compelling mix of types and typology offered the new, if only dimly perceived, notion that America was, indeed, a polyglot society, far different from the monolithic WASPality presented as TV's norm.

"Of the two characters, Tod was the more intellectual," recalled Milner in a recent interview. "He came from a well-to-do family and was college educated, optimistic and a liberal who always believed in doing the right thing . . . (He) had

163

"How Much A Pound Is Albatross?": Maharis' Buz and Newmar's Vickie outside Tucson.
(Hollywood Book & Poster)

inherited some money from his father in order to buy that first Corvette.

"Now Buz, on the other hand, was a real street kid. He was a bad boy from the ghetto—from Hell's Kitchen—and had been involved in crime. His adopted father had died in his arms of an overdose, and Buz had truly seen the worst part of life."

This juxtaposition, later to be flogged into irrelevance in countless buddy cop variations, served the show's central conceit well, providing different, and often divergent, worldviews to the week's unfolding drama. It was an ambivalence uneasily articulated by the show's creators: whether they knew it or not, they were grappling with the conundrums later to divide the nation and the generations. For while Tod and Buz could, and regularly did, descend to the level of mobile Mary Worths, fixing people and their problems before gunning it into the sunset, the very best of *Route 66* dealt with the clash of conflicting values: freedom vs. responsibility; an individual's desires and society's pliers; touseling your toddler's hair or letting the wind blow through yours.

The paradox was best presented in Silliphant's purple prose. Two of the writer's classic episodes, "How Much A Pound Is Albatross?" and "Ever Ride The Waves To Oklahoma?" (the titles themselves gloriously evoke Silliphant's visionary pretensions) are delightful relics from a dawning age of self-discovery.

In "Albatross," Julie Newmar plays Vickie, a proto-flower child who blows into Tucson where she's promptly arrested for, as much as anything, being enigmatic. "'Who Am I?'" she responds to a police query. "I ask myself that a thousand times a day. A gallery of people, somewhere between thought and naught . . . but which one?" Has she ever been arrested before? "I'm arrested by everything I see, everything I touch." Small wonder Buz promptly falls for this blithe spirit, while practical Tod remains dubious, especially after his partner puts up the 'vette to bail out the misunderstood vixen.

But just how misunderstood? After various meandering plot twists, Vickie ends up in court, where a stern judge rides a familiar hobby horse. If everyone acted like her, he admonishes, what would happen to our society and, by extension, our precious way of life? Vickie's response is a typically over-the-top Silliphant tone poem. "It's not easy being a pilgrim or a rebel," she says. "But how else can you give yourself to life?" Significantly, the judge is denied his curt rejoinder and the question is left hanging. How indeed? For Buz and Tod, escorting Vickie to the outskirts of town, the answer lies just around the next bend.

The postulate is given another startling twist in "Ever Ride The Waves To Oklahoma?," another of Silliphant's sterling immersions in wild style. Here it's Buz who disapproves of the footloose dalliances of a gang of exceptionally clean cut surfers. After the pier-shooting death of an earnest gremmie, Buz is determined to put Hob, the local hotshot (Jeremy Slate), in his place, and exposes the surfer king's lowly day job as a busboy. In the ensuing fracas, Hob delivers an impassioned plea for the Surfer Life. "You're just another wave, man," he tells the fuming Buz, "and I'm gonna let you roll by."

By the hour's conclusion, in a remarkable reversal of prevailing convention, it's Buz who sees the light. Maybe, he ponders, surfers are just like other people. "And if they're people, and they're getting ready to make their moves, when they make their moves, good or bad, right or wrong . . . that's between a man and himself."

On *Route 66*, an entire society was getting ready to make its moves.

ROAD SIGNS: The series' last regular appearance was on Nick at Nite (late Eighties), and where it'll turn up next is anyone's guess. When it does, look especially for the episodes "Who Will Cheer My Bonnie Bride?" (a violent proto- *Bonnie & Clyde* feat. Rip Torn and Albert Salmi), "Birdcage On My Foot" (Buz helps Robert Duvall kick a habit), and "Welcome To The Wedding" (a psycho chiller starring Rod Steiger as an escaped con).

HIP CITY U.S.A.?

Natch, there're plenty more *obvious* cool capitals. Tourist mobs will never dim the eternal hipness of S.F or N.O. Still, overexposure has rendered both a bit too holy and Home on the Range-ish. Contrarywise, P-burgh's industrial armpit rep pisses off its many denizens who *know* they're boss and *dig* having a place called The Iron And Glass Bank. Homeboy Gary Koteski thinks the town's frigid because, after working the night shift, steelworkers "go home and watch *Leave It To Beaver* reruns."

Civic jingoism like that is one of the requisites of a cool place. Recently, I called up a friend in Mobile and told him I was in town. "Why?" he asked. Such a response is unthinkable in P-burgh, where almost 85% of the population remains native-born (even a lot of the ones who split come back). For the record, the other coolville requirements are mixed population, unpretentiousness, and, most of all, idiosyncratic regionalism in every area of life. This last feature Pittsburgh possesses to dizzying degrees. I wouldn't even be surprised if they don't have their own sexual positions. They

sure have their own way of talking, a kind of chewed-up nasal drawl that combines East, Midwest and Southern dialect. A sentence like "You go five miles down the road" comes out "Y'go fahv mahls donner rud." Once heard, never forgotten, like one's first view of the city itself.

A real E ticket entry is to blast through Fort Pitt Tunnel and shoot across the bridge into the nineteenth century. Rows of once smoke-belching factories are jammed under the steep hills, connected by a series of antique bridges (1700 in Allegheny County, and Pittsburgh has more than any town except Venice, Italy). Set as it is inside the fork made by the Ohio, Allegheny and Monongahela, it's possible, as the Greater Pittsburgh Office of Promotion claims, for a visitor to jet-ski around downtown.

They'd probably also like you to know that their town has one of the best salary-to-housing ratios in the U.S., and is the birthplace of such established *artistes* as Hank Mancini, Shirley Jones, Michael Keaton, Martha Graham and Gene Kelly.

IT'S THE PITTS!

by Dick Blackburn

New Pittsburgh Publications

That's the official line. But what about wacko's like playboy mental case Harry K. Thaw, the son of a railroad and coke magnate who, in '06, blew away architect Stanford White on the roof of Madison Square Garden, over Floradora beauty Evelyn Nesbitt? Or gone eccentrics like method actor/parodist/ *Batman* Riddler Frank Gorshin, and grand old diesel Gert Stein whose "a rose is a rose is a rose" sort of sums up the town's no-jive attitude. Once, workers had to take an extra shirt to those factories, because the joints turned the skies and everyone under them into soot-blackened moles. Old pix of P-burgh at noon, from the Fifties, look like midnight in a *film noir*. But the smoke laws hanged that; today, urban workers who've moved into redone factory-cat homes take one of two inclines down steep Jefferson Hill and stroll across the bridge to their gigs. When they return, their pinpoint oxfords are still snowy white.

The town's topography of trees, brick, water and steel is constantly being captured by as-yet-nationally-undiscovered home talent such as photographer Mark Parrot who digs P-burgh for its "grit and grime against the glitter," and painter Bob Qualters who calls his city "dramatic, full of contrast, atmosphere. When I was a kid, it was dark and spooky, massive and theatrical." Qualters renders the Triangle City in an earthy Reginald Marsh style that feels just right to enthusiasts who, so far, can still afford his canvases. Critics bug him to junk such a "gauche and ordinary" subject and move to fame and bucks in the Apple. Qualters won't budge.

He'd miss the endless conjectures about local legends. Like that time in the early Fifties when a B-25 bomber crash landed in the Monongahela and was never found. Cover-up? Of what? Nobody knows. And Qualters'd probably get homesick for the landmarks: the world's largest analog clock on the old Duquesne brewery, a handsome piece of deco, and Wholey's (pronounced "Wooley's") neon fish, visible from any downtown bridge.

Some of the real Pittsburgh has made it onto film. Not the old studio stuff like *Valley Of Decision*

167

(1945), a historically interesting Greer Garson potboiler, or even the on-location *Flashdance* (1983), an I-gotta-be-me glitzcapade. But more memorably in the work of George Romero. His *Martin* ('78), a contemporary vampire story, uses the minimalist gothicism of the place as a supporting character. James Foley's *Reckless* ('84) sold the city as a blue collar poem. *Slap Shot* ('77), George Roy Hill's best film, rendered the special ambience less self-consciously than Michael Cimino's hysteric but still impressive *The Deer Hunter* (1978). (These flicks had some real manic characters. Real Pitts folk aren't as overamped. Andy Warhol, Perry Como and Mister Rogers were/are natives, all of them so amazingly laid back that George Westinghouse, whose main plant was here, could've had 'em air-conditioned.)

Pittsburgh's history—besides labor riots and the Slav steelworker version of Paul Bunyan, Joe Magarac, is full of unpretentious innovations.

SOOT SUIT: Women shop downtown, masked for smog, 1946. Courtesy Carnegie Library of Pittsburgh.

Among its famous firsts: the Ferris Wheel (1893), indoor ice rink, and pro hockey game (1894), the banana split (1904), service station (1914), Bingo (early Twenties), and the first armored car robbery (1927).

An obsessive chronology of movies and musicians who've played the Iron City, *Key to the City, Vol. 1: 1928-54* (1985) highlights the town's entertainment history. Author Dave Goodrich, when he's not reigning as a radio trivia expert ("The Doctor of Rock & Roll"), is night manager of the colorful Edison Hotel on Ninth Street downtown, where he works a strip show featuring the likes of Toppsy Curvey. Just your average P-burgh guy.

Music? The story of the black Hill district, where great jazzbo's like Mary Lou Williams, Erroll Garner, Ahmad Jamal, Stanley Turrentine and divers *autres* pounded, plucked and blew, is the subject of a local documentary, *Wylie Avenue Days*. And retired *Pittsburgh Courier* photographer Teenie Harris lensed beacoups sepia acts during his 50 years with the paper. Native Billy Eckstine gave the world soul balladry *and* the famed Mr. "B" collar, that aerodynamic flared wonder, developed, legend has it, to prevent restricting the singer's swelling pipes. Doowop from Iron City is represented on countless dreamy & drivin' discs: the Del-Vikings' cosmic "Whispering Bells" and "Come Go With Me" (1957), and the Marcels' turbo-charged rending of "Blue Moon" (1960). For still deeper digs, check sides by the Diadems, Four Dots, El Venos and Chapellaires. As for whiteboys, there's the duly celebrated Lou Christie (who debuted with local group Luigi & the Lions), and the Skyliners, whose soaring "Since I Don't Have You" is arguably the sharpest teen ballad ever waxed. And dig 'liners lead singer Jimmy Beaumont's hometown accent when he rhymes desires ("desahrs") with hours ("ahrs"). Rocker Buddy Sharpe cut blasters "Bald Head Baby" and "Fat Mama Twist" in P-burgh, as well as the ultra gone

Joe Magarac bends P'burgh iron.
Courtesy University of Pittsburgh / Westmorland Museum of Art, Greensburgh, PA.

"Please Please Please Please" (described in *Kicks* magazine as sounding "like Larry Williams being eaten alive by Tony the Tiger from a mile-high weather balloon"). In the Sixties, the Swamp Rats waxed the wildest versions of both "Louie Louie" and the Sonics' "Psycho," and Pittsburgh psychedelia flew high with the Marshmallo' Steamshovel's "Mister Mole." More recently, happening locals the Cynics have recut the Sixties (Texas) punker "I'm In Pittsburgh And It's Raining."

The town also copped honors for having the world's first radio station (KDKA signed on in 1920). But a year before, a guy named Frank Conrad had been spinning platters from his garage on Penn Ave., making him *the world's first deejay*! Ever

New Pittsburgh Publications

PORKOLOGY
Featuring PORKY CHEDWICK
With BILLY PRICE
AND THE KEYSTONE RHYTHM BAND

PORKY'S RAP: "More jams than Smuckers, more lines than Bell Telephone."

since, jocks here have been heavy business. While doing a live broadcast in front of the Stanley Theater, Porky Chedwick, the "dapper rapper, porkulatin' papa and daddio of the raddio," urged everyone to "come on down!" Thousands jammed the Stanley. Ten thousand more mobbed the streets, forcing cops to close down a totally gridlocked city. Chedwick, one of the original badboys of the air, played dirty "race records" when it was a no-no, beseeching his faithful to "Climb the walls!," "Pound the boards!," and, at the start of a raucous sax break, "Blow the horn!" On at least one occasion, tuned-in drivers complied literally with the latter, leaning on their car horns and creating civic cacaphony. On their first U.S. tour in 1964, the Rolling Stones drew a scant 300 locals to their West View Park show. Platter pusher Mad Mike's swingin' soiree the same night drew 2000.

Today, P-burgh deejays continue "breaking" old wax years after it was pressed. Locally sought singles featuring odd vocal groups, blazing instros, and anything with lyrics about cars or booze are known to rare vinyl dealers across the country as "Pittsburgh records." Mad Mike, Porky and Charlie Apple blast the discs to devoted listenerships, jealously keeping their obscuro "finds" from each other; Mad Mike even released a series of lps on the sleeves of which he changed the names of the artists, to confound his competition.

Not content with its many firsts, Pittsburgh is also the last bastion of "Telephone Music." This archaic phenomenon, kicking from the Thirties to early Fifties, lets bar patrons drop their coins right into the slot of a jukebox, phone their selections into a central switchboard hooked up through old turntables, to the bar's juke. The deejay can even give a dedication over the bar's speakers before scratching the wax. In T-Music's heyday, the phone jocks were all young frails, and part of the novelty's appeal was a husky hint of softcore phone sex. Not long ago, the basic Telephone Music system had become so antiquated that its 66-year old owner Helen Reitzel was about to shut it down for good. Then she had a premonition, about a way to electronically update the curious P-burgh institution. It worked, and today Telephone Music flourishes in eight Iron City bars. Reitzel, appropriately, moonlights as a dream analyst on local radio.

Frankie Capri's a far more *outre* hero. He performs every Friday eve at the Liberty Bell Lounge on East Carson St., the second Sunday of the month at the McKeesport AmVets hall, and the third Sunday of the month at the Elks Lodge in Lincoln Place. Frankie's act? Singing and playing guitar, piano, accordion and kazoo, backed by two ventriloquist dummies, a life-size plastic Snow White dwarf and countless wind-up musical monkeys. An adept Elvis impersonator, he can sing in any style from Dean Martin to the Bee Gees and dons a different hat for each number. Complimented on his talent, Capri modestly replies, "God made the pizza. I just deliver it."

Indeed, Pittsburgh itself delivers some of the world's great junkfood. It's the home of Heinz' 57 varieties, as well as the Clark Candy Company (producers of the groovalacious Zagnut bar). The Potato Patch, found inside the fab Kennywood Amusement Park (Frankie Capri performs there on Italian Day), processes and french-fries endless spuds (dig the spicy garlic variety). Among other regional specialties: chipped ham, Rolling Rock

Sign of good taste. Photo by P.J. McArdle.

"WHOSE IS THE SAUSAGE-WITH-MUSHROOMS?" Frankie Capri.

beer, Klondike bars, City Chicken (veal cubes breaded, fried and baked on skewers), and the world's bossest pop: Tommy Tucker Old Southern Style Mint Ginger Ale (locals use it to cook kielbasa).

Lest P-burghers be accused of living in the past, consider the concessions to life's quickening pace made by the Primanti Bros. Tavern and Restaurant, located down by the river warehouses in the Strip district where the truckers roll in from all points. Because these guys-on-the-go need at least one hand on the wheel, the Bros. have pushed the fast-food envelope to its limit: viz. the mighty Primanti Bros. Sandwich—why put slaw and fries on the side when you can shoehorn 'em in on top of the homemade sausage, cheese, ham or whatever?

And, yeah, the aforementioned Kennywood Park still boasts one of the country's few remaining wooden rollercoasters (dig that jerky, clickety clack, non-machine-tooled ride). But it also houses the awesome Thunderbolt, one of the world's few monstro 'coasters to require riders to have their necks strapped to the seat, since the 'bolt hits speeds of 80 m.p.h. Wicked.

PITTS SHOP: Porky Chedwick's patented rap is preserved on a 45 r.p.m. single, "Porkology" (Green Dolphin Records), available with picture sleeve, from P.J. McArdle Productions, 310 Barnes St., Pittsburgh, PA 15221.

Pittsburgh's Greatest Hits, a cd compilation of golden-age P'burgh hits, is available from Itzy Records, PO Box 8799, Pittsburgh, PA 15221. Phone: 412-241-4626.

LOU CHRISTIE

Courtesy Harry Young, Lou Christie Fan Club.

Nobody's going out of his way to nominate Lou Christie for the Rock 'N' Roll Hall of Fame, or any other career honors. Lugee Alfredo Giovanni Sacco looked like one of the long line of Italianate pouter pigeons with a forte of feeble Fabianisms. He sounded like a shriller Frankie Valli, and he's thought of (if at all) as a second-rater below the Bobbies and Frankies who, the consensus has it, dominated early Sixties pop.

A grave injustice. From "The Gypsy Cried" on, the records of this multi-talented Pittsburgher (who actually collaborated with a Gypsy woman, Twyla Herbert, with 20 years on him) featured a weird keening edge and frequent musical innovation (check the proto-reggae rhythms of 1963's "Two Faces Have I") that set them apart.

By his 1966-67 peak, Lou's songs typically swelled from modest beginnings to thunderous orchestral climaxes. As he effortlessly alternated between his pleasant, slightly orotund tenor and that piercing trademark falsetto, even higher-pitched background vocalists wove in Tourette's Syndrome whoops, witches' babble, and Greek-chorus admonitions aimed at the woebegone singer as he wallowed in the most extraordinary morass of tortured jealousy, revenge fantasies, wounded macho pride, betrayed trust and guilt-edged lust.

Vivid metaphors sliced through the emotional wreckage—love as a "Trapeze," those lubricious lightning strikes, or the talking windshield wipers of "Rhapsody In The Rain" (extended to an entire automobile in the boggling, mini-operatic "If My Car Could Only Talk").

By Mid-1967, with "Back To The Days Of The Romans," Lou was parroting conservative cant about Sixties America recapitulating Caligulan decadence, while warning "Don't laugh at the devil's existence." Considering also the flipside, the suicidally frustrated "Don't Stop Me (Jump Off The Edge Of Love)," a chilling chunk of cod-psychedelia cash-in even bleaker than the Supremes' awesome "Reflections," Lou must have known he'd pushed the parameters of pop torment as far as he could. Conventionality (relatively speaking) and obscurity followed, but don't overlook the rhapsody of his reign.

True Lou: *Enlightnin'ment: The Best Of Lou Christie* (Rhino).
For more, Harry Young publishes a newsletter, *Lightning Strikes*: write him c/o the Lou Christie Official Fan Club, P.O. Box 748, Chicago, IL 60690-0748.   - Ken Barnes

Shake's Hamlet hipped Horatio that "There are more things in heaven and earth than are dreamt of in your philosophy." The cool world, too, comprises more things than we could dream up chapters for. Hence, this randomly accessible blend of style substances . . .

BEEFHEART'S SWEET TOOTH. Presley hankered for a "Big Hunk 'O Love." Big Maybelle crooned for "Candy." But the real sugar pops are Captain Beefheart & His Magic Band, who banged the gong for corn syrup and partially hydrogenated vegetable oils on two consecutive albums. The amazingly sensuous peanutbutter-filled taffy bar Abba Zabba inspired Cap's tale of a psyched-out Nature Boy on *Safe As Milk* (1966). Brach's honey-enriched Halloween pellets sparked the trippy deconstructed blues "Kandy Korn" on *Strictly Personal* (1968). Try both: let what was on CB's mind melt in your mouth.

MOYERS' AMERICA: '64 AND THE LIVING IS EASY. Bill Moyers, a deacon and veritable beacon for inquiring PBS minds, did the right thing once (1984), producing a one-hour documentary series called *A Walk Through The Twentieth Century*. The episode we're concerned with deals with Americans and their cars.

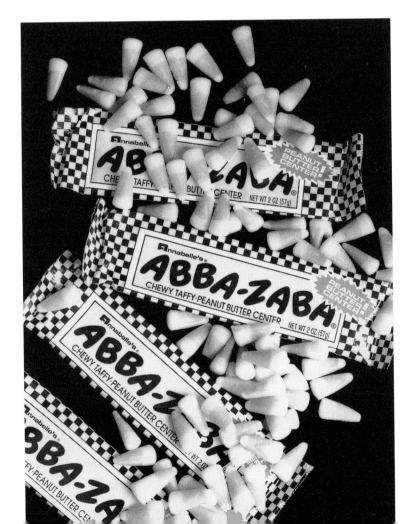

Illustration: Carol Lay

Clean style, with no energy return systems.

Scroll back a bit, through the early days of automotive Americana. Here's a serious look at the country's auto attachment, Henry Ford's Model T assembly line, the early days of motor touring, Fifties dream-mobiles, America as a drive-in culture, and then, whisked in on the bulging bodywork of a Corvette Stingray filtered through the dense (even then) Southern California air, something quintessential appears. It's rough amateur filmwork, scenes shot from a corner: American teenagers on the cruise in Southern California. in their cars.

Ever look at one of those early Beach Boys or Jan and Dean album covers (maybe *Drag City* or *Shut Down Vol. 2*) and wish that you cut with that kind of style? Just an immaculate white T-shirt, levis, navy blue deck shoes: perfect. We're talking about a time when there were only a few basic haircuts, when athletic shoes didn't contain energy return systems, when American cuisine was exemplified by a casserole of noodles, hamburger, green beans and Velveeta. In Moyers' brief luminous footage that feeling is definitively captured. It depicts American youth at the peak of adoles-

cence, like the glimmer of an idea for *American Graffiti*. Here we see teenage males standing on the sidewalk, reaching as the girls roll by, popping with an outrageous come-on ("Hey, I wanna marry you!") and inflicting the toughest put-down they can muster ("Daddy's car, Daddy's car . . . rank!"). Finally, they get a ride.

Earlier in the tape Moyers had talked about how important his '52 two-door Chevy was, and quoted Sinclair Lewis saying that the filling station had become the crossroads of America. He even went on about how we had invented machines that were capable of fulfilling human longing and fantasies. We all know better. It really has to do with fun and attitude, and in a brief moment in Moyers' very thorough documentary, we can see it again, in those grainy hand-held black and white frames of anonymous adolescents in the California sun.—Mike Koehn.
A Walk Through The 20th Century— America on the Road; 55-minute videocasstte available from Pacific Arts Video Publishing, 11858 La Grange Ave., Los Angeles, CA 90025. 1-800-538-5856.

Warner animator Chuck Jones' "One Froggy Evening" pushes the hip amphib further into his role as mischievous square-baiter. Here, a construction worker opens a box he finds at a demolition site and discovers a hammy vaudevillean frog who belts opera and cavorts like George M. Cohan. Sensing big bucks, the guy takes his novelty act to movie agents, bookers, even rents a hall to introduce the world to his singing frog. Unstoppable in private, each time he's called to perform for anyone other than the construction worker, the croaker clams up. The worker is finally driven mad and places his find back in its box, which he stashes in a fresh building site. In the year 2056, a new fool falls by to open the box and restart the cycle.

It's the early Fifties TV series *Andy's Gang*, though, that introduces Froggy the Gremlin, a disruptive rubber wiseass whose pranksterism regularly sent pre-teen studio audiences into screaming frenzies. Froggy's antics: sticking words in the mouths of the show's pompous storytellers, replacing a music teacher's throat spray with glue, mouthing off to host Andy Devine ("You tiny little rascal!" chuckles ruboid Andy. "You great big square!" croaks Froggy). Ladling out plot points like cold porridge, Billy Gilbert inches up to the punchline of "Goldilocks And The Three Bears": "First she tasted the big bear's bowl, but it was too hot . . . Then she tasted the middle-sized bowl, but it was too cold . . . Then she tasted the smallest bowl and said-" "Dig this, it's *reeaal* cool!" blurts Froggy in pure *Trout Mask* growl, sabotaging story, show and decorum . . . From there, it's but a jump to Clarence Henry, the Doors' plagiaristic "Peace Frog" (a rip of Donovan's "Barabajagal"), and S. Clay Wilson's Checkered Demon, an unsettling horned toad who shrinks bikers till they're small enough to fall into their own Tree Frog Beer cans and twists their arms into handlebars. Ribbit! (Jones and Disney cartoons are rentable. For *Andy's Gang* episodes, see mail-order houses in our TUBE Shop Around guide. Ken Grahame's *Willows* can be found in most libraries.)

Chris Cooper

THE HIP AMPHIB. Stealth and poise long ago knocked the cat its status as official mascot of cool, and who'd want to change mascots this late in the game? But you do have this lunar two-legger over here, green with envy and mottled with credentials. His first big gig was in Kenneth Grahame's 1908 kidsbook *The Wind in the Willows*. There, and in Walt Disney's cartoon adaptation, Mr. Toad's mode is High Goof. He's impulsive and incorrigible, hungry for speed and action. After his wild-ride flip-out (a speeding motorcar knocks him and his pals in a ditch, he's smitten and buys his own short to tear up the countryside in), Mr. T's guardians lock him in a room where he tries to shake his wheel-kick cold turkey. "When his violent paroxysms possessed him," Grahame writes, "he would arrange bedroom chairs in rude resemblance of a motorcar and would crouch on the foremost of them, bent forward and staring fixedly ahead, making uncouth and ghastly noises, till the climax was reached, when, turning a complete somersault, he would lie prostrate amidst the ruins of the chairs, apparently completely satisfied for the moment."

THE MUSEUM OF JURASSIC TECHNOLOGY. Nestled between a burger stand and an Indian grocery store in a seedy neighborhood on the fringes of Venice, California, a non-descript brick building houses either an elaborate spoof, a baffling art installation, a sly commentary on the frangible nature of truth, or all of the above . . . depending, of course, on the eye, attitude or inclination of the beholder.

The imposing sign hung over the storefront, announcing with brass-bound solemnity The Museum Of Jurassic Technology, should be enough to spark the curiosity of anyone with even a passing interest in those warehouses of anti-quity called museums (or, depending on the marble-carver's penchant, mvsevms). And if, while entering the porticos of this tidy trove, one wonders what, exactly, could be technical about a geologic age characterized by the emergence of dinosaurs, the helpful guide and serene aura within will put such momentary qualms to rest.

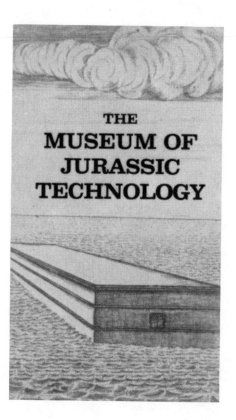

So too will the sonorous piped-in baritone and dreary slide show that "orient" the visitor to the Museum and its ostensible purpose. Anyone who has fidgeted through such pedantic presenta-tions during school outings or rainy Tuesday afternoons will feel right at home. Never mind that after ten minutes you may be more confused about the Museum's *raison* than when you walked in. Isn't that all part of the reverent experience unique to historical repositories?

It's not until one wanders into the Museum's muted halls that a curious sense of dislocation sets in. Here, for instance, is an obfuscating exhibit on a small rodent known as the "European Mole," replete with tiny skeleton. Next to it, a detailed account, including maps cross-hatched with bewildering troop movements, of an ancient battle between two hitherto unknown civiliza-tions, the purpose and outcome of which remains a complete mystery. Turn a corner and you're faced with an elaborate exhibition of "man-made gems," which includes a minutely detailed machine, consisting of a tiny brass hammer which is regularly lifted and dropped on an unknown substance to no apparent purpose.

Down the hall is a glass case holding an apricot pit into which has been purportedly carved a fanciful menagerie as well as, according to its long-winded plaque, "a particularly brutal depiction of the Crucifixion." Despite the small mirror, handily angled to allow viewing of the back of the pit, none of this is readily apparent. Perhaps it's just the light . . . muted and reverent as any cloistered reliquary should be.

But what, then, is to be made of the exhaustive exposition dealing with the construction of Noah's Ark, complete with a beautifully crafted balsa wood model, in eerie suspension on a velvet backdrop behind what seems to be bullet-proof glass? Or how about the diorama of the "famous" waterfall of Paraguay's Paranha River, with real water trickling over painted plaster-of-paris?

A joke? A hoax? The curio emporium of some demented collector? After a visit to the Museum Of Jurassic Technology, the mystery endures. So too, does the lingering conviction that all the past's priceless and carefully preserved artifacts are only as real as we're prepared to pretend them to be. D.S.

The Museum Of Jurassic Technology. 9341 Venice Blvd., Los Angeles, CA 90232-2621. Phone: 310 836-6131.

Cool Fuel: White Pie, Black Joe

by Petaluma Pete

When it comes to foodstuff, two staples from the Mediterranean hold the record for providing stimulus and sustenance to generations of hipsters . . .

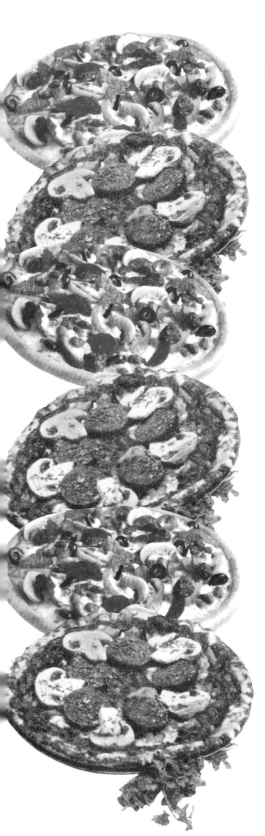

Look, I'll grant you, Pizza Hut's not cool; Domino's is definitely not cool, but pizza itself, at a mom-and-pop pizzeria that usually doesn't have much else on the menu (a couple of appetizers, a salad that *must* come with fluorescent yellow-green semi-hot pickled pepper, probably lasagne, spaghetti and meatballs, and, at the shore, spaghetti and clams), a place where they still use chopped garlic soaked in olive oil instead of garlic powder, and homemade sausage from the neighborhood butcher, and where there is invariably a painting of Lake Como on the wall — in America, it doesn't get much better than that.

Pizza is the story of Italian immigrants taking a common snack food from the old country and turning it into a fortune. Whenever possible, the first Italians here would never *buy* bread, they'd build a little wood-fired bakehouse in the back yard and make it there. Add some olive oil to the bread-dough, squeeze some tomatoes on top, throw some oregano and garlic and cheese onto it and presto! Something for the kids. In the cities, there was no room for a bakehouse, so commercial bakers made pizza and its cousin focaccia, a non-topped hearth-bread. The first pizzeria per se opened in Brooklyn (hi, Spike!) just after the turn of the century, and the Thirties saw Lupo's open in San Francisco, introducing the pie there. Tommasso's, which is the successor business in the same premises (1042 Kearny, just below Broadway), continues to make what might be the best pizza in the U.S.

But for my money, the hoppin'-est pizza place in the country is the Wyoming Valley of Pennsylvania. There, in 1926, Philip Senape, a Hazleton baker, was asked to contribute something to his church fair, so he rolled out some dough in an 18 x 24-inch pan, squeezed some tomatoes on it, and sold the results as "Pitza." Now, 65 years later, there are no fewer than 14 different styles of pizza for sale between Hazleton and Scranton, including the indigestible Sizzle-Pi (fried pizza), sauce-on-top-of-cheese style, cheese-on-top- of-sauce style, "Brooklyn" style (round), and white pizza, unique to this region of the country. In its classic form, epitomized by the pie at Arcaro & Genell's in Old Forge, white pizza is like this: a layer of dough on one of Senape's 18 x 24 pans, followed by the secret five-cheese mixture (provolone, brick, mozzarella, mozzarella *scamuzz'*, and the mystery cheese), and then, if you've ordered the white pizza with broccoli like you should, a layer of finely-chopped broccoli that's been sauteed in heavily garlic-scented olive oil goes on, then another layer of dough, which is brushed with olive oil and sprinkled with a fine dust of herbs, including rosemary, oregano, and marjoram. A couple of "cuts" (don't call them slices) of that, and you'll realize that it's worth the trip to Scranton.

Chicago's stuffed pies are another American glory, cheese and mushrooms and spinach inside, tomato and herbs on top, and I'd love to go to New Haven solely for the famous white clam pizza at Pepe's. Someday, though, I shall go to Naples, where it all started. Ah, pizza in Naples! A dream.

* * *

These days, among the people I know, it's the drug of choice. It's got the jolt of cocaine, but it doesn't tear up your nose or have that annoying come-down. It lacks amphetamine's rough edges, although it's somewhat addictive. There are times when I sit and wonder what it means, that so many people I know have gone from pot to coke to alcohol to . . . cappuccino. I've always loved the story of the discovery of coffee, the Ethiopian goatherd who noticed that his goats got friskier when they ate red berries off of a certain bush. Right, so then, I suppose, he picked some, roasted them, ground them, and poured boiling water through them. Well, whatever he did, good for him, because he jump-started the whole human race with those red berries.

The trouble is, though, that we drink really horrible coffee in the U.S. We seem to have developed a bean that is bitter, thin-tasting, but packed with caffeine. Like the terrible beer we brew, it seems to be means to an end, evil-tasting medicine to be swallowed for the effect. The world's coffee-drinking cultures, the Arabs, the Turks, the French, and especially the Italians, disdain us for it, and usually when Americans of taste visit one of those cultures, they see the light.

No wonder that, for years, America's bohemia has been drawn to European-style, usually Italian, coffee-shops. They fill one with the tradition that stretches back to the joints where Sam Johnson held forth, where the French Revolution was plotted, where the artistic youth who were their spiritual forebears gathered in Vienna, Budapest, Berlin, Milan, Paris, and Rome to foment the artistic and intellectual advances that brought us into the modern era. And no wonder these artistic and intellectual achievements sprang forth over cups of the goatherd's brew, whether in one of those bathtub-sized cups of *cafe au lait* they serve in Berlin or one of those antiseptic-white Italian cups with three ounces of evil black liquid with dark-brown froth around its edges. Because coffee makes you want to talk, and that's where ideas come from. And maybe that's good news about my friends: pot gave them ideas that weren't as good as they seemed at the time, and which they forgot in the morning; coke gave them ideas that were too grandiose to realize, and made them too busy to even start; and alcohol was about forgetting that you had ideas in the first place.

Even so, we've got so much to learn. I was initiated into the after-dinner espresso by a Sicilian-American gentleman who got his demi-tasse with a fingernail-sized piece of lemon rind in the saucer. Pressing down hard, he would work this around the lip of the cup, and then, twisting it, drop it into the coffee. (I know, it sounds weird, but it's really delicious.) Years later, I found myself in San Francisco, yearning to be cool, and so I went to one of the Italian coffee-shops in North Beach. The espresso I ordered, though, came without the lemon, so I called the waiter back over asked for it. "Oh," he boomed, for the benefit of the hipper types at neighboring tables, "you should have ordered *caffe Romano!*" He then walked the entire length of the cafe, slowly, and came back, bearing my tiny lemon sliver on a clean white plate. "*Caffe Romano!*" he intoned. And a friend who's just back from Italy tells me she counted 19 kinds of coffee in one place. "The names for the different preparations change from town to town, too," she said. Her favorite? "*Caffe perfecto,*" she said. "That's with a big slug of *grappa.*" Mmmm! Signore! Signore!

Jim "Ernest" Varney's
5 Favorite Junk Foods

Chocolate Chocolate	Chocolate	Chocolate Chocolate

19ᵀᴴ CENTURY BREAKDOWN:

A Hundred Years Ago Today, Some Mad Lads Made with the Wildest Style and Wiggage

By Dick Blackburn

Joris-Karl Huysmans tried to figure out how to live decadently on a civil servant's salary.

Sure, the current century gets the highest coolness rating. But its predecessor also moved mightily, as seen in the assorted tics and thrill-quests of those who chose to groove where none had grooved before . . .

French Kicking

Gerard de Nerval (1808-1855) was a member of *Les Bousingos* (the Wildmen), a group of poets that included Petrus "Le Lycanthrope" Borel and Philothee O'Neddy (who wore glasses in his sleep to see his dreams). After debating in the buff, these guys found some dolls, downed rum punch in skulls, fired off pistols, and bopped till they dropped to the "gallop infernal," which littered the pad-floor with unconscious bodies. But Gerard, an eventual suicide, out-weirded 'em all when he began taking his lobster-on-a- pale-blue-ribbon for a shuffle through the Jardins de Tuileries. When passersby asked why he had such a bizarro pet, Ger' blithely replied "Because he comes from the depths of the ocean and never barks."

"Nature is only interesting when she is sickly and desolate," wrote the king of decadence, Joris-Karl Huysmans (1848-1907) in *Parisian Sketches* (*Croquis Parisiens*, 1880), grooving on industrial pollution *and* the smell of women's armpits before penning his magnum flip-top *Against Nature* (*A Rebours*, 1884). The *Nature* boy is an aristo perv who surrounds himself with monstrous flowers, a "mouth organ" (liqueurs whose tastes correspond to musical instruments), a bejeweled tortoise, and a ship's cabin on springs set within a room to imitate the motion of the sea. When it comes time for him to travel, he puts off his trip, preferring to groove on fantasy over reality.

Penniless nobleman Jean-Marie-Philippe-Auguste, Comte de Villiers de L'Isle-Adam, was on the same wavelength as Huysmans. In his play *Axel's Castle*, a novitiate renounces her vows and crashes out of a nunnery to the basement of a chateau where she meets a no-dough aristo-cat. They fall for each other, live an entire fantasy lifetime in minutes, swallow poison and kick. "But what about living?," she asks, going under. His answer? "Our servants can do that for us." *Cruel Tales* (*Contes Cruels*, 1883), his other boss *oeuvre*, was way ahead of its time. In one eternally cool piece, an author unsuccessfully swears he's a no-talent hack to a paranoid publisher who's terrified of hiring uncommercial geniuses. In 1889, Villiers, worn out by being too hip for the room, married his cleaning lady on his deathbed. R.I.P. Jean-Marie.

All of these guys managed to blow some great riffs before finally shuffling off to St. Pete's rent party. Tristan Corbière (1845-1875), felled by TB on a yacht in the Mediterranean, laid out such word jazz as "Paysage Mauvaise" (Evil Landscape):

> Flopping onto an old white-boned beach
> Exhausted tides gasp in fright
> Seeing the moon gulp giant worms
> To make it through the pale marsh night.
>
> Little croaking toads
> Bitch and moan
> Oozing thick bile
> To poision their mushroom thrones

Translation: D.B.

So sayeth Tristan.

On the Gaulic rhyme-front, all the *poetes maudites* tried to out-decadent Chuck Baudelaire's *Fleurs du Mal*, scribbling twisto verse and blasting "abs", the slang term for absinthe. The "green hell" liqueur was so popular that the term *heure bleu* (crepuscular early evening dusk) was changed to *heure vert* 'cause so many cafe habitues and people off work were getting zonked. Absinthe even came with its own ritual. A special silver slotted spoon holding a sugar cube was balanced over a glass half full of abs while water, from a carafe placed at the imbiber's elbow, was dripped through the tube, turning the liquor milky and opalescent. *Malheursement* abs got the "Just say no" treatment by the early 1890's, due to the effects of cheap brain-rot publicized by vintners tired of having their product undersold by absinthe, and by the military, who didn't want the infantry crocked during World War I. Today abs is outlawed in every country except Spain.

All the fixin's for a glass of 'green hell.'

'Abs' enhances imbiber's reaction to 19th century Art Buchwald.

The Dream King

LUDWIG II OF BAVARIA
BY WILFRID BLUNT

Mechanical bunnies and peacock thrones: King-freak Luddy.

Health kicks of the Big Nineteenth were no less gone than the era's substance abuse. For a time it was *chic* for anemic chicks to make it down to the neighborhood abbatoir to down a steaming blood cocktail from just-slaughtered ox. It was just such behavior that helped spread the vampire myth of the day.

The Too Much Teuton

Around the same time, to the east, the original Walt Disney, Mad King Ludwig II of Bavaria (1864-1886), was wiping out his country's treasury, building castles that outgrooved Sleeping Beauty's Fantasyland crib big-time. In Linderhof, after overdoing the cherub decorations, Luddy installed weighted trap doors so gourmet meals

184

prepared by unseen servants could magically appear. An early animal-rights advocate, he hunted track-run mechanical bunnies from a horse-drawn sleigh. In an artifical grotto, Ludwig would drift about in his swan boat serenaded by a string quartet concealed inside a papier-mâché rock, or set a spell on his massive Peacock Throne awaiting inspiration. He got it, commissioning an inventor to come up with an aircraft so Lud could do the wing thing over the mountains. To the Chamber of Councillors this was firm proof that the monarch was mad. Finally, his indigent countrymen rose up and drowned him in a lake. Ten years later the first airplane flew. A hundred years later, the Mad King's realized dreams are the region's biggest tourist attraction.

England's Garb Gang:
Flipped, Fop and Fly

A couple years before Ludwig's scene, Britain's style-obsessed Beau Brummel had kicked off dandyism, using up countless yards of stiff linen to get the perfect knot in his cravat. "By using a few hours in each day, which would otherwise be wasted, you may hope to have excellent cravats in middle life. The whole knack lies in pointing your chin to the sky, and then arranging your folds by the gradual descent of your lower jaw." This from *Rodney Stone*, A. Conan Doyle's (1896) novel of the Regency. Connie's young hero is encouraged to cultivate an eccentricity to launch himself in society. "Do you think that you could engage to climb round the furniture of an ordinary room without setting foot upon the ground?" The speaker, a famous exquisite, is later socially ruined when he tragically chooses Isinglass over starch as a cravat stiffener.

By mid-century, the Victorian clothes horse had become a fantasy figure for the masses. Music hall audiences dug The Great Vance (1838-1888), a monocled swell who sang about his East End tailor in order to obtain free "clobber," in a verse style that uncannily prefigures Lord Buckley or Forties bopster Babs Gonzales . . .

Now kool my downy kicksies, they're the style for me
Built on a plan very naughty
The stock around my squeeze is a guiver colour, see!
And the vestat with the bins so rorty!
My tailor serves you well
From a perjure to a swell
At Grove's you're safe to make a sure pitch
For ready venom down,
There ain't a shop in town
Can lick Groves in the Cut, as well as Shoreditch.

By the *fin de siecle* things had gotten out of hand. Henry Cyril Padgett, fifth Marquis of Angsley (1875-1903), was a fopped-out gem freak. To dig his dazzlers, he'd drape his nude young wife from head to toe in them, and ogle her. When their marriage was annulled for non-consummation, "the Dancing Marquis" toured in his own amateur theatricals, where he fluttered about doing "The Butterfly Dance," a pre-"Bird" step of his own creation, in bejeweled costumes costing up to 40,000 pounds. By 1901, the Dancing Marq was tripped up for good, owing creditors over half a million pounds. It took 40 days to sell all his vines, stones, dogs, horses and carriages, yachts, motor cars and gem-encrusted walking sticks.

The Last Victorian:
Big Sal with the Shoe Hat

While chronology keeps him out of the era (b. 1898, d. 1980), Salvador Dali demonstrated a real spiritual affinity with the Big Nineteenth eccentrics. He copped Huysmans' jeweled tortoise lick, but did him one better by mounting an ashtray on the creature's back. Some of Sal's other cool moves: predicting that everyone would eventually have their thumbnails replaced by tiny TV screens. Inventing the Self-Irrigating Taxicab full of seaweed, mannequins and snails. Baking long and longer loaves of bread, leaving them in public places while the media went crazy trying to figure out what his message was. Inventing the High-heel Shoe Hat. Creating "heart jewelry" that actually beat. Labeling Mondrian a maker of Linoleum. Writing an unfilmable script for the Marx Bros. Digging Dan's Do-Nut Drive-in off the San Diego Frwy in L.A. Having a long, unusually thin window built in his bathroom so he could sit on the toilet and watch the red descent of the sun like mercury in a thermometer. Getting naked, covering himself with olive oil, and waiting till he no longer felt the flies before starting to paint . . .

DEAN VS.

ERNIE

by Nick Tosches

In the fall of 1958, Dean Martin, *principe della cool*, sold his name and likeness to Liebmann Breweries in New York, makers of cheap beer: "'You may need good luck on the links,' says the famous crooner, 'but not at the nineteenth hole. You always score with Rheingold Extra Dry.'"

Globe Photos

Thus Dino joined the company of Ernest Hemingway, who, six years before, had sold his name and likeness, as well as his prose, to another brewery. "How would *you* put a glass of Ballantine Ale into words?" asked the advertising copy. "Here— Ernest Hemingway turns his famous hand to it." Hemingway, who by then had perhaps chased after one marlin too many, took the task to heart: "I would rather have a bottle of Ballantine Ale than any other drink after fighting a really big fish."

Whose beer-prose was finer, Dean's or Ernie's? Ezra Pound, T.S. Eliot, and Sinatra stood in silence and took no side. It was, in all honesty, close to a stand-off, with deciding points going to Dean, whose brevity and choice of metaphor outclassed those of the over-the-hill Nobel-winner.

On March 19, 1959, a few months after the Rheingold ads ran, Dean and Ernie squared off once again, as a *Playhouse 90* production of Hemingway's *For Whom the Bell Tolls* shared a television evening with *The Dean Martin Show*.

Harriet Van Horne of the *New York World Telegram* found the Hemingway production "a mas-

sive accomplishment." Dino, on the other hand, was "a rather offensive young man." But massive was no match for cool and offensive. Another New York reviewer, hepster Jack O'Brian of the *Journal-American*, found the Hemingway "hopelessly confused, pretentious, dated." Dino, however, with "no pretenses at art or esthetics . . . was thoroughly pleasant."

Beaten now by Dean in both the literary and television arenas, Hemingway's final two years on earth became a slow, sad march to the grave.

THREE SHOWS A NIGHT

The Consecration of Nick Apollo Forte

By Chris Davidson

Canova + Martin + Cole + Sorvino.

Like a tour guide in Duluth, Nick Apollo Forte works alone. Ten fingers, 88 keys and a few hundred bucks—that's all he needs. Being the backup band for Nick Forte is like being Orson Welles' decathlon coach or William Shatner's wig washer. It's just not done.

Figuring the sorry state of lounge acts nowadays (my town's most popular singer does John Denver imitations to a disco beat), Nick's the real deal. He even managed to make a Woody Allen movie funny. Check out *Broadway Danny Rose*, with Nick as Lou Canova, a real ice singer/swinger/boozehound in a clingy tux and blow-dried cut. Like a tipsy Frankie Laine, Lou sings about indigestion and knows a version of "My Funny Valentine" with special lyrics about the moon landing.

Watching Nick perform today, he's a mixture of Lou (he does his movie tunes sandwiched between "Summer Wind" and "The Wonder of You"), Dean Martin (Nick's "That's Amore" is music parmigiana), Nat Cole (his piano jumps like butter on a hot griddle) and Paul Sorvino (Nick's about as built as the *GoodFellas* big daddy). Nick played a recent gig in New Haven, Connecticut (the urban equivalent of cruising in a K car), and showed the locals that the guy who recorded "Scungilli Song" in the Seventies, now 55 years young, still had the power to cook on all burners.

The lounge tore a page out of Atlantic City high fashion. Tall windows overlooking a busy street; signed pictures of John Davidson and Meat Loaf (with clothes, thankfully); a wooden bar heavy enough to collapse on; red vinyl booths along one wall; small wooden tables scattered around; a parquet dance floor with a stained-glass ceiling above. It was dark enough to avoid seeing your date.

Nick sat at a small piano between the bar and dance floor, looking healthier (green T-shirt, white pants, white slip-on shoes, dark tan) than the whole crowd put together. He'd been playing for hours as it closed in on midnight, mixing and matching verses and harmonies like Elton John's wardrobe designer on a shopping spree.

He'd already done about 100 songs, and he was peaking.

It started innocently enough with "San Francisco." Then Nick cranked the electric rhythm machine, and an Andy Gibb/heavy-metal beat pounded from the speakers. He whooped out some nonsense lyrics and jumped up beside the piano. A second later, he was sitting again. The crowd brought out utensils, and proceeded to eat him

for dinner. Nick looked over at the bar, said, "You knew I was crazy," and dove straight into the next batch of songs.

For the rest of the night, there would be no question why he chose "Apollo" for a show biz name: Nick was the god of lounge singers.

The audience dug him even more. Old guys pouring on the sauce for young women, men with big rings talking louder than the music, a couple in matching warmup suits drinking scotch, two jazz nuts keeping time on the table with a spoon, a few old timers dancing to the slow numbers. They knew greatness had driven to New Haven, parked and walked inside.

Young couples at a function in the next room went to the bar and watched for a minute as their drinks were being made. One cat clapped above his head when Nick sang "Agida" from his movie. Nick could have finished the night with 80 choruses of "Kumbaya." He could commit no crime.

With almost 40 years of show business stashed away, Nick's definitely had hotter nights, playing for wilder crowds in better joints. But he's surely had worse, when opening for a juggler sounded good. Nick's still keeping audiences awake better than Johnny Carson, and for that (not to mention he hawks his own records between sets) he deserves a spot beside the immortals. As Lou Canova once said, "Big gun, big gun. No two ways about it."

Apollonian Audio: *Songs From 'Broadway Danny Rose' And Other Pearls Of Culture* (Milan lp).

JIVE'S

Screamin' Jay Hawkins'
5 Coolest Operas/Arias

Figaro
Ravel's 'Bolero'
Pagliacci
Old Man River
   (Robeson)
Be My Love (Lanza)

SWINGING

by Chris Davidson

Lounge vinyl is impossible to find in good shape. Mostly, you come across albums in people's basements, covered in the residue of rec room parties (onion dip smeared into the grooves, sleeves used as coasters). With the compact disc

takeover, lounge music has been pouring out faster than Jackie Gleason could swill G-and-T's. Reissue programs have now made it possible for you to blow half your check on original Mel Torme albums, with money left over to stock up on Sammy's Decca and Frank's Columbia recordings. So lounge hounds, hug a record exec today, and dig these great cd reissues the next time you're ragging about the LP's demise. And if you find it, buy *Crooners of the Century* (Goodtimes Home Video, about $10), a compilation of clips featuring most of the fellas below.

Tony Bennett: *I Left My Heart In San Francisco* (Columbia Records/CBS). You've seen this album stuffed into a card board box at a million yard sales. But pick it up and discover Tony's world of stingy brim hats, narrow pants and girl watching from the front steps of your apartment. If you've got the lettuce (about $50), CBS' Bennett box set teaches an important lesson. Somewhere in those grooves, you'll learn why Sinatra still calls his only real competition "Mister Tony Bennett."

Jack Jones: *Greatest Hits* (Curb Records). Jack's not the total sap you may have thought (singing the theme from *Love Boat* is one accomplishment you hope he did for the bread). In the Sixties, he was a lounge kingpin, having hits like "Wives And Lovers" and "The Impossible Dream" and always looking a bit overly blow-dried. As usual, don't expect much from Curb's packaging job; just look for the cd that resembles a TV dinner.

Dean Martin: *Swingin' Down Yonder* (Capitol Records). He had a cute side, dragging Jerry Lewis around the stage by his front teeth, but Dean was also smoother than marinara sauce, especially on vinyl. And biggies like "That's Amore" could have been flubbed in many less-capable, more Al Martino-like hands. On this album, Dean strolls below the Mason-Dixon, and comes back with a batch of Southern faves, proving a concept album doesn't always need to end up lining your puppy's training cage.

Frank Sinatra: *In The Wee Small Hours* (Capitol Records). Sinatra's magic has helped guys score with their dates more than anything, except perhaps dishonesty. In *Tin Men*, for example, Richard Dreyfuss plays this album, then needs a crowbar to pry off Danny DeVito's wife (Babs Hershey). Tell your school: Guidance counselors should have a stack of these on hand for kids who are having trouble finding a girl for the prom. But be careful: in some neighborhoods, giving a gal *The Capitol Years* box set is seen as a bigger move than popping the question.

ashtrays by." This collection is pure Roselli, recorded in a time vacuum only Vic Damone could pierce. If your lungs can stand it, listen to this three times in one night, and be cleansed. in a weird sort of way. C.D.

Louis Prima: *Zooma Zooma* (Rhino Records). To many, Louis is the first, last and every in-between word in hepcat singers, lounge or otherwise. With a voice like gravel shovelled into a dumpster, Louis and his crackerjack band, the Witnesses, ruled Vegas during the years when nightlife and sunglasses meant the same thing. College credit should have been given for deciphering the meaning of his Capitol recordings, a volume of work easily as important as man's struggle against man, or at least man's struggle against having his sideburns shaved off while sleeping.

Jimmy Roselli: *3 a.m.* (M&R Records). Jimmy Roselli fans practice a brand of social suicide unlike, say, fans of synthesizer groups from England. What kind of person would actually admit he or she likes a singer whom most regard as a third-rate Sinatra? It's obvious, though, these detractors are blind to the true Jimmy Experience: a guy so in love with the aura surrounding lounge singers that his albums could all be subtitled "Music to fill

HICK HANDLES

On the first encounter, Elvis Presley's name was at least as exotic as his singing. Little did citizens above the Mason-Dixon suspect that they weren't dealing with an isolated phenom. Narvel Felts and Hasil Adkins are only slightly better known than the wildly handled gents listed below, most of whom were single shot, no-hit rockabilly cats. These boys did not need to be renamed Conrad Birdie.

Melrose Bagby	Elroy Dietzel	Merdell Floyd	Chandos McRill	Bozo Ratcliff
Hindle Butts	Huelyn Duval	Arbis Hanyel	Titus Odermatt	Braxton Shooford
Deral Clour	Dwarless Fearsley	Beecher Hickman	Shadie Oller	D.B.

In the early Sixties, art/film critic Manny Farber wrote a piece called "Termite Art vs. White Elephant Art." The former was ostensibly lowbrow, hidden in pulp genres, its meaning often obscured by plot conventions. The latter was middle-brow, exposed in best-seller hot air, its meaning always on the surface and drawing attention to itself as officially cultural. On the cool plane, the termite artists fly higher. You'll see what we mean when you climb into the cockpit with

Chester Gould, 1978.
Richard Pietrzyk.

CHET & JACK

By Dick Blackburn

Chester Gould and Jack Webb's ultra-conserv right-winger surfaces thinly disguised what were essentially two radical surrealists. Their superego cop automatons—Dick Tracy and Joe Friday—were as rigid and affectless as their villains were grandiose and hysterical. Reassurance, maybe, that irrational feelings/emotions could be controlled. The exaggerated tension between craziness and control is why we love 'em both today. That, and because we sense their obvious identification with weirdos.

Tombstones to Hambones

Consider: Chester had a little graveyard in his backyard made up of miniature tombstones. Each one bore the date of a villain's intro and outro in the Tracy strip. Is this affection or what? And some of his comic good guys inadvertently blow the status quo as much as the crooks do. Bandleader Spike Dyke (Jones) or Vitamin Flintheart, a pill-popping healthnut/hambone actor, is the worst judge of character on God's globe. B.O. Plenty, a skinny briar patch in a hat, hasn't the combined IQ of the fleas in his beard, and is always screwing up. Diet Smith, billionaire industrialist, is a physically powerless infant king, constantly burping and scarfing baby food for his ulcer.

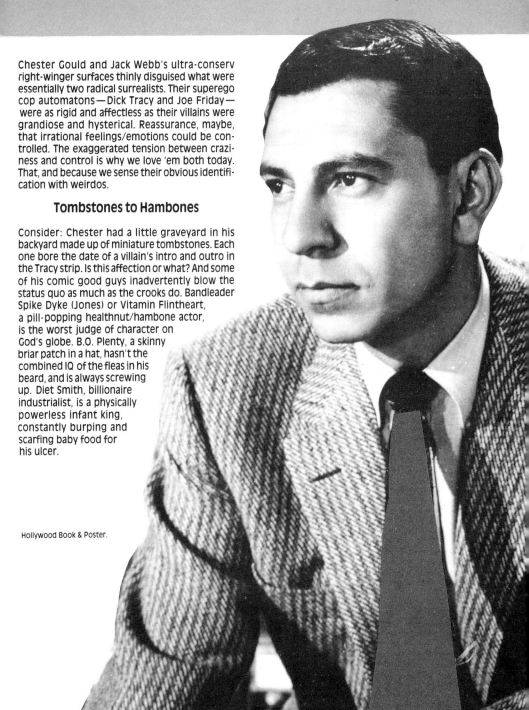

Hollywood Book & Poster.

Consider this as well: Webb's barely controlled fury and righteous seething against the forces of evil was like a personal dialogue—as if he was going to fly off the handle and slug himself. Check him out in *The D.I.*, a movie that predates Stan "The Man" Kubrick's *Full Metal Jacket* by more'n 30 years. Jack musta written his dialogue all in CAPS: it's all shouted. In one scene, he grabs his leading lady, smashes his mouth onto hers and snaps his head back as if he wanted to kill sex before it starts. Anti-Whap-A-Dang.

A Little Doll And A Drowning Mask

Chet Gould was like the Little Engine That Could. An early lack of success turned him into a tireless workaholic who lived to draw. Ultimately, he parlayed a lack of draftsmanship into one of the most powerful graphic styles comics have ever seen. His stark blacks and whites perfectly complemented Gould's Manichean universe of light and dark.

The German sixteenth century artist Matthais Von Grunewald painted a pus-filled, lacerated Crucifixion to contrast the mortification of earthly flesh with divine salvation. Gould, too, reveled in physical suffering. Dick Tracy, battered, shot, suffocated ad nauseum, is constantly dying for our sins and rising from the dead. A comic strip Jehovah, Chet digs destroying/cleansing by fire. By the late 1940s, his Tracy-tormenting agents of evil had grown so bizarre that villain Sketch Paree, for instance, was a psycho dress designer (fear of foreigners, madness, gays) who spoke to a little doll in his pocket and wore a water-filled mask to drown his victims! The livin' endpoint of all this was probably Rhodent, a man with the face of a rat and parents (literally) blind to his physical and moral abnormality. Finally, the earthly horrors became too much for Chet. After a few interviews, in which he came off somewhere to the right of Yosemite Sam, he took off for the moon prophesying that "He who controls magnetism controls the universe."

Jack Webb's career was a series of reversals. In the late Forties, he wrote, directed and starred in a San Francisco radio show, *Pier 51*, later renamed *Pat Novak For Hire*, in which his baroque Chandleresque voiceover ("Her hair was the color of a brush fire just barely under control," "The

© 1990 Tribune Media Services, inc.

© 1989 Tribune Media Services, Inc.

neon motel sign looked like icing on a cheap wedding cake") became so clotted they buried the plots. Most stories involved a husky-voiced, come-hither "nightclub thrush," a sex fantasy Jack later made real by marrying songstress Julie London. By the early Fifties, Webb was a young actor portraying both punks and killers (*Dark City* and *Appointment With Danger*), as well as vaguely left-leaning intellectuals and H'wood bohos (*The Men* and *Sunset Boulevard*). But it was his first film, an obscure B police procedural — *He Walked By Night* (1948) — based on an actual LAPD case, that inspired *Dragnet*.

Later For Pronouns

Suddenly, left went right. Decadent Chandlerisms were replaced by a classic Hammett style so tight-lipped it made The Master himself seem prolix. And Jack's Hemingwayesque repetitions make conversations sound like ping-pong matches played inside coffee percolators. The Webbed One was the first in tube talkdom to obsessively leave off the personal pronoun ("Didn't say. Left yester-day. Didn't say a word," etc.), and to close scenes with the pre-packaged zinger ("You think he'd see me?" "He's not seeing anyone." "How do you know that?" "He's dead"). When *Dragnet* went to TV,

Webb's abstract minimalist style ("visual shouting and verbal whispering," wrote film crit Andrew Sarris) was seen as realism instead of a Kabuki drama on Thorazine. The banter between Joe Friday and his partner(s) Frank Smith/ Bill Gannon sounds like two deejays trying to keep awake on the night shift. By the end of his career, Webb had played Friday too long. When not knocking 'em back at the red leatherette Cock N' Bull restaurant on Sunset Strip, he was monitoring police calls and showing up at crime sites. Dom da dom dom.

CHET & JACK:
As of this writing, Gladstone Publishing has purchased the rights to many of Gould's Dick Tracy strips which ran origi-nally in the *Chicago Tribune*, and reprints them in a variety of formats. Gladstone: 212 S. Montezuma, Prescott, Arizona 86303.

Radio Yesteryear sells cassettes of Webb's original *Dragnet* radio shows: Box C, Sandy Hook, CT 06482. Phone: 1-800-243-0987.

Chillin' With the True Jesus of Cool

By Jim Trombetta

QUINN THE ESKIMO
(The Mighty Quinn) by Bob Dylan

Everybody's building ships and boats
Some are building monuments, others jotting down notes
Everybody's in despair, every girl and boy
But when Quinn the Eskimo gets here,
Everybody's gonna jump for joy

    Chorus: Come all without.
              Come all within
              You'll not see nothing
              Like the mighty Quinn

I like to do just like rest, I like my sugar sweet
But guarding fumes and making haste just
ain't my cup of meat
Everybody's 'neath the trees, feeding pigeons
on a limb
But when Quinn the Eskimo gets here
Them pigeons gonna go to him.

    Chorus

A cat's meow, a cow's moo, I can recite 'em all,
But tell me where it hurts and I'll tell you who
to call
Nobody can get no sleep when someone's on
everyone's toes
But when Quinn the Eskimo gets here,
Everybody's gonna doze.

    Chorus

The end of the world ain't what it used to be. Back in the boom times of the cold war, one push of the well-known button would send everything up like your father spraying too much charcoal-lite on the grill some Sunday—now *that* was an *apocalypse*. That 30-mile H-bomb blast radius makes the words *nowhere to run* really mean something. Oh, the end is still stalking us now, it just seems less dramatic, a slow and lingering thing like a real bad sunburn or a nasty *bug*... crueller maybe in that it gives us all the more time to *worry*...

Which is why it still seems timely to listen to the crazed carol printed above, a gone gospel beamed direct from the Bermuda Triangle, a prophecy of the advent of... what, an eschatological *Eskimo*? Well, every apocalypse deserves its own messiah, and its own prophet too, in this case a kind of John Q. Public who "likes to do just like the rest." Speaking through this regular Joe, Biblical Bob presents the tale of people obsessed not just with creating memorials but with "building boats"... like old man Noah. Because the end is nigh... right?

Except pretty soon we're slipping and sliding on the black ice of these words. Like "come all *without*." Without *what*? Well, without *whatever*, I guess. Or just, *outside*. Then, "you'll not see nothing like the mighty Quinn." A heavy pronouncement, but... Hold on a minute, Bob, let me get this straight: we'll *never* see *anything* like him? Which is to say, we'll never see anything as... impressive? Or, is this an assurance that we'll at least see *something* (that is, *not nothing*)... Or, simply, we'll never actually see the big guy at all?

Or what?

Well, it's an absolute statement that pulls the rug out from under itself... executing a pratfall in the midst of a never-ending cosmological ping-pong of *all* and *nothing* (with major supporting players *some* and *one*) that bounces through the whole song... suggesting that no one thing is ever absolutely all or nothing.

As for Quinn, what is known about him? Not much. But as an Eskimo he does have a certain claim to coolness... even to a state of being coolest... to find a being cooler than Quinn would be like going north of the North Pole. You can't get there from here. And you don't need to, because he's coming this way... in his own good time. Bringing...

Yawn. A predisposition to "doze." Hard to get excited about that... seems a little *anticlimactic*. But when the climax in question is the Absolute

End—or absolute zero—a little anticlimax might hit the spot. In a world where the sirens never quit, so jammed up that you not only have to be on your toes, but those of everybody else in the vicinity, it might be nice to... *chill out*.

Or as Mr. Zimmerman sings elsewhere, "Genghis Khan could not keep/ All his kings supplied with sleep."

Such is the Cool of which the mighty Quinn is the avatar: a balm against the fire-breathing, the righteous and the trigger-happy; a polar opposite to the merely hip, to the Mohawked doorman checking out the fit of your bicycle shorts before he lets you into the new hot place; a victory over anxiety by plain old daily life.

> "*Quinn the Eskimo*, I don't know. I don't know what that was about. I guess it was some kind of nursery rhyme."
> —Bob Dylan, notes to *Biograph*

(Chill with Dyl: "Quinn the Eskimo" is featured on the CBS/ Sony cd's *Biograph* and *Self Portrait*.)

"DA CAT"

Tale of the Young Surf Rebel

By Domenic Priore

LOS ANGELES (1963). What we are talking about here is far more than a sport, or a lifestyle, or a facet of regional pop culture. This is a view of the world at large from the p.o.v. of punters weary from the banality of the most idyllic reality in God's wide world. You have a flourishing clutch of like-minded kids inhabiting the southwest coastal region of this most prosperous and otherwise four seasonal nation. Well-toned strongmen carrying 100-pound wooden planks into the water are being joined by a more diminutive species using the lighter foam surfboards just invented. You've got teenagers, disposable income, health, energy, and restless natural surroundings, an environment where a creeping sense of the stress and burdens inherent in the outside world is to be held off for maybe the last time.

I'm talking about surfing waves, surfing boards, surfing trunks, surfing hair, surfing wagons, surfing language, surfing music, surfing dances, surfing magazines, surfing comics, surfing films, surfing exploitation movies, surfing products and surfing bandwagons. That's where it was at in the late Fifties and early Sixties in teenage Southern California.

The sport is for young people. There are thousands of these kids, millions of them, all over the world like polliwogs. It was different in my day. It was a small community and everyone respected each other. Now that world and life are gone forever. Off the face of the earth. What's to discuss?
—Mickey Dora, *California* magazine 1983

This doesn't exist in the here and now. No more can one live in that simple world defined by Rick Grffin's "Murphy" art, the crude lunacy of Ed "Big Daddy" Roth's etchings, or countless 45's by the Chantays, Surfaris, Lively Ones, etc. Publisher John Severson long ago sold out *Surfer* magazine and left his primevally perfect surf filmmaking behind.

Dora, '67
Ron Stoner, courtesy *Surfer* magazine.

DA BLUE CAT is an annual award, presented to one individual, who has exhibited the most valor and gallant chivalry in standing up to the enemy power structure with cool, clear courage. Unfortunately for the year 1966, there were no qualifiers. All nominees disintegrated under the weight of the establishment, caving in under pressure, copping out at the moment of truth; so once again this cherished award remains dormant as DA CAT awaits the development of the potential award winner. Perhaps 1967 will be the year, SO CLEAN YOURSELVES UP YOU CREEPS, SHAPE UP YOU PHONIES, DA CAT is giving you another chance.

da Blue Cat

But all the *Beach Party*'s, *Surf Party*'s and *Swinging Summer*s could never cover up or rub out the most enigmatic representative of this billboard and advertisement inspiration: The Surfer. And no one better spans the birth and death of this lost creature better than Mickey Dora.

It was around 1955 and Dora was quickly becoming the local legend in Hawaii's sport of kings. It was essentially his trailblazing and unique style of manipulating a wave that accounted for the essence of surfer cool from which all other action emanated. The theater for his inimitable brilliance

da CATS' Theory of Evolution

RETARDESS KOOKUS	PIGMIO PHAINAS	MALIBUIS MASOCHSCUS	VALLEI SAN FERNANDO	HOMO COOPERI
The earliest stage, unworthy of discussion.	Characterized by small structure and jerky, uncoordinated movements, little ability.	Recognized by determined expression on face, but no ability. This short structured musclehead resorts to throwing of objects and threats abortive attempts to make waves.	This small-brained inland migrant is only mentioned because of the peculiar habits they have of traveling in packs and futile attempts to look skilled on waves over one foot. It is hoped that they will soon become extinct.	The first stage with This form was unable in a limited way . . . this form was unable pete with the earl and became extinct.

was Malibu, the site of Jan & Dean's *Surf City* promotional film, and the namesake of Chevrolet's '65 fastback. The terrain of this particular stretch of beach was singularly special, and spots discovered around the world were appropriately judged by how much they were "like Malibu." To match its flowing grace and consistent break, Mickey Dora developed a style that conformed to, rather than fought against, nature's perfection. His genius at wave riding, presenting himself at the perfect spot on a wave in a manner unimaginable to even the most skilled riders, gave rise to the perpetual question: "How did he *think* of that?" The answer, of course, was "He didn't ... He's just 'there.'"

My whole life is this escape, my whole life is this wave. I drop into 'em, set the whole thing up, pull out the bottom turn, pull up into it, and shoot for my life, going for broke, man. Behind me, all the shit goes over my back. The screaming parents, teachers, police, priests, politicians, kneeboarders, wind-surfers, they're all going over the falls into the reef—head first into the fucking reef—and I'm shooting for my life, and when it starts to close out, I pull out the bottom, out to the back, and I pick up another one, and do the same goddamn thing.
—Dora, *Surfers: The Movie*, 1989

Many believe that Mickey Dora singlehandedly began the whole mystique of the surfer lifestyle. His unique West Coast surf dialect will forever be misrepresented by advertisers of contemporary T-shirt logo design, despite the plethora of "surfing dictionaries" thrust upon the public since the early Sixties. Dora used this pointed slang in communication with peers and as a foil in confusing outsiders. He was different, one step ahead of the rest. His style, the way he lifted his sunglasses, the way he moved, the way he surfed, the way he liked to ride the nose, everything he did was uniquely Dora and young impressionable kids around Malibu began copping his style, his phrases becoming their own.

Such charisma eased Mickey Dora into a fleeting association with the film industry, as a technical adviser on scores of beach movies, standing in as an extra and surf stunt double. It was naturally assumed by the producers of Columbia Pictures' *Ride The Wild Surf* that Dora was a big-gun wave rider, when he actually had no experience handling Waimea's 25-foot monsters. The *normal* tactic for riding such waves is to beat the white water crunch by reaching the bottom of the wave as quickly as possible, far out ahead of the imposing danger. Dora, on the other hand, shot straight through the *middle* of Waimea's tumultuous sweep as if it were the four-foot perfection of Malibu, inventing a whole new way of riding big

waves that winter. Dora was well aware of media manipulation. He knew such cultural overexposure was ruining the sacred sport and, though he grabbed his cut, he all the while proselytzed the reality of the ridiculous. At one surf-flick premiere, he unleashed a jar of moths to converge on the projector light. His agreement with Greg Noll's surfboard company to design, model and advertise a signature "da Cat" surfboard is another example. Dora's sly ad copy for his boards said it all . . .

> . . . For shaking up the status quo and stepping on the wrong toes at the right time, strange things begin to happen. When these things occur you know you're beginning to hit home and the foundation is starting to split. Da Cat was here before and will be here after. The more it's put down, the stronger it gets. The moons and the finks and the rest of you deadbeats will always be washed up because you're nothing and you stand for less and there are a few of us left who know who you are.

Such self-promotion soon turned into true surfing prophecy. Mickey Dora rode for pleasure only. Invited to enter contests for prize money, his reply was a flat "No thanks." This was in line with his "illusionary prosperity" theory, detailed in an elaborate graph he drew in a late Sixties issue

of *Surfer*. At the time, such prosperity must have seemed like a far-off dream to the just-emerging surf-industry professionals. But the glow boys of the neon wetsuit persuasion today are living proof of Dora's fatal vision; the essential concern of the contemporary surf thrasher is sponsorship — recognition from manufacturers who churn out soulless product to landlocked America and coastal cretins alike, fashions as grotesque and murky as the East River. (The "rad" subversion of surf cool even extends to the music used in surfing films, which absolutely robs the action onscreen of its Astronautical potential.)

Dora, as always, got it right.

> Professionalism will be completely destructive to any control an individual has over the sport at present. The organizers will call the shots, collect the profits, while the waverider does all the labor and receives little. A surfer should think carefully before selling his being to these 'people,' since he's signing his own death warrant as a personal entity. Practically speaking, if any of this makes sense to someone, all my mail will be forwarded to my retreat in Madagascar.
> —Dora, *Surfer* magazine, 1969

With these words, Mickey Dora split from the face of Malibu and his inadvertent surfer godhood. As his prediction of the cataclysm of surfing came to pass, Dora's contact with the world at large receded. Realizing the peak had passed, Dora had the dignity to walk away. As time went on, sightings of Mickey Dora across the globe read like the legends of Loch Ness, Big Foot and flying saucers. Rumors of his exploits in exotic locales around the world occasionally surfaced, including a scandal involving a major hotel in Buenos Aires being renamed The Gran Hotel Dora . . . or Dora crashing a $10,000-a-ticket governor's ball much in the same way he crashed a Beatles party in Hollywood in 1964. Over the next 20 years, Dora was in France, no, Dora was seen in Bali, Peru, Costa Rica, New Guinea, in Namaqualand, in Tybarao, anywhere his thirst for surf took him.

What eventually brought Dora back to California was the antithesis of such freedom: prison. Leaving a string of credit-card forgings and probation jumps behind him, he was arrested in France in 1982 and apprehended by FBI agents upon his return to California. He spent the Eighties haggling with various jails and legal systems, then, in July 1989, faced the surfing world again in a *Surfer* article wherein he explained his "absence" . . .

From 1974 to 1981 I covered well over 200,000 miles over four continents, 90% of the time reconnoitering the coastal areas of India, Africa, the Far East, Indonesia, Australia, New Zealand, South America, and hundreds of

A style that conformed to nature's perfection.

Courtesy *Surfer* magazine.

islands. Only in Europe did Interpol or the Feds ever get close. Only after five passports and millions of taxpayer dollars wasted on the hunt did I, with a gun pointed at my head, volunteer to return to the USA (just visiting, thanks), thus ending the most extraordinary surfing odyssey in the history of mankind.

With his return, he appeared for a public interview for the first time since 1969, in the documentary *Surfers: The Movie.* The years and experience had vastly widened Dora's view of the planet, while leaving intact his distinct character and penchant for prophecy. Dora was the first in his field to scrutinize the behavior and temper of his environment, to react and report on the situation to a blissed-out public; a foretelling of surf rapture that will endure as long as his legend.

* * *

The greatest artifact of the vibe, music and humor of surf cool is captured in Bruce Brown's film *The Endless Summer* (1966), which features footage of Dora surfing Malibu. It's available (separately, or as part of the *Bruce Brown Golden Years of Surf Collection*) from Pacific Arts Video, 11858 La Grange Ave., Los Angeles, CA 90025. Phone: 1-800-538-5856.

"Where Are They Now?"

A highly selective low-down on recent & reissued cool-works covered in the *Catalog of Cool*. Think of these as desert-island durables...

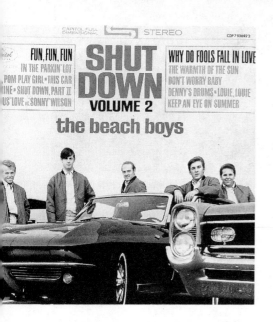

All The Best: Steve Allen TV Shows (Fox Hills Video)

Harvey Pekar's American Splendor (newly collected edition from Four Walls, Eight Windows Publishing).

THE BEACH BOYS: Capitol's Collectors Series features 2 original lps on each of eight cds; *Brian Wilson* (Sire).

LENNY BRUCE: Fantasy Records offers volumes 1 and 2 of *Lenny Bruce Originals* (two original lps on each cd).

LORD BUCKLEY: *A Most Immaculately Hip Aristo-crat* (Enigma/Retro cd).
Lord Buckley Live cassette (Shambhala Lion Editions, Boston).

CAPTAIN BEEFHEART: *The Best Beefheart* (Pair cd); plus two-fer cd's on Reprise.

JAMES BROWN: *The CD of JB—Vols I and II* (Polydor).

THE CRAMPS: *Stay Sick!* Enigma cd.

MILES DAVIS: *Birth of the Cool* Capitol cd.

BO DIDDLEY: Chess 3-cd box set.

DION: Various Ace import cd's; *Bronx Blues: The Columbia Recordings 1962-65* (CBS)

Dr. No (MGM Home Video).

Doctor Strangelove (RCA / Columbia Home Video).

BOB DYLAN: *Biograph* and *The Bootleg Series* (CBS).

EC COMICS: *Tales From the Crypt* and *Vault of Horror* published regularly by Russ Cochran publishing.

DUKE ELLINGTON: *Reminiscing In Tempo* (Legacy cd); *Sophisticated Lady* (Bluebird); *The Young Duke* (Pearl).

ESQUERITA: *Esquerita* (Capitol Collectors Series cd).

RICHARD FARINA: *Been Down So Long It Looks Like Up To Me* (Penguin paperback reissue).

FLESHTONES: *Best Of* (IRS cd)

The Honeymooners (MPI Home Video)

CHESTER HIMES: Various novels available through Vintage Black Lizard.

HOSTESS TWINKIES: Convenience stores in most cities.

HOWLIN' WOLF: Three-cd box set (Chess box/MCA).

LEE KONITZ WITH LENNIE TRISTANO: *First Sessions* (Prestige lp).

ERNIE KOVACS: *TV's Comedy Wizard* and other collections (Video Treasures); *Best of Ernie Kovacs* (White Star Video).

JERRY LEE LEWIS: *Live at the Star Club in Hamburg* (Rhino cd).

Lolita (MGM Home Video).

MAD MAGAZINE: Four bound volumes reprint the first issues, 1952-54 (Russ Cochran)

Our Man Flint (Fox Home Video).

LOUIS PRIMA: *Zooma Zooma* (Rhino cd).

Prime Cut (Key Video)

The Prisoner: Several volumes available on MPI Home Video.

RAMONES: Two volumes of *All The Stuff (And More)* (Sire cds).

ROCKY & BULLWINKLE: *The Adventures of Rocky & Bullwinkle* (Buena Vista Home Video).

ROLLING STONES: *The Singles Collection* 3-cd box set (Abkco).

SOUPY SALES: *Best of the Soupy Sales Show* (Rhino Home Video).

PHIL SPECTOR: *Back To Mono* 4-cd box set (Abkco).

SINATRA: *The Capitol Years* cd set; *Reprise Collection* cd box.

TERRY SOUTHERN: *Red Dirt Marijuana* (Citadel Underground paperback).

JIM THOMPSON: Various novels through Vintage Black Lizard.

BIG JOE TURNER: *Greatest Hits* (Atlantic cd).

The Editors

GENE SCULATTI edited the *Catalog of Cool*, and has written *San Francisco Nights: The Psychedelic Music Trip* (with Davin Seay) and *Popcorn* (with Marsha Meyer). He co-created and hosted the music-and-comedy radio program *The Cool and the Crazy* (1984–88, KCRW FM, Santa Monica), and is currently Director of Special Sections for *Billboard* magazine.

DICK BLACKBURN makes films (*Legendary Curse of Lemora, Eating Raoul*), writes (*L.A. Weekly, Village Voice*, et. al.), and compiles albums (Rhino's *Excello Story* and others).

BOB MERLIS was a contributor to the *Catalog of Cool*. His articles have appeared in *Los Angeles, L.A. Style, California, Oui*, and the *L.A. Weekly*; his Car Culture column appears in *L.A. Style*. Mr. Merlis' idols are Little Richard, Raymond Loewy and Walker Percy.

DAVIN SEAY is an author and journalist whose work has appeared in the *Los Angeles Times*, the *San Francisco Chronicle*, the *Philadelphia Inquirer, People*, and *National Review*. He is the co-author of *San Francisco Nights* and *The Wanderer: Dion's Story* and author of *Stairway To Heaven*.

A graphic designer by trade, RONN SPENCER was responsible for art-directing the Sex Pistols' American campaign. He co-created and hosted *The Cool and the Crazy* radio show. Not long ago, Mr. Spencer moved deep into the Arizona desert, 100 miles from the nearest city. On a recent trip back to Los Angeles, he inadvertently heard a Sinead O'Connor record. He is thinking about moving 100 miles further out.

JIM TROMBETTA is a writer in film and television, whose credits include multiple episodes of *Miami Vice, The Equalizer* and *The Flash*, and original screenplays.

TOM VICKERS is an A&R man for Mercury Records. An avid boogie-boarder, TV watcher and lover of the inane, insane and all-out absurd, he is currently searching for the next big musical thang.

DANNY WEIZMANN used his bar mitzvah money to publish the punk-rock fanzine *Rag In Chains* under the nom de plume Shredder. He has since written for *Flipside*, the *L.A. Weekly*, and *California*. New Alliance Records recently released his first spoken-word album, *The Wet Dog Shakes*. He digs pinball and off-ramps.

INDEX

Following is a selective listing of names and titles appearing in *Too Cool*. For a guide to general subjects covered, see the Table Of Contents.

A

B